MW01686589

THE ABUNDANT LIFE BIBLE AMPLIFIER

MATTHEW

GEORGE R. KNIGHT

THE ABUNDANT LIFE BIBLE AMPLIFIER

MATTHEW

The Gospel of the Kingdom

GEORGE R. KNIGHT
General Editor

Pacific Press Publishing Association
Boise, Idaho
Oshawa, Ontario, Canada

Edited by Marvin Moore
Designed by Tim Larson
Typeset in 11/14 Janson Text

Unless otherwise noted, all Bible quotations in this book are from the New International Version, and all emphasis in Bible quotations is supplied by the author.

Library of Congress Cataloging-in-Publication Data:

Knight, George R.
Matthew: the Gospel of the kingdom / George R. Knight.
p. cm. — (The Abundant life Bible amplifier)
Includes bibliographical references.
ISBN 0-8163-1216-8.
1. Bible. N. T. Matthew—Criticism, interpretation, etc.
2. Bible. N. T. Matthew—Study and teaching. I. Title. II. Series.
BS2575.2.K55 1994
226. 2'07—dc20 93-50866
CIP

94 95 96 97 98 • 5 4 3 2 1

CONTENTS

DEDICATION

Dedicated
to George C. and Betty A. Knight,
two very special
parents

GENERAL PREFACE

The Abundant Life Bible Amplifier series is aimed at helping readers understand the Bible better. Rather than merely offering comments on or about the Bible, each volume seeks to enable people to study their Bibles with fuller understanding.

To accomplish that task, scholars who are also proven communicators have been selected to author each volume. The basic idea underlying this combination is that scholarship and the ability to communicate on a popular level are compatible skills.

While the Bible Amplifier is written with the needs and abilities of laypeople in mind, it will also prove helpful to pastors and teachers. Beyond individual readers, the series will be useful in church study groups and as guides to enrich participation in the weekly prayer meeting.

Rather than focusing on the details of each verse, the Bible Amplifier series seeks to give readers an understanding of the themes and patterns of each biblical book as a whole and how each passage fits into that context. As a result, the series does not seek to solve all the problems or answer all the questions that may be related to a given text. In the process of accomplishing the goal for the series, both inductive and explanatory methodologies are used.

Each volume in this series presents its author's understanding of the biblical book being studied. As such, it does not necessarily represent the "official" position of the Seventh-day Adventist Church.

It should be noted that the Bible Amplifier series utilizes the New International Version of the Bible as its basic text. *Every reader should read the "How to Use This Book" section to get the fullest benefit from the Bible Amplifier study volumes.*

Dr. George Knight, a professor of church history at the

Seventh-day Adventist Theological Seminary at Andrews University in Berrien Springs, Michigan, is the general editor for the entire Bible Amplifier series. Over the years he has made a deep personal study of the book of Matthew (see the Author's Preface). He is an experienced writer and the author of many books, including *Angry Saints*, *My Gripe With God*, *The Pharisee's Guide to Perfect Holiness*, and *Millennial Fever and the End of the World.*

AUTHOR'S PREFACE

In 1980 I began an intensive, verse-by-verse study of the Bible that I estimated would take thirty years to complete. The first New Testament book that I studied was the Gospel According to Matthew. At that time, I had no idea that the twelve months I spent with Matthew would have any results beyond personal edification.

But that expectation began to change in February 1989, when the late Eugene Stiles, then president of Pacific Press Publishing Association, first unveiled to me Pacific Press's intention of developing a major series of books to help people understand the Bible better. That introduction to the series eventually led to the opportunity to write this volume on Matthew.

Developing this study of the first Gospel has been one of the joys of my life. The research and writing have provided me with the rare opportunity to live on a daily basis with both Matthew and his Lord in an intensive way. My hope is that the readers of this volume will receive a portion of the blessing from reading it that I did from writing it. My prayer is that each of you will have a closer walk with Jesus because of this book.

Several people contributed to this volume, whom I would like to acknowledge. Not the least of those is Bonnie Beres, my hard-working secretary, who translated my handwriting into readable copy. I would also like to thank Marvin Moore of Pacific Press for both helping in the conceptualization of the format for the Abundant Life Bible Amplifier series and for editing the present volume. In addition, I would like to express my appreciation to those administrators of Pacific Press Publishing Association who had the foresight and vision to sponsor the Abundant Life Bible Amplifier series. Chief among those administrators are the late Eugene Stiles (past president), Robert E. Kyte (current president),

B. Russell Holt (vice-president for editorial), and Robert H. Gorton (vice-president for marketing). As usual, I would also like to express my appreciation to the administration of Andrews University for providing me with time and an atmosphere conducive to research and writing.

I trust that *Matthew: The Gospel of the Kingdom* will be a blessing to its readers as they seek to learn more about their Lord and as they put that knowledge into practice in walking in an ever closer way with both Jesus and their "neighbors."

George R. Knight
Berrien Springs, Michigan

How to Use This Book

The Abundant Life Bible Amplifier series treats each major portion of each Bible book in five main sections.

The first section is called "Getting Into the Word." The purpose of this section is to encourage readers to study their own Bibles. For that reason, the text of the Bible has not been printed in the volumes in this series.

You will get the most out of your study if you work through the exercises in each of the "Getting Into the Word" sections. This will not only aid you in learning more about the Bible but will also increase your skill in using Bible tools and in asking (and answering) meaningful questions about the Bible.

It will be helpful if you write out the answers and keep them in a notebook or file folder for each biblical book. Writing out your thoughts will enhance your understanding. The benefit derived from such study, of course, will be proportionate to the amount of effort expended.

The "Getting Into the Word" sections assume that the reader has certain minimal tools available. Among these are a concordance and a Bible with maps and marginal cross-references. If you don't have a New International Version of the Bible, we recommend that you obtain one for use with this series, since all the Bible Amplifier authors are using the NIV as their basic text. For the same reason, your best choice of a concordance is the *NIV*

Exhaustive Concordance, edited by E. W. Goodrick and J. R. Kohlenberger. *Strong's Exhaustive Concordance of the Bible* and Young's *Analytical Concordance to the Bible* are also useful. However, even if all you have is Cruden's Concordance, you will be able to do all of the "Getting Into the Word" exercises and most of the "Researching the Word" exercises.

The "Getting Into the Word" sections also assume that the reader has a Bible dictionary. The *Seventh-day Adventist Bible Dictionary* is quite helpful, but those interested in greater depth may want to acquire the four-volume *International Standard Bible Encyclopedia* (1974-1988 edition) or the six-volume *Anchor Bible Dictionary.*

The second section in the treatment of the biblical passages is called "Exploring the Word." The purpose of this section is to discuss the major themes in each biblical book. Thus the comments will typically deal with fairly large portions of Scripture (often an entire chapter) rather than providing a verse-by-verse treatment, such as is found in the *Seventh-day Adventist Bible Commentary.* In fact, many verses and perhaps whole passages in some biblical books may be treated minimally or passed over altogether.

Another thing that should be noted is that the purpose of the "Exploring the Word" sections is not to respond to all the problems or answer all the questions that might arise in each passage. Rather, as stated above, the "Exploring the Word" sections are to develop the Bible writers' major themes. In the process, the author of each volume will bring the best of modern scholarship into the discussion and thus enrich the reader's understanding of the biblical passage at hand. The "Exploring the Word" sections will also develop and provide insight into many of the issues first raised in the "Getting Into the Word" exercises.

The third section in the treatment of the biblical passages is "Applying the Word." This section is aimed at bringing the lessons of each passage into daily life. Once again, you may want to write out a response to these questions and keep them in your notebook or file folder on the biblical book being studied.

The fourth section, "Researching the Word," is for those students who want to delve more deeply into the Bible passage under study or into the history behind it. It is recognized that not everyone will have the research tools for this section. Those expecting to use the research sections should have an exhaustive Bible concordance, the *Seventh-day Adventist Bible Commentary*, a good Bible dictionary, and a Bible atlas. It also will be helpful to have several versions of the Bible.

The final component in each chapter of this book will be a list of recommendations for "Further Study of the Word." While most readers will not have all of these works, many of them may be available in local libraries. Others can be purchased through your local book dealer. It is assumed that many users of this series will already own the seven-volume *Seventh-day Adventist Bible Commentary* and the one-volume *Seventh-day Adventist Bible Dictionary*.

In closing, it should be noted that while a reader will learn much about the Bible from a *reading* of the books in the Bible Amplifier series, he or she will gain infinitely more by *studying* the Bible in connection with that reading.

INTRODUCTION

The Gospel of Matthew

One of the best ways to study a book of the Bible is to read it thoughtfully and prayerfully from beginning to end in as short a time as possible. The following suggestions will help you to get the most out of a thoughtful reading of Matthew.

1. **As you read Matthew's Gospel, list on a page in your Matthew notebook what you consider to be the main point or idea for each chapter. How does that point or idea contribute to the book's developing theme?**
2. **For each chapter, list or underline at least one idea or text that is of special importance to your spiritual journey. Why is that thought so special or precious to you?**

Most Christians have a favorite Gospel. Some prefer John for its simple language and profound spiritual insights about the life and ministry of Jesus. Others relate most easily to the quick-flowing action of Mark, while some favor Luke's focus on human interest.

Many readers, however, are drawn to Matthew for his masterful presentations of the Lord's teachings. Such Christians may even agree with Michael Green, who has suggested that "the Gospel according to Matthew is perhaps the most important single document in the New Testament, for in it we have the fullest and most systematic account of the birth, life, teaching, death and resurrection of the founder of Christianity, Jesus the Messiah" (M. Green, 1).

One of the first things a reader notes about the four Gospels is that they are both alike and different at the same time. Similarity is most evident in the Gospels of Matthew, Mark, and Luke. Those three, broadly speaking, each give an account of the same events in Jesus' life. Beyond that, they use much the same language and largely adhere to the same order of events.

Matthew, Mark, and Luke are commonly known as the Synoptic Gospels. The word *synoptic* comes from two Greek words that mean "to see together." Hence the term *Synoptic Gospels*—Gospels that set forth the life and teachings of Jesus from a common perspective.

John's Gospel, on the other hand, exhibits the life of Christ from a distinctly different viewpoint. It adds much material not included in the Synoptics. In addition, John's Gospel tends to go deeper than the others as it searches out the spiritual meaning of what Jesus did and said.

The Synoptics, however, are not carbon copies of each other. Each writer had his own purpose. As a result, the four Gospels supplement each other in filling out a portrait of Jesus. Each Gospel presents a portrait in itself, but combined they offer the fullest representation.

Frank Colquhoun helps us see the unique contribution of Matthew in the Gospel collage of Jesus:

> "In *Matthew* we see him in his messianic role as the promised *king*, fulfilling the Jewish scriptures.
>
> "In *Mark* we see him in his ceaseless ministry as the Lord's *servant*, obediently treading the appointed path of suffering and sacrifice.
>
> "In *Luke* we see him in the perfection of his manhood as the *saviour* of the world and friend of sinners.
>
> "In *John* we see him in his self-humiliation as the everlasting Son of the Father, made flesh for us" (Colquhoun, 82, 83).

Matthew's Purpose

Unlike the other Gospels, as noted above, Matthew was especially written for the Jewish community. A major goal of Matthew was to set forth Jesus of Nazareth as the promised Messiah of the Old Testament. That is one reason for the first Gospel's extensive use of Old Testament quotations—more than sixty in all. Beyond quotations, Matthew contains innumerable single words and allusions that echo the Old Testament. This "Jewishness" is also seen in Matthew's interest in Christ's genealogy, the law, the traditions of Judaism, and fulfilled prophecy.

A second purpose of Matthew was to present the significant events in the life of Jesus from His birth to His death and resurrection. While not a biography in the modern sense, the first Gospel presents the essential outline of Christ's life in the context of growing antagonism on the part of the Jewish leaders and developing faith among the disciples. Jesus' teachings are embedded within the biographical narrative of His life.

A third purpose of the first Gospel was to provide a teaching manual for the Christian community. In that role, Matthew became the first systematizer of Jesus' teachings. That resulted in his presentation of the Lord's teachings on various topics in the five great blocks that are listed under "Structure" below.

The teaching function of the first Gospel is also highlighted by the accent placed upon teaching in the great commission, where part of Jesus' final command to His followers was to "go and make disciples of all nations, . . . *teaching* them to obey everything" He had commanded (28:19, 20).

To facilitate his teaching goal, Matthew arranged materials in a way that made memorization easier. Thus he not only presented Jesus' teachings in subject-matter blocks, but he arranged things in groups of threes and sevens. The genealogy that begins the Gospel with its three groups of fourteen names is a good example of Matthew's technique. Fourteen, incidentally, is the numerical significance of David's name in Hebrew. The first Gospel is notable for both its systematization and its use of devices that make memorization and teaching easier. That was an especially important contribution in a culture that passed on teachings in largely oral, as opposed to written, form.

While the first Gospel, like the other three, is anonymous, there are internal hints that Matthew, the tax collector who became one of the twelve, was its author. That position was held by the early church.

Indications also exist that Matthew's Gospel was put into writing before the fall of Jerusalem in A.D. 70. One of the most forceful of those indications is that it seems quite evident that the temple had not yet been destroyed at the time of writing.

The Gospel's Structure

Many scholars have marveled at the literary skill that the book of Matthew exhibits. Indicators of Matthew's literary skill are the dramatic and complex development of the story of Jesus in the context of His relationships to His disciples and His detractors, the Gospel's clearly marked sections, the utilization of repeated formulas, and the grouping of materials in such a way that one episode throws light on another.

Matthew's Gospel as the developing story of Jesus is divided into three sections by the twice-repeated phrase "From that time on Jesus began" (4:17; 16:21). Up through 4:16, Matthew's focus is the person of Jesus the Messiah.

But a major shift in the presentation is signaled by 4:17—"From that time on Jesus began to preach, 'Repent, for the kingdom of heaven is near.' " Thus the focal point of the Gospel's second section (4:17–16:20) is the proclamation of Jesus the Messiah.

The next major shift in the narrative is 16:21, where Matthew writes: "From that time on Jesus began to explain to his disciples that he must go to Jerusalem and suffer many things . . . , and that he must be killed and on the third day be raised to life." Thus the emphasis in part 3 of Matthew's Gospel (16:21–28:20) is the suffering, death, and resurrection of Jesus the Messiah. At the climax of each of the Gospel's three major sections is the declaration that

Jesus is "the Son of God" (3:17; 16:16; 27:54).

Another conspicuous organizational feature in the book of Matthew is the repeated use of the phrase "when Jesus had finished saying all these things" (7:28; 11:1; 13:53; 19:1; 26:1). That phrase, with slight modifications, is repeated at the end of each of Jesus' five major teaching discourses. Each discourse centers on the kingdom of heaven. They may be listed as follows:

1. The Sermon on the Mount, or the principles of the kingdom (5–7).
2. The duties of the leaders of the kingdom (10).
3. The parables of the kingdom (13).
4. Greatness and forgiveness in the kingdom (18).
5. The coming of the kingdom (24, 25).

Each of these five discourses is set between narrative sections that picture Jesus "*teaching* . . . , *preaching* the good news of the kingdom, and *healing* every disease and sickness among the people" (4:23; see also 9:35; 11:1). Thus the five major sections at the heart of Matthew's Gospel are alike in structure, with each narrative section covering Jesus' ministry being followed by an instructional section that presents His teachings.

While there is no one approach to the structure of Matthew's Gospel that adequately answers all the questions that can be raised in regard to it, enough has been said to indicate that the first Gospel is a carefully crafted and structured piece of literary artistry. We now turn to Matthew's major themes.

Matthew's Major Teachings

1. One of the most obvious themes in Matthew is that *Jesus and His ministry are a fulfillment of the Old Testament prophecies.* While all the Gospel writers give some attention to that topic, Matthew goes out of his way to set forth the significant events of Jesus' life as fulfillments of prophecy.

Falling into that category are His birth (1:23), His birthplace

(2:6), the return from the Egyptian sojourn (2:15), the killing of the Bethlehem babies (2:17, 18), His residence in Nazareth (2:23), the work of the forerunner (3:3), the location of His principal labors (4:15, 16), His healing ministry (8:17), His demeanor as God's servant (12:17-21), His lack of reception from the Jews (13:14, 15), His use of parables in His teachings (13:35), the manner of His entry into Jerusalem (21:4, 5), His arrest (26:56), and the price of His betrayal (27:9).

The above texts emphasize the fulfillment of prophecy, with ten employing the verb *fulfill*. For Matthew, Jesus—as the fulfillment of Old Testament prophecy—was the promised Messiah.

2. A second Matthean theme is Christ Himself. As noted above, *the entire Gospel focuses the reader's attention on Christ*: first on His person (1:1–4:16), then on His public ministry (4:17–16:20), and finally on His death and resurrection (16:21–28:20).

Matthew sets forth Jesus as the expected Messiah (*Christos* in Greek, 1:16, 18). Literally, the term means "the anointed one." Closely connected with the idea of Messiah was the fact that the Coming One would be a Son of David (1:1, 16, 17, 20, 25). But to the Jews, that title signified mere descent from David, not a heavenly being (Jer. 30:9; Ezek. 34:23, 24; 37:24; Hos. 3:5). In first-century Judaism, there was both great expectation of the coming Messiah as a deliverer and confusion over the exact nature of His mission.

It is therefore of the utmost significance that Matthew sets forth Jesus as "Immanuel . . . 'God with us' " (1:23). The Messiah is not merely the Son of Abraham or the Son of David, but the divine Son of God. That insight will dominate Matthew's presentation of the Gospel. Jesus Himself is the fulfillment of all God's promises. Thus He is the true foundation of all faith in God.

For Matthew, Jesus is also the divine King. From the very beginning of his Gospel, Matthew sets forth Jesus as being in the line of royalty (1:1-17). Even the wisemen came looking for the "king of the Jews" (2:2). And Jesus accepts the title of King before Pilate (27:11). The Gospel closes with Jesus having divine kingly power (28:18).

3. Closely related to the concept of the divine Messiah-King in Matthew is a third major theme—*the kingdom of heaven.* The Gospel's central emphasis is found in "the good news [gospel] of the kingdom" (4:23; 9:35; 24:14).

The good news is that the reign or rule of God has arrived in history through the presence of Jesus. Everything in Matthew's Gospel relates in one way or another to the kingdom-of-heaven theme.

It should be noted that Matthew presents the kingdom of heaven as both present (12:28) and future (20:21; 24:1–25:46). Thus Jesus not only can rule in human lives in the present age, but He will rule in an even fuller manner at His second advent.

4. Thus *eschatology*, the doctrine of the return of Christ at the end of the age, provides a fourth theological emphasis in Matthew. His special interest in eschatology can be seen from the extended treatment he gives to the topic in chapters 24 and 25 and in 13:24-30, 47-53; 20:1-16; and 22:1-14.

Much of Matthew's treatment of eschatology is related to Christian conduct in the light of future judgment. Thus, as Matthew presents it, eschatology is important not only to understanding but also to discipleship.

5. That brings us to a fifth Matthean emphasis—*the ethical implications of the kingdom of heaven.* Matthew's Gospel uses the Greek words for discipleship more than any other Gospel. Discipleship means following in the steps of Jesus.

Matthew is clear that following Jesus means both a repudiation of old ways and behavior and an acceptance of the law of the kingdom of heaven. The love and forgiveness that brought a person into the kingdom are to be passed on to his or her neighbor (7:12; 18:21-35).

Matthew teaches that the gospel and ethics cannot be separated. And the ethic of the kingdom is clearly spelled out in the Sermon on the Mount (5:1–7:29). If the Master took up His cross and became a Servant, so must His followers. Self-crucifixion and servanthood stand at the center of kingdom ethics (10:38, 39; 16:24-26; 20:26, 27; 23:11, 12). People have choices as to how they will live their lives (7:13, 14, 24-27).

6. The idea of choices brings us to a sixth Matthean theme—the reality of *conflict between the kingdom of heaven and the kingdom of the evil one* (13:31-43). The conflict begins with the attempt of ruthless Herod to destroy Jesus, moves into the wilderness temptation, and culminates in Gethsemane and Calvary.

Matthew traces the conflict along three major lines: (1) conflict with the Jewish leaders, who finally put Jesus on the cross; (2) conflict with the disciples as they struggle to appropriate the lordship of Jesus through faith, and (3) the conflict of Jesus Himself as He struggles to accept death on a cross. All three conflicts come to resolution in Matthew's final chapters.

All of Christ's disciples must face these struggles and conflicts in every age. All disciples are faced with the moral decisions set forth in Matthew's Gospel. In the conflict of good and evil, every person is presented with the choice of building on the rock or on the sand (7:24-27); of choosing the narrow or the broad gate (7:13, 14); of opting for the kingdom of heaven or the kingdom of the evil one.

7. A seventh theme in Matthew's Gospel is a concern for the *salvation of the Gentiles*. While the first Gospel is written mainly for the Jews, from its first chapter to its last, it sets forth an undercurrent of hope for all people.

Thus, we find several Gentile females in Jesus' ancestral background in chapter 1, the wise men from the East as "believers" in chapter 2, and Christ's great commission to present the gospel message to all the world in the book's closing verses. And interspersed throughout Matthew are verses demonstrating Gentile faith and Gentiles being invited into the kingdom (e.g., 8:5-13; 15:21-28; 21:33-43; 22:1-10; 24:14).

8. An eighth item to note about Matthew's Gospel is that it is the only one to contain the Greek word for *church* (16:18; 18:17). Beyond that, the entire Gospel is organized as a teaching tool for the developing Christian community.

9. Last, as with the other three Gospels, Matthew's book climaxes with *Jesus' death and resurrection*. That theme is first hinted

at in 12:40, but Jesus' death and resurrection dominate the narrative after Peter's confession in 16:16 that Jesus is "the Christ, the Son of the living God."

Outline of Matthew

I. The Person of the King (1:1–4:16)
   A. The King's human and divine credentials (1:1-25)
   B. The King's childhood (2:1-23)
   C. The King's forerunner and anointing (3:1-17)
   D. The King's test (4:1-16)
II. The Proclamation of the King (4:17–16:20)
   A. The King's early ministry (4:17-25)
   B. Principles of the kingdom (5:1–7:29)
   C. The King's authority demonstrated (8:1–9:38)
   D. The King's authority delegated (10:1-42)
   E. Varying responses to the King (11:1–12:50)
   F. Parables of the kingdom (13:1-53)
   G. Varying responses to the King's teachings and miracles and the King's withdrawal (13:54–16:20)
III. The Suffering, Death, and Resurrection of the King (16:21–28:20)
   A. Glimpses of the cross and the kingdom (16:21–17:27)
   B. Qualifications for citizenship in the kingdom (18:1–20:34)
   C. The King's return to Jerusalem (21:1-22)
   D. Controversies between the King and the Jewish leaders (21:23–23:39)
   E. The destruction of Jerusalem, the return of the King, and the coming of the kingdom (24:1–25:46)
   F. The King's arrest, trial, death, and resurrection (26:1–28:15)
   G. The King's last command (28:16-20)

For Further Reading

1. For a general survey of issues relating to Matthew as a person and to his Gospel, see D. A. Carson, "Matthew," in *The*

Expositor's Bible Commentary, 8:3-57; G. W. Bromiley, ed., *International Standard Bible Encyclopedia*, 3:280-288; F. D. Nichol, ed., *Seventh-day Adventist Bible Commentary*, 5:271-275.

2. For extended treatments of the first Gospel's theme and structure, see J. D. Kingsbury, *Matthew as Story*; J. D. Kingsbury, *Matthew: Structure, Christology, Kingdom*; R. T. France, *Matthew: Evangelist and Teacher*.
3. For a helpful overview of the distinctiveness and interrelatedness of the four Gospels, see F. Colquhoun, *Four Portraits of Jesus: Christ in the Gospels*.

LIST OF WORKS CITED*

Albright, W. F., and C. S. Mann, eds. *Matthew*. The Anchor Bible. Garden City, N.Y.: Doubleday, 1971.

Barclay, William. *The Gospel of Matthew*. 2d ed. 2 vols. The Daily Study Bible. Edinburgh: Saint Andrew Press, 1958.

Beasley-Murray, G. R. *Baptism in the New Testament*. Grand Rapids, Mich.: Eerdmans, 1973.

Bonhoeffer, Dietrich. *The Cost of Discipleship*. New York: Collier Books, 1963.

Bromiley, Geoffrey W., ed. *International Standard Bible Encyclopedia*. Rev. ed. 4 vols. Grand Rapids, Mich.: Eerdmans, 1979-1988.

Brown, Raymond E. *The Gospel According to John*. 2d ed. 2 vols. The Anchor Bible. Garden City, N.Y.: Doubleday, 1966, 1970.

Bruce, Alexander Balmain. "The Synoptic Gospels." In *The Expositor's Greek Testament*, edited by W. Robertson Nicoll, 1:1-340. Grand Rapids, Mich.: Eerdmans, n.d.

Bruce, F. F. *New Testament History*. New York: Doubleday, 1971.

Bruner, Frederick Dale. *Matthew: A Commentary*. 2 vols. Dallas: Word, 1987, 1990.

Carson, D. A. "Matthew." In *The Expositor's Bible Commentary*, edited by Frank A. Gaebelein, 8:1-599. Grand Rapids, Mich.: Zondervan, 1984.

Colquhoun, Frank. *Four Portraits of Jesus: Christ in the Gospels*. Downers Grove, Ill.: InterVarsity, 1984.

Davies, W. D., and Dale C. Allison, Jr. *A Critical and Exegetical Commentary on the Gospel According to Matthew*. 2 vols. The International Critical Commentary. Edinburgh: T & T Clark, 1988, 1991.

*This list does not include classical works that utilize standard referencing systems across various editions.

Denney, James. *Jesus and the Gospel.* London: Hodder and Stoughton, 1908.

Filson, Floyd V. *A Commentary on the Gospel According to St. Matthew.* Black's New Testament Commentaries. London: Adam & Charles Black, 1960.

France, R. T. *The Gospel According to Matthew.* Tyndale New Testament Commentaries. Grand Rapids, Mich.: Eerdmans, 1985.

______. *Matthew: Evangelist and Teacher.* Grand Rapids, Mich.: Zondervan, 1989.

Gibson, John Monro. *The Gospel According to St. Matthew.* The Expositor's Bible. New York: George H. Doran, n.d.

Green, Joel B., and Scot McKnight, eds. *Dictionary of Jesus and the Gospels.* Downers Grove, Ill.: InterVarsity Press, 1992.

Green, Michael. *Matthew for Today.* Dallas: Word, 1989.

Guelich, Robert. *The Sermon on the Mount.* Dallas: Word, 1982.

Gundry, Robert H. *The Use of the Old Testament in St. Matthew's Gospel, With Special Reference to the Messianic Hope.* Leiden: Brill, 1975.

Hare, Douglas R. A. *Matthew.* Interpretation: A Bible Commentary for Teaching and Preaching. Louisville, Ky.: John Knox, 1993.

Hengel, Martin. *Crucifixion in the Ancient World and the Folly of the Message of the Cross.* Philadelphia: Fortress, 1977.

Horn, Siegfried H., et. al. *Seventh-day Adventist Bible Dictionary*, rev. ed, edited by Raymond H. Woolsey. Hagerstown, Md.: Review and Herald, 1979.

Jeremias, Joachim. *The Parables of Jesus.* 2d ed. New York: Charles Scribner's Sons, 1972.

Johnson, Sherman E. "The Gospel According to St. Matthew: Introduction and Exegesis." In *The Interpreter's Bible*, edited by George Arthur Buttrick. New York: Abingdon-Cokesbury, 1951, 7:250-625.

Kiehl, Erich H. *The Passion of Our Lord.* Grand Rapids, Mich.: Baker, 1990.

Kingsbury, Jack Dean. *Matthew: Structure, Christology, Kingdom.* Minneapolis: Fortress, 1989.

______. *Matthew as Story*. 2d rev. and enl. ed. Philadelphia: Fortress, 1988.

Knight, George R. *My Gripe With God: A Study in Divine Justice and the Problem of the Cross*. Washington, D.C.: Review and Herald, 1990.

______. *The Pharisee's Guide to Perfect Holiness: A Study of Sin and Salvation*. Boise, Idaho: Pacific Press, 1992.

Lenski, R. C. H. *The Interpretation of St. Matthew's Gospel*. Minneapolis: Augsburg, 1961.

Lloyd-Jones, D. Martyn. *Studies in the Sermon on the Mount*. 2 vols. Grand Rapids, Mich.: Eerdmans, n.d.

Moltmann, Jürgen. *The Crucified God: The Cross as the Foundation and Criticism of Christian Theology*. New York: Harper & Row, 1974.

Moore, George Foot. *Judaism in the First Centuries of the Christian Era: The Age of the Tannaim*. 2 vols. Cambridge, Mass.: Harvard University Press, 1946.

Morris, Leon. *The Gospel According to Matthew*. Grand Rapids, Mich.: Eerdmans, 1992.

______. *Testaments of Love: A Study of Love in the Bible*. Grand Rapids, Mich.: Eerdmans, 1981.

Mounce, Robert H. *Matthew*. A Good News Commentary. San Francisco: Harper & Row, 1985.

Neufeld, Don F., and Julia Neuffer, eds. *Seventh-day Adventist Bible Students' Source Book*. Hagerstown, Md.: Review and Herald, 1962.

Nichol, Francis D., et al. *Seventh-day Adventist Bible Commentary*. Rev. ed., 7 vols. Hagerstown, Md.: Review and Herald, 1976-1980.

Plummer, Alfred. *An Exegetical Commentary on the Gospel According to St. Matthew*. London: James Clarke, n.d.

Ridderbos, H. N. *Matthew*. Bible Student's Commentary. Translated by Ray Togtman. Grand Rapids, Mich.: Zondervan, 1987.

Schweizer, Eduard. *The Good News According to Matthew*. Translated by David E. Green. Atlanta: John Knox, 1975.

Stott, John R. W. *Christian Counter-Culture: The Message of the*

Sermon on the Mount. Downers Grove, Ill.: InterVarsity, 1978.
______. *The Cross of Christ*. Downers Grove, Ill.: InterVarsity, 1986.
Tenney, Merrill C. *The Reality of the Resurrection*. New York: Harper and Row, 1963.
Thielicke, Helmut. *Life Can Begin Again: Sermons on the Sermon on the Mount*. Translated by John W. Doberstein. Philadelphia: Fortress Press, 1963.
Warren, Max. *I Believe in the Great Commission*. Grand Rapids, Mich.: Eerdmans, 1976.
White, Ellen G. *Christ's Object Lessons*. Washington, D.C.: Review and Herald, 1941.
______. *The Desire of Ages*. Boise, Idaho: Pacific Press, 1940.
______. *Education*. Boise, Idaho: Pacific Press, 1952.
______. *The Great Controversy*. Boise, Idaho: Pacific Press, 1950.
______. *Thoughts From the Mount of Blessing*. Boise, Idaho: Pacific Press, 1956.

PART ONE

The Person of the King

Matthew 1:1–4:16

CHAPTER ONE

Jesus the Promised King

Matthew 1, 2

The first two chapters of Matthew's Gospel set the stage for Jesus' ministry. Chapter 1 introduces us to Jesus and presents both His human and divine credentials. We discover that He is not only the promised Messiah-King in the line of David, but that He is also the divine Immanuel—"God with us." Matthew's first chapter also marks the all-important announcement of the true nature of Jesus' mission.

Chapter 2 takes us rapidly through the childhood of Jesus by way of three "snapshots": the Magi seeking out the "king of the Jews," the Egyptian sojourn, and the return to Nazareth. In addition, Matthew 2 presents three responses to Jesus and thereby sets up themes that will be developed throughout the rest of the Gospel.

These two chapters prepare the reader for the public "coming out" of Jesus and the beginning of His public ministry in chapters 3 and 4.

■ Getting Into the Word

Matthew 1

Read Matthew 1 through two times. On the second reading, begin to deal with the following questions:

1. Would you start a book with a genealogy? Why do you think Matthew began his Gospel that way? In particular, according to verses 1 and 17, what is he seeking to prove

by his genealogy?

2. **Read the genealogy of Jesus in Luke 3:23-38. In what ways are Matthew's and Luke's genealogies alike, and how do they differ? In particular, note the earliest (in terms of history) name in each genealogy. Why do Matthew and Luke start the ancestry of Jesus with different men? What might that say about the differing audiences of their Gospels?**
3. **What four women (excluding Mary) do you find in Matthew's genealogy? List them on a piece of paper. Now, through the use of a concordance and/or your Bible's marginal cross-references, see what you can discover about these women in the rest of the Bible. In particular, what kind of people were they? What were their racial backgrounds? What were their professions or ethical experiences?**
4. **Was it common for Jews to include women in their genealogies? In answering that question, you may want to examine such Old Testament genealogies as those found in Genesis 10 and Ezra 2. Why do you think Matthew included the particular women he selected, rather than people like Sarah, Rebekah, or Rachel?**
5. **As you read verses 18 to 25, pick out the text that you believe comes closest to stating the mission of Jesus. What connection, if any, do you think there might be between that text and the four women listed in Matthew's genealogy?**
6. **What are the implications of Jesus being "God with us"?**

■ Exploring the Word

A Strange Way to Start a Book: The King's Credentials

One of the most amazing things to the modern reader is the way Matthew begins his book. Who wants to read a long list of names before getting to the story? For a twentieth-century author, such a procedure would guarantee that his or her manuscript would end up on the editor's scrap heap.

To a Jew, however, beginning the story of a person's life with a genealogy was the most natural and the most interesting way. When Josephus, a first-century Jewish historian, wrote his autobiography, he began it with his genealogy, which he most likely found in the public records kept by the Sanhedrin.

The Jewish interest in racial pedigree stemmed from the fact that the Jews placed great store on the purity of one's lineage. A priest, for example, needed to produce an unbroken record of his pedigree back to Aaron. After the Babylonian captivity, certain families could not serve as priests because they "searched for their family records, but they could not find them and so were excluded from the priesthood" (Ezra 2:62).

Herod the Great, being Idumean, was so embarrassed that his name was not in the official genealogies that he ordered their destruction.

A first-century Jew would not only find a genealogy at the beginning of a biography to be natural and interesting, but would consider it to be essential. That would especially be true for a book claiming that its subject was the *Christ* (the Greek word for the Hebrew *Messiah*). And Matthew makes this claim in his first verse: "A record of the genealogy of Jesus Christ the son of David, the son of Abraham." If Matthew could not prove the purity of Jesus' ancestry, he might as well not write the rest of his Gospel, because no Jew would read it.

Matthew's task, however, was not only to demonstrate Jesus' racial purity, but also to demonstrate that Jesus had particular ancestors. First, the Messiah would have to come from the line of David. " 'Your house and your kingdom,' " God had told David through Nathan the prophet, " 'will endure forever before me; your throne will be established forever' " (2 Sam. 7:16). It was widely held by the Jews that that promise pointed to the coming Messiah.

The New Testament repeatedly stresses the fact that Jesus was a descendant of David. Peter emphasized this in the first recorded

Christian sermon (Acts 2:29-36). Paul sets forth Jesus as "of the seed of David" (Rom. 1:3; 2 Tim. 2:8, KJV). And the next-to-the-last words of Jesus in the Bible are, " 'I am the Root and the Offspring of David' " (Rev. 22:16). In addition, Jesus is repeatedly addressed as the Son of David in Matthew's Gospel—especially by those recognizing the Messianic overtones of His ministry (12:23; 15:22; 20:30, 31; 21:9, 15).

It is also important to Matthew that he prove that Jesus is a son of Abraham. Not only is Abraham the father of the Jewish race, but God promised that He would bless all the people of the earth through him (Gen. 12:1-3). Thus Matthew emphasizes that his genealogy is that of "Jesus [the] Christ [Messiah] the son of David, the son of Abraham" (1:1). In other words, because Jesus is of the lineage of both David and Abraham, He qualifies for the role of Messiah. The rest of Matthew's genealogy demonstrates that dual sonship.

This brings us to a comparison between the genealogies of Matthew and Luke. One of the most interesting differences is that Matthew traces the lineage of Jesus back to Abraham, while Luke goes clear back to Adam. One reason for this significant difference is that Matthew is primarily writing for Jewish readers, while Luke (the only Gentile author in the New Testament) is writing for a non-Jewish audience.

The two authors will drive home their different focuses in the development of their books. Matthew, for instance, repeatedly sets forth Jesus as the fulfillment of Old Testament prophecy—an emphasis lacking in Luke. Luke, on the other hand, is the Gospel writer who gives us such stories as the good Samaritan (a contradiction in terms to a Jew) and who highlights the fact that Elijah was helped by a Sidonian (rather than a Jewish) widow and that Elisha healed "only" Naaman the Syrian, even though many lepers lived in Israel (Luke 10:30-37; 17:11-19; 4:24-27; see also 13:29).

The point is that Matthew's primary emphasis is Jesus as the promised Messiah-Saviour of the Jews, while Luke's primary focus is Jesus as the Saviour of all the peoples of the world. Thus

Luke traces Jesus' genealogy all the way back to Adam, while Matthew only goes back to Abraham.

For many of the major differences between the two genealogies, there is no entirely satisfactory answer, given our inability to research records that were destroyed in the Jewish calamities of the first century. On the other hand, it probably would have been possible to verify both genealogies at the time the Gospels took shape.

Two especially plausible explanations exist for the differences between Matthew's and Luke's genealogies. The first is that Matthew traced Joseph's ancestry, while Luke traced Mary's. According to this view, Joseph became the legal son of Mary's father (Heli) through provisions in Jewish marriage laws given through Moses.

A second explanation for the differences holds that both genealogies are those of Joseph, with Luke giving the actual blood descent and Matthew providing his descent by adoption into a related family line. Thus Joseph could be both the son of Jacob and the son of Heli.

While the discrepancies between the genealogies are problematic to modern people, they undoubtedly created no difficulty for their first-century readers, who understood more fully the rules of making genealogies and had access to the official family lists. Each Gospel writer carefully developed his material to prove his point. Both writers were undoubtedly successful with their first readers.

Another thing to note about Matthew's genealogy is the artistry with which he developed it. Note, for example, the subtle move in verse 16, where Matthew ever so gently shifts the flow of his material from Joseph to "Mary, of whom was born Jesus, who is called Christ." That shift is crucial, because Jesus is not the son of Joseph, but of the Holy Spirit and the "virgin" Mary (vss. 18, 23).

If that is true, we are compelled to ask, why does Matthew make such a point of developing the pedigree of Jesus through Joseph? "The answer," suggests Michael Green, "is that Matthew is . . . not interested in strict biological descent but in legal standing.

Legally Jesus was the son of Joseph, and inherited his pedigree. Biologically, Matthew maintains, he was not. He was born of the virgin Mary through the direct intervention of the Holy Spirit" (M. Green, 42).

A second facet of Matthew's artistry and method is that he divides his genealogy into three sets of fourteen generations. Also of interest is that each set ends with the name of a pivotal king in Jewish history.

> The first section ends with David—the king who brought the Jewish kingdom to its peak.
>
> The second section ends with Jeconiah—the king who lost the kingdom.
>
> The third section ends with "Jesus, who is called Christ"—the King who is to restore the kingdom.

The arrangement of the three groups into fourteen each was apparently a teaching device to make the list easier to memorize. Ease of memorization, it should be noted, was of crucial importance before the age of printed books.

The number 14 is also of interest as an aid to memorization, because it represents the numerical significance of David's name. The consonants for David's name in Hebrew (a language lacking vowels) are *D W D*. Not having separate signs for numerals, Hebrew letters also had numerical significance, with *D* standing for *4* and *W* for *6*. Thus *D W D* stands for *4 + 6 + 4*, which adds up to 14. Thus even the arrangement of Matthew's genealogy helps us see him as a teacher seeking to develop his Gospel as a manual of instruction for the growing Christian community.

One last thing we will note about Matthew's genealogical list is that it is incomplete, although it claims that "there were fourteen generations in *all* from Abraham to David, fourteen from David to the exile to Babylon, and fourteen from the exile to the Christ" (vs. 17).

The plain biblical fact is that there were more than fourteen in at least one of those divisions. A comparison with Old Testament genealogies indicates that in verse 8 three names have been omitted between Jehoram (Joram) and Uzziah—Ahaziah, Joash, and Amaziah (2 Kings 8:24; 1 Chron. 3:11; 2 Chron. 22:1, 11; 24:27). In addition, Jehoiakim has been dropped out between Josiah and Jeconiah (also known as Jehoiachin) in verse 11 (2 Kings 23:34; 24:6, 14, 15). The apparent reason for the deletions was to make each section come out to fourteen generations.

So, we must ask, How can Matthew say there are fourteen generations "in *all*" in each of the three genealogic sections? The expression must mean all the generations included in *his* genealogy, rather than all the generations in the absolute historic sense of the most complete genealogies.

The lesson in all this for modern readers is that we need to read the Bible according to the ground rules of the people who wrote the Bible, rather than imagining that those writers were operating under the logical rules of twentieth-century usage. One of the most difficult of all lessons is to learn to read the books of the Bible from the perspective of their authors. Matthew obviously selected the names in order to arrive at his fourteen-times-three system so that Jewish students could memorize the list more easily. He operated "according to the rules" of his day, in spite of the fact that modern readers may have difficulties with his use of evidence.

A second lesson to be gained from Matthew's deletions from Joseph's genealogy is that we should be cautious in our use of biblical texts to prove this or that historical point, however interesting that point may be to modern readers. It is safer and truer to the Bible itself to read the Bible for the point its authors were seeking to make in each passage rather than the point we want them to make. The obvious truth to be gained from Matthew's genealogy is that Jesus is the son of both David and Abraham (vss. 1, 17). Thus He possessed qualifications that were essential in order to be accepted as Israel's Messiah-King. The genealogy itself is proof of that fact, while its organizational format is a memory device to help teachers pass on the genealogy in a largely oral culture.

The Case of the Four Ladies and the Purpose of Matthew

While Jews would not find it strange to begin a book with a genealogy, they would certainly be shocked to read a book that began with a genealogy containing women. It was quite unusual to find the names of women in Jewish genealogies. A woman had no legal rights; she was regarded as a thing rather than a person, a possession of her father or husband. Jewish males, in their morning prayer, thanked God that they were not Gentiles, slaves, or women.

Even at that, given the fact that Jewish genealogies, including Matthew's, were provided to demonstrate the purity of a person's heritage, one might not be too shocked to find that Jesus had such female ancestors as Sarah, Rebekah, or Rachel. But one would hardly expect to find the four selected in Matthew. As one author put it in his discussion of the women in the genealogy, "One gets the impression that Matthew pored over his Old Testament records until he could find the most questionable ancestors of Jesus available" (Bruner, 1:6).

It is important to remember that Matthew's Jewish readers knew their history. Not only would the inclusion of women in his genealogy strike them like a jolt of electricity, but the four selected would give that jolt the force of a lightning bolt. Let's look at these four women.

The first is Tamar (vs. 3). We do not generally recite her story to our children for evening devotions or cover it in their Sabbath School lessons. But Matthew's readers recognized Tamar immediately. Her story is told in Genesis 38.

This Canaanite woman had been married sequentially to Judah's two oldest sons, in harmony with Near Eastern custom. They both died in wickedness while she was childless. Judah, in harmony with the marriage laws of the time, then promised her marriage to his third son when the boy grew to marriageable age. Meanwhile, Judah sent Tamar back to her father's house to live as a widow until his son came of age.

As the years passed, however, Tamar came to realize that her father-in-law had no intention of honoring his promise. She therefore disguised herself as a prostitute and had sex with the unsuspecting Judah. Several months later, when her pregnancy became evident, Judah was overjoyed that she had been caught in sin and that he could, as stipulated by contemporary legal practice, "have her burned to death" (vs. 24).

But, to Judah's shock, when she was brought before him for sentencing, she was able to demonstrate that he—Judah himself—was the father. At that point, he exclaimed, "She is more righteous than I" (vs. 26).

To tell the truth, it is difficult to find much righteousness on either side of the Tamar/Judah episode. Yet Matthew, under the guidance of the Holy Spirit, selected her for his all-important genealogy!

The second female in Matthew's pedigree of Jesus is Rahab (1:5). Rahab, of course, had two counts against her in the eyes of most Jews. First, she was a prostitute by profession. Second, she was a Gentile (Joshua 2:1-21; 6:22-25).

Matthew's third female candidate seems to be virtuous enough in character, but she came from an especially despised racial strain. Ruth was a Moabitess (Ruth 1:4). Her people were the product of the incestuous relations of Lot with his oldest unmarried daughter. In order to preserve the family line, each of the daughters got their father drunk and caused him unknowingly to have sexual relations with them. The son produced by the older daughter was Moab, father of a people who became one of Israel's most implacable enemies (Gen. 19:30-37).

Following the suggestion of Balaam, the Moabites later seduced the Israelites into licentiousness and idolatry in the great apostasy of Baal-Peor (Num. 22–25). As a result, no "Moabite or any of his descendants," God proclaimed through Moses, "may enter the assembly of the Lord, even down to the tenth generation" (Deut. 23:3-6; Neh. 13:1, 2). While Ruth was not a prostitute or an adulteress, her racial background, in the eyes of the Jews, was just as serious.

The fourth female Matthew put in Jesus' ancestral list is in many ways the most interesting of all. Part of that interest stems from the fact she is not even listed by name.

If Matthew had called her Bathsheba, he would have brought to mind her adulterous affair with King David. But by calling her the one who "had been Uriah's wife" (vs. 6), Matthew raises two more points. First, the fact that Uriah is generally referred to as Uriah the Hittite (2 Sam. 11:3; 23:39; 1 Chron. 11:41) implies that, although born an Israelite, legally, she was probably considered a Gentile through marriage.

Second, and more significantly, the intrusion of Uriah's name into the story as Bathsheba's former husband raises the issue of the multiple murder perpetrated by David to cover up his sin of adultery. Of course, his preferred way of handling the problem was not murder but deception. With that in mind, David had Uriah, an officer in his army, sent home from the front, ostensibly to present a report. While in Jerusalem, it was expected that Uriah would sleep with his wife and thereby come to think that he fathered the child Bathsheba had already conceived through her affair with David.

But David's plan misfired. He had not taken into account the faithfulness and moral code of this Hittite officer. In fact, given the king's sexual weaknesses, David probably couldn't even imagine Uriah's course of action.

It soon came out that Uriah did not go home, as David suggested, but slept at the entrance to the palace. When questioned by the astounded David, Uriah—pictured as the most faithful of men—said that he could not pamper himself when his men were sleeping in tents on the field of battle.

That night, the increasingly frustrated king "made him drunk," but even then, the exemplary Uriah kept his wits and maintained his principles. Once again, he slept at David's palace with the servants.

David, seeing the scandal of his own "Watergate" on the horizon, felt forced to move from the milder expedient of deception to that of murder. The main thing was to cover up his sin. In the process, he merely multiplied it.

In the end, David decided to let Uriah carry his own death warrant back to the field of battle. David's letter to General Joab instructed him to "put Uriah in the front line where the fighting is fiercest. Then withdraw from him so he will be struck down and die" (2 Sam. 11:14). Only after that was Joab to press for victory.

The plan worked. Uriah was killed in the battle along with, undoubtedly, many of his battalion (vss. 16-24).

Thus, with a stroke of his pen, Matthew brought to his readers' minds not only the adultery of Israel's leading king but also his ruthless coverup. It must never be forgotten that Matthew's audience was quite familiar with the stories alluded to by the genealogy's four women. For them, that history—especially given the background of the women—was a message blazed across Jesus' pedigree. Three of the four were involved in gross sexual sin, and three were definitely despised Gentiles, with the fourth probably regarded as such. They were women who would not easily be accepted into first-century Judaism—a culture that had little use for either Gentiles or sinners.

Then why, we are forced to ask, did Matthew, who was writing for Jewish readers, deliberately add these women to his genealogy? After all, he could have proved his point without listing them.

Part of the answer is found in one of the great texts of the first Gospel. Speaking of the fifth woman in his list (Mary), Matthew penned: "She will give birth to a son, and you are to give him the name Jesus, because *he will save his people from their sins*" (vs. 21).

Jesus is the Greek form of the Hebrew name *Joshua*, which means "Yahweh saves" or "God saves." But, we ask, who are "his people"? What kind of people can Yahweh save through the One born of Mary? The answer flashes through from the genealogy: Jesus can save people like Tamar, Rahab, Ruth, Bathsheba, and David. He can save Gentiles, prostitutes, adulterers, deceivers, and murderers. He can save anyone! Thus we find Matthew preaching the gospel even in his genealogy.

Another important point to note about Matthew 1:21 is that it is a revolutionary proclamation of the Messiah's mission. Matthew had plainly set forth Jesus from verse 1 onward as the Messiah and the Son of David. In the Jewish mind, both titles had political overtones. The two titles came together in the vision of an earthly king. David had been an illustrious conquering warrior, and first-century Jews expected their Messiah-King to carry out the same program. The Messiah, or Christ, was to be a national deliverer.

For example, in a book called the Psalms of Solomon (written during the period between the Old and New Testaments), the anointed Son of David is a king who will arise from among the people to deliver Israel from its enemies. This Davidic king is to be endowed with supernatural gifts. "With a rod of iron he shall break in pieces all their substance, he shall destroy the godless nations with the word of his mouth" (Ps. of Sol. 17:26, 27). Likewise, in Fourth Ezra (a first-century A.D. apocalypse), the Messiah reigns over a temporary Messianic kingdom for some four hundred years (4 Ezra 7:28, 29).

There had been three great bondages in Israel's history: the Egyptian, the Babylonian, and now, the Roman. The first two had had political solutions. For first-century Jews, a Messiah who did not at least deliver the nation politically could hardly be considered a genuine Messiah. The Messianic hope of the Jews was built upon a king of David's line who would free them from the oppressor. It is in that light that we need to see the revolutionary significance of Matthew 1:21. With one inspired sentence, Matthew overturns the whole Jewish concept of the Messiah. *The Christ, he asserts, did not come to save His people from their Roman overlords but from their sins.* The fact that Jesus as the anointed Son of David did not come to save people from their enemies came as a terrible disappointment to the Jews of Christ's day, including the disciples. (It still comes as a disappointment to many.) One of Matthew's major tasks is to teach the true nature of Jesus' Messianic kingdom to a people who prefer the conquering-king model.

There is a sense, however, in which Jesus did come as a conquering king. He came to "save his people from their sins." Herman Ridderbos is undoubtedly correct when he writes: "Here the word 'sins' must be understood in its broadest sense, not only as the guilt and penalty of sin, but also its power and its consequences" (Ridderbos, 28).

In other words, Jesus did not come to save people *in* their sins but *from* their sins. A prominent focus of Jesus' work in Matthew's Gospel is to liberate His people from the imperialism of their own sins, from the control of sin over their daily actions.

Jesus came to enable us to conquer sin in our lives. That takes place at three levels. First, through His sinless life and His death on the cross, He saves His people from the penalty of sin. Ellen White puts this thought nicely when she writes that "Christ was treated as we deserve, that we might be treated as He deserves. He was condemned for our sins, in which He had no share, that we might be justified by His righteousness, in which we had no share. He suffered the death which was ours, that we might receive the life which was His. 'With His stripes we are healed' " (White, *Desire of Ages*, 25).

Second, Jesus saves His people, as we noted above, from the power of sin over their lives.

And third, Jesus will eventually save His people from the presence of sin, when He returns in the clouds of heaven to give them their eternal reward. All three of these "salvations" from sin are evident in Matthew's Gospel. Truly, Matthew's revolutionary Son of David-Messiah is One who "will save his people from their sins."

God With Us

Another revolutionary contribution of Matthew's first chapter is that the Messiah is " 'God with us' " (vs. 23). Earlier in his first chapter, Matthew has indicated that Jesus is the Messiah, the Son of David, and the Saviour from sin, with the last descriptor being a distinct modification of the militant Jewish concepts related to the Messianic reign of the Son of David. Matthew's fourth title for Jesus—Immanuel—also modifies those concepts. By the time of Jesus, the ideas of the Messiah and the Son of David had been combined in various ways into the hope of a powerful, kingly Davidic Messiah who would overthrow Israel's enemies, but the Jews looked for a literal descendant of David rather than a divine King.

Matthew's particular view of the divine Sonship of Jesus the Messiah-King is without parallel in the Old Testament. According to Matthew, Jesus is not the Son of God in the manner that the ancient Davidic kings, or Israelites in general, were sons of God. Rather, Jesus is the Son of God in that He was conceived by the Holy Spirit in the womb of a virgin.

Matthew's readers had been set up for that idea in Matthew 1:16, where Matthew concludes the earthly pedigree of Jesus by subtly shifting the line of thought from Joseph to Mary, the only human parent of Jesus.

The second half of Matthew 1 leaves Jesus' human pedigree and moves to His divine ancestry, plainly stating that His "Father" is the Holy Spirit. Thus Jesus is not exactly like other children. He is the God-Man. Being born of the Holy Spirit and the virgin Mary (vss. 18, 20, 23, 25), He is both divine and human.

Matthew claims that Jesus is the ultimate fulfillment of Isaiah 7:14. Jesus is Immanuel, or " 'God with us' " (vs. 23). That is perhaps the greatest claim in the New Testament. And the recognition that Jesus is truly the Son of God is a central point in the Gospel of Matthew (see, for example, 3:17; 16:16).

The apostle does not present Jesus as merely a great teacher. For Matthew, Jesus is no guru or seer, nor is He God's messenger in the sense that Mohammed is the messenger of Allah. No! Matthew is emphatic: Jesus is " 'God with us.' " Christianity is built upon that essential claim. It cannot be abandoned without totally abandoning the faith.

Nor does Matthew present Jesus as the God above us. God in the Old Testament is often pictured as above humanity. He is the God of the unapproachable Most Holy Place. But from the very first chapter of the New Testament, we begin to get another view, a fuller revelation of the Old Testament God. He is no longer the God *above* us but is present, through Jesus, as "God *with* us." Jesus, through His preaching, teaching, and healing acts of kindness, becomes the fullest revelation of the character of God. "Anyone," Jesus claimed, "who has seen me has seen the Father" (John 14:9). As Paul put it, God in Christ "humbled himself" and became a human being (Phil. 2:6-8). In the words of John, " 'God so loved the world that he gave his one and only Son' " (John 3:16).

In that only Son, we have "God with us," the Son of David and the Heir to David's throne and God's promises to David; we have the Messiah of God, the Child born of the Holy Spirit and the virgin Mary, One whose mission is to "save his people from their sins." That divine One is the theme, not only of Matthew's first chapter, but of his entire Gospel.

■ Getting Into the Word

Matthew 2

Read Matthew 2 through twice. On the second reading, begin to look for answers to the following items:

1. **In what way(s) is Matthew 2 a continuation of chapter 1? In answering that question, look for patterns that Matthew is developing. What is the significance of that continuation and those patterns?**
2. **One of Matthew's major themes begins to develop in chapter 2. That theme is varying responses to the "king of the Jews." Matthew 2 presents at least three possible responses to Jesus in the form of three sets of people (not including His parents). List those three groups, and outline the response of each. Are there other possible responses to Jesus? If so, what are they?**
3. **In what ways is "the great controversy" (or conflict) between Christ and Satan evident in Matthew 2?**
4. **Matthew 2 begins to introduce us to some of the principal people and places in Jesus' life. Some understanding of these people and places will better enable us to**

understand the Bible. Locate Bethlehem and Nazareth on the map of Palestine in the time of Jesus in the back of your Bible. Using the mileage indicators, approximate the distance of each of these cities from Jerusalem, remembering all the while that Jesus will walk between these cities many times during His ministry, and that most of the events of Jesus' life take place in the rather geographically restricted limits of Palestine. While Nazareth is not mentioned in the Old Testament, it is mentioned several times in the New Testament as the home of Jesus. Read John 1:46 to discover Nazareth's reputation among the Jews. What does that text signify about Jesus' hometown? With the help of a concordance, discover those New Testament texts that clearly indicate the Jewish understanding that the Messiah was to come from Bethlehem.

5. **You will understand Matthew 2 much better if you have some grasp of its main characters. Look up in a Bible dictionary Herod the Great and Archelaus. In what ways do their personal characterizations help you to comprehend Matthew 2? You may also want to use a Bible dictionary to see what you can discover about the Magi.**

■ Exploring the Word

Recognition of the King: A Mixed Bag

One of the most obvious things a reader notices about Matthew 2 is that it is a continuation of chapter 1 in its presentation of Jesus as a fulfillment of Old Testament prophecy. Thus, while Matthew's first chapter presents Jesus as the Son of both David and Abraham and as "Immanuel" or " 'God with us,' " his second chapter presents Jesus as a fulfillment of prophecy in that He was born in Bethlehem, was called out of Egypt and grew up in Nazareth. Matthew even indicates that the slaying of Bethlehem's baby boys was a prophetic fulfillment.

At every possible point, Matthew drives home the items most

important to his Jewish readers. He is out to demonstrate that the Old Testament prophecies are fulfilled in Jesus, who thereby qualifies as the promised Messiah that the Jewish nation has been looking for.

While that fact is still of utmost interest and importance to modern readers, Matthew 2 has another emphasis that is especially relevant for current students of the Gospel; namely, the varied responses to the kingship of Jesus. That topic is important, because every person, when confronted with His claims, must respond to Jesus in one way or another. Matthew 2 presents three possible responses to Jesus' kingship. Those responses form a developing theme in Matthew's Gospel—the reception and rejection of Jesus as the Christ.

The first response is that of King Herod (73–4 B.C.). The Bible says Herod was "disturbed" when the Magi (wisemen) came seeking " 'the one who has been born king of the Jews' " (vss. 3, 2).

Any king would have been disturbed by the report that a child who was to occupy his throne had been born, but Herod had more reasons to be upset than most. For one thing, Herod the Great was not even Jewish by birth, but an Idumean (one of the descendants of the ancient Edomites). His Gentile blood, of course, made Herod suspect in the eyes of the Jews, who, as we noted above, had an obsession with racial purity.

Herod, however, was a Jew by religious profession and citizenship. Beyond that, Rome had appointed him to be king of the Jews in 37 B.C. In order to make himself more acceptable to the Jews he ruled, Herod married Mariamne, heiress of the Jewish Hasmonean royal line.

Another example of Herod's desire to please the Jews was his reconstruction of the temple in Jerusalem. He began that project in 20 B.C. and kept at it until his death in 4 B.C. The rebuilding continued for some six decades after that, coming to completion shortly before the fall of Jerusalem in A.D. 70.

That Herod the Great was not all bad is evidenced by the fact that in 25 B.C. he melted down his own gold to purchase food for starving Jews. In addition, he was a great builder of cities and public buildings. These projects provided work for a large number of Jews. Nothing, however, could enable Herod to overcome Jewish animosity toward his birth.

He was, therefore, in an unstable political position. That insecurity, when linked with an inordinate desire for power and an almost insane suspicion of others, made him ruthless when he sensed any threat to his power.

Anyone who threatened Herod was promptly eliminated. Thus, soon after making Aristobulus (his brother-in-law through his marriage to Mariamne) high priest, Herod had him "accidentally" drowned in the palace pool, when he realized the youth's popularity as the last male of the Hasmonean family. Herod later provided Aristobulus a magnificent funeral, at which the king pretended to weep.

Mariamne, Herod's favorite wife, soon shared her brother's fate, when Herod suspected her of plotting against him. That same fear led to the death of her grandfather and two of Herod's sons. Five days before his death (soon after Jesus was born), he had a third son, his oldest and thus his heir, executed. During his reign, Herod purged all who had any royal Hasmonean blood in their veins. Roman Emperor Augustus bitterly claimed that it was safer to be Herod's pig than his son.

Here was a king who would brook no challenge or threat to his authority. And it was in Herod's territory that Jesus was born in Bethlehem! It is little wonder that Herod was "disturbed" at the wisemen's question, "Where is the one who has been born king of the Jews?" Nor should we be surprised to find him killing all the male children in Bethlehem under two years of age in an attempt to eliminate a potential rival.

One of the greatest evidences of Herod's ruthlessness is that he had Jerusalem's most distinguished citizens imprisoned shortly before his end. He knew no one would mourn his own death, so he gave orders for execution of the prisoners the moment he died. In that way, Herod believed he could guarantee weeping rather than rejoicing at his death. Such was the nature of Judea's ruler when Jesus was born in Bethlehem as "king of the Jews." The killing of twenty to thirty children in Bethlehem was in keeping with everything we know about Herod the Great.

Herod's response to Jesus was one of rejection and murder. Fortunately, that was not the only reaction.

A second response to the birth of He "who has been born king of the Jews" was that of "the Magi from the east" (vs. 1). The Magi of Matthew 2 probably came from Persia, where they formed the priestly class. These men were learned for their day, being skilled in such areas as philosophy, medicine, and natural science.

One of their main interests, however, was astrology. Although frowned upon by the Old Testament, astrology was prevalent throughout the ancient world as a way of discerning the purposes of the gods. Thus when the Magi saw the supernatural "star" (vs. 2), they set out to discover its significance.

We do not know exactly how they came to connect the special star with the birth of the "king of the Jews," but there are several indications. For one thing, those Jews who did not return from the Babylonian captivity in the sixth century B.C. were still scattered in communities throughout the Near East and the Mediterranean world. And since the second century B.C., these scattered Jews had had a Greek (the universal language of the time) translation of the Bible. Thus learned men—especially priestly types—would have had access to the Septuagint (Greek) version of the Old Testament.

Of special significance to the astrological interest of the Magi would have been the words of another Gentile Magi in Numbers 24:17, where Balaam declared: "A star will come out of Jacob; a scepter will rise out of Israel." That very text was being interpreted by many Jews about the time of Jesus' birth as a prediction of the coming Messiah.

That specific expectation and the more general Jewish expectation of the coming Messiah-King apparently led to a widespread belief in the Roman Empire that a world ruler would arise in Palestine. Thus the Roman historian Suetonius (c. A.D. 100) could write: "There had spread over all the Orient an old and established belief, that it was fated at that time for men coming from

Judea to rule the world" (*Life of Vespasian*, 4:5). Tacitus (c. A.D. 55–120), another Roman historian, wrote that "there was a firm persuasion . . . that at this very time the East was to grow powerful, and rulers coming from Judea were to acquire universal empire" (*Histories*, 5:13).

With these thoughts in mind, it should not seem too unusual that the Magi followed the star in their search for "the one who ha[d] been born king of the Jews" (vs. 2). In addition to the above information, we should keep in mind the possibility that the God who "warned" the Magi "in a dream not to go back to Herod" (vs. 12) may also have given them dreams concerning the "star" and its significance before they began their search.

The important point in the story is that the wisemen responded positively to God's guidance. They followed the star and found the "king of the Jews."

And after finding Jesus, they "bowed down and worshiped him" (vs. 11). This fact is crucial in Matthew's portrayal, because, according to the Ten Commandments, the Jews had been commanded not to "bow down" or "worship" anything but God Himself (Exod. 20:3-5). By emphasizing the Magi's bowing down and worshiping in a book written for Jews, Matthew is plainly claiming that Jesus the Christ is none other than " 'God with us' "—a theme he began to emphasize in chapter 1 and will continue to highlight throughout his Gospel.

The Magi's interchange with Jesus did not end with their bowing down in adoration, but extended to the more tangible presentation of their gifts of wealth to Him (vs. 11). Worship never takes place just in our minds. To the contrary, it spills over into the world of everyday life as men and women, following the example of the Magi, give themselves and their wealth in response to Him who "so loved the world that he gave his one and only Son" (John 3:16).

The Magi's giving was as much an act of worship as was their bowing. Beyond that, their giving provided the much-needed means for Joseph to take the young King to Egypt, where He would be safe from the evil intentions of Herod the Great.

A third response to Jesus in Matthew 2 is that of the Jewish leaders. Matthew tells us that "all Jerusalem" was "disturbed" by the arrival of the Magi and their statements and questions regarding the birth of the "king of the Jews" (vss. 2, 3). The Jewish leaders understood the import of the Magi's mission and were able to pinpoint the fact that according to Micah 5:2, the Messiah would be born in Bethlehem (vss. 4-6).

The great tragedy of Matthew 2, however, is that the Jewish leaders were apparently "disturbed" because of their fear of what Herod might do, rather than being excited about the possible arrival of the Messiah. Matthew paints their response to Christ as one of utter indifference. They made no trips to Bethlehem; they gave no evidence of Herod's fear and hate, nor did they display the interest of the worshiping Magi. *They didn't care.*

Thus Matthew skillfully presents the three possible responses to "Jesus, who is called Christ" (1:16): violent rejection, worship, and indifference. With that portrayal, Matthew advances several themes that he will more fully develop as he moves through his presentation of Christ's life.

One of those themes is that the coming of Jesus always divides people and brings conflict. Confronted by His life, teachings, and claims, every person is forced into responding in terms of (1) praise and welcome, (2) hatred and opposition, or (3) cold indifference.

A second Matthean theme highlighted in chapter 2 is that of Gentile acceptance and adoration of Jesus the King versus Jewish rejection. Both are paradoxical. While a reader might expect the Jews to anticipate and welcome their King, one would hardly expect a Gospel that was written to convince the Jews of Jesus' Messiahship to paint the Gentile Magi in such a favorable light.

In fact, nowhere else in the New Testament are Magi spoken of in favorable terms. In many ways Matthew's presentation of the Magi in chapter 2 is as startling as his treatment of the four women in chapter 1. Magicians and astrologers were just as despised by the Jews as were prostitutes and profligates. Yet Matthew presents them as entering the kingdom, while the Jews are left on the outside. This theme also extends throughout his Gospel—a Gospel that closes with a command by Christ to His followers to "make disciples of all nations" (28:19).

A final theme in Matthew that is related to the responses to Christ in chapter 2 is the idea that "Herod is not merely the Gospel villain; he is Everyman" (Bruner, 1:51). There is a Herod in each of us. The essence of "Herodism" is that he was king of his realm and life, and he permitted no competition from Christ or anyone else. Herod's problem is the core problem of sin.

Every sinner desires to be his or her own king, his or her own God. Self-centeredness stands at the center of sin. Thus crucifixion of the egocentric self is a prerequisite for citizenship in the kingdom of heaven. Matthew will more fully develop that theme throughout his Gospel as Christ moves toward His cross and repeatedly tells His disciples that they must also submit to a crucifixion (16:21-28; 10:38, 39).

When the Herod in me (or you) meets God in Christ Jesus, something must give way. Either we will eventually crucify Him, or we will let Him crucify us. In the long run, there is no middle ground with King Jesus. "No one can serve two masters" (6:24).

■ Applying the Word

Matthew 1, 2

1. **What lessons can I gain from the story of the four women (excluding Mary) in Matthew 1 for my personal life?**
2. **If I had lived in Jesus' day, what kind of king would I have wanted? Why? If I am *honest* with myself, do I most want a king who can give me material wealth or one who can save me *from* my sins? How is that value expressed in my everyday life?**
3. **What is my personal response to King Jesus? Is it that of Herod or the Magi, or have I put off my response through indifference?**
4. **What "gifts" do I have that I can offer to Christ? In what ways can I better express my offering this very day?**

5. Do I really have a "Herod" in me? If so, what am I doing about it?
6. If God let Jesus grow up in a place like Nazareth (John 1:46), why do I sometimes excuse my shortcomings by blaming them on my birthplace or my lack of advantages?
7. What lessons can I learn from Matthew's genealogy about the "naive" use of texts to prove this point or that? What can I learn about reading the Bible from the genealogy?

■ Researching the Word

1. Compare Matthew 1:22, 23 with Isaiah 7:14 in the New International Version. Compare the same texts in the Revised Standard Version or the New English Bible. Compare your findings with the translation of Isaiah 7:14 in other modern translations. Look up the Hebrew meaning of the word *virgin* in Isaiah 7:14 in the *NIV Exhaustive Concordance* or *Strong's Exhaustive Concordance*. What does the *SDA Bible Commentary* say about this word in Isaiah and Matthew? How can this brief study help you to be more sensitive to problems in Bible translation? What does it teach us about the New Testament writers' use of Old Testament words?
2. Each of the four Gospels presents the birth and early years (up to age thirty) of Jesus from a different angle. Read the accounts in each Gospel. Then on a clean page in your Matthew notebook, make four vertical columns (one for each Gospel). Next, outline the contribution of each Gospel in its respective column. Why do you think the writers took such vastly different approaches? Is the variety good or bad? Why?

■ Further Study of the Word

1. For general insight, see E. G. White, *The Desire of Ages*, 19-92.
2. For more information on Matthew's use of Old Testa-

ment quotations, see R. H. Gundry, *The Use of the Old Testament in St. Matthew's Gospel.*

3. For more information on the relationship between Matthew's and Luke's genealogies, see F. D. Nichol, ed., *Seventh-day Adventist Bible Commentary*, 5:721-722; 276-282; D. A. Carson, "Matthew," 8:63-65.

CHAPTER TWO

Preparing the King for Service

Matthew 3:1–4:16

Matthew's first two chapters present us with Jesus' human and divine credentials and set forth three possible responses to Him. They also indicate that the focal point of Jesus' work will be to "save his people from their sins" (1:21).

The next two chapters resume the story of the divine/human Messiah-King after He has reached maturity and is ready to enter upon His public ministry. Chapter 3 introduces us to John the Baptist and the baptism of Jesus. The first sixteen verses of chapter 4 take us through Jesus' temptations and lead us up to the beginning of His preaching ministry and the calling of the first disciples.

Thus Matthew 3:1 through 4:16 forms the crucial bridge between the infant narratives of King Jesus found in Matthew 1 and 2 and the beginning of His public ministry in 4:17-25 and the enunciation of the principles of His kingdom in chapters 5 to 7. Matthew 3:1–4:16 might best be thought of as the final steps in both the preparation for *and* of *the King before He begins His all-important public ministry.*

■ Getting Into the Word

Matthew 3

Read through Matthew 3 two times. During the second reading, begin to wrestle with the following questions and issues.

1. We left Jesus in chapter 2 as a young child. Now He is thirty years old. He will die at age thirty-three. Examine the second chapter of Luke to discover the *only* story preserved by any of the Gospel writers from the missing years in Jesus' life. Why do you think Matthew skipped over nearly the entire earthly life of Jesus? In a short paragraph, explain what you think this means concerning the difference between Matthew's Gospel (or any other of the Gospels) and a more traditional biography. How does that difference relate to the difference in purpose between a Gospel and a traditional biography?
2. Make a list of the personal characteristics of John the Baptist. How would you characterize John as a person? Use the marginal reference to 3:4 to unlock the symbolic significance of John's clothes. For the full implications of that symbolism, look up the references to Elijah in Malachi and Matthew in a concordance.
3. Through the use of your Bible's marginal reference, find the Old Testament location for the quotation in 3:3. What major change related to the individual in the last line of that quotation did Matthew make? What is the implication of that change?
4. List the major characteristics of John's message in 3:2-12. What do you consider to be the two most important focal points of that message? Why did you select those two as being more significant than other aspects of his message?
5. An understanding of certain key words in Matthew 3 will help you understand the chapter better. Look up such words as *repent*, *kingdom of heaven*, *baptism*, *Pharisee*, and *Sadducee* in a Bible dictionary.
6. Why did Jesus need to be baptized? In a paragraph or two, describe how Jesus' need to be baptized differs from ours.
7. List the major events that took place at Jesus' baptism in verses 16 and 17. In a few sentences, explain the significance of *each* of those events for the Gospel story and the plan of salvation.

■ Exploring the Word

The King's Forerunner

"In those days," claims Matthew 3:1, "John the Baptist came, preaching." With that short phrase, Matthew skips over nearly ten-elevenths of Jesus' entire life. Missing entirely is any account of His childhood, youth, or early adulthood. Chapter 2 left Him as a young child in Nazareth, and chapter 3 picks up the story at the time of His baptism by John, when, Luke tells us, He was "about thirty years old" (Luke 3:23).

The only story any of the Gospel writers give us about Jesus in the thirty-year interim is Luke's contribution of the incident of the Boy Jesus in the temple, when He declared to Joseph and His mother that He had absented Himself from them because He needed to be in His "Father's house" (Luke 2:49) or, alternately, to be about His "Father's business" (KJV). The only other thing the New Testament tells us about the missing years of Jesus' life is that He "grew in wisdom and stature, and in favor with God and men" (Luke 2:52).

The total silence of Matthew, Mark, and John and the almost total silence of Luke on most of Jesus' life tells us something about the nature of the Gospels: They are "abnormal biographies." Matthew's Gospel, like those of the other three evangelists, is not a well-balanced account of Jesus' life. Rather, it is an "unbalanced" account that, as we shall see, gives a disproportionate amount of space to the events leading up to Jesus' death and resurrection. Whereas "normal" biography focuses on the total life span of the central figure and may give a very small portion of pages to the hero's death, Matthew and his fellows turn those proportions on their head. Why, we might ask? The reason is that Jesus was no ordinary person. Thus His biography could not be an ordinary biography. Rather, it would be the story of the God/man who came to earth to "save his people from their sins" (1:21) by dying for the sins of the world (26:28; 16:21). This disproportion is due to the fact that Jesus' death and His victory over death form the crucial part of the story. Without His death and resurrection, there would be no need to tell the rest of the story.

From beginning to end, the Gospel focus is on the hopelessness of sinful human beings and God's remedy for that hopelessness through Jesus. As a result, Matthew selects the content for his Gospel on the basis of its contribution to an understanding of the saving mission of Jesus.

One crucial element in that understanding is the role of John the Baptist as Jesus' forerunner. Four hundred years before the birth of Jesus, the prophet Malachi set forth the idea that a forerunner would usher in the Messianic age. Malachi prophesied that the forerunner would be the prophet Elijah (Mal. 4:5). Matthew picks up on that allusion to the forerunner when he pens that "John's clothes were made of camel's hair, and he had a leather belt around his waist" (vs. 4). It is no accident that 2 Kings 1:8 gives the same description of Elijah's clothes. In effect, Matthew, through his description of John's dress, identifies him as the prophesied forerunner of the Messianic kingdom and its King. Matthew will return to that theme in 11:14.

Meanwhile, Matthew couples the Elijah symbolism with a second allusion to the forerunner that he gleaned from the Old Testament. In verse 3 Matthew quotes Isaiah 40:3 and identifies it as a prediction that John would come as " 'a voice of one calling in the desert, "Prepare the way for the Lord, make straight paths for him." ' " The imagery in Isaiah's word picture is the preparation of roads in anticipation of a visit from the king. That, suggests Matthew, is John's function. He is a preparer of the way.

The point to note about Matthew's use of Isaiah 40:3 is that he provides a major shift in the prophet's meaning. Whereas Isaiah says that the paths are to be made straight for "God," Matthew replaces "God" with "him"—that is, Jesus. Thus Matthew's readers are getting another dose of the teaching he first set forth in 1:23—that Jesus the Christ is really " 'God with us.' " In simple yet skilled ways, our writer will continually drive home the major themes of his Gospel.

Matthew's overall picture of John's clothing and diet is one of simplicity. His lifestyle is well in harmony with one preaching a message of repentance.

But while the Baptist's lifestyle may have been simple, his message is both complex and profound. It includes at least six elements. First and foremost, John's message is a call for repentance (vs. 2). That very call once again places John in the line of the prophet Elijah, whose ministry centered around his confrontation with Ahab, Jezebel, and an apostate priesthood as he called both Israel and its leaders to repent of their ways.

The Greek words for *repentance* can be translated as "to change one's mind" or "to change one's way of thinking." But in John's mind, and throughout the New Testament in general, repentance implies not only a change of mind but also a changed life. As a result, John demands that his hearers "produce fruit in keeping with repentance" (vs. 8). Mental convictions of right are not enough. John is calling for a change in the orientation of his hearers' entire lives that results in lives lived according to God's principles.

A second element in the Baptist's preaching is that " 'the kingdom of heaven is near' " (vs. 2). That announcement implies that the fulfillment of prophecy is at hand, that God will once again reveal Himself as Israel's King, as the prophets have foretold (see, for example, Mic. 4:7; Zech. 14:9). The end of one age has arrived. The next will soon begin. The heavenly kingdom will soon break into the earthly realm; God's salvation and judgment will soon confront the nations of the earth.

These ideas were common in Jewish thinking before John. His contribution to the topic was the *nearness* of the kingdom.

The nearness in itself would not have been so frightful, but in Jewish thought, the arrival of the kingdom would be a time of judgment as God punished the wicked and rewarded the just. And that judgment element forms a third and indispensable aspect of the Baptist's message. As a result, he can speak of " 'the coming wrath' " (vs. 7), the ax already being " 'at the root of the trees' " (vs. 10), and the One to come as One who would " 'gather his wheat into the granary' " but burn the chaff " 'with unquenchable fire' " (vs. 12, RSV).

It is in light of both the nearness and the magnitude of the coming kingdom that John cries for his hearers to produce both repentance and "fruit" (lives) in line with that repentance.

Unfortunately, as John sees it, the Jews and their leaders do not understand either the depth of the needed repentance or the meaning of the needed fruit. They have misunderstood the terms of salvation. This brings us to a fourth element in John's frightful message: the uselessness of religious pedigrees. Being children of Abraham will not be sufficient to get anyone through the coming judgment (vs. 9). To many Jews, it was unthinkable that the great patriarch's descendants should be excluded from God's blessing.

The Jews are not the only people to have imbibed that thought. Many Christians in their various strands (e.g., Catholic, Baptist, Adventist, and so on) have had similar thoughts. But all such thinking is fallacious. After all, " 'out of these stones God can raise up children for Abraham' " (vs. 9). God was not dependent upon the children of Abraham to accomplish His purposes in the time of John, nor is He dependent upon any certain group in the twentieth century. What counts with God, according to John, is a repentant heart and a life that is characterized by healthy fruit bearing.

Thus the fifth aspect of John's message is confession and baptism (vs. 6). The populace has responded to his preaching. They have gone "out to him from Jerusalem and all Judea and the whole region of the Jordan" (vs. 5). In the Baptist they sense the power and characteristics of Elijah and the prophets. They sense the genuineness of both John's person and his message. Even the religious leaders of the day (the Pharisees and Sadducees) are inspired to make their appearance and undergo John's ministrations, only to be challenged by the Baptist's condemnation of them. It is after their arrival that John gives his speech about Abraham. Apparently the lay and clerical religious leaders of the Jewish church have been especially prone to take confidence in their denominational affiliation.

John's demand for all those who came to him was for confession of sin and baptism. Now, baptism was nothing new to the Jews. They regularly employed baptism in admitting Gentiles as converts to Judaism. But John took the process a giant step forward in calling for Jews by birth to be baptized. That was the shocking part of his work. The unprecedented baptism of Jews undoubtedly gave John notoriety and brought many to hear him.

In effect, he was saying that it is not enough to merely be born a child of Abraham. Jews also must confess their sins and be washed clean from their past by the cleansing waters of baptism. Thus many "were baptized by him in the Jordan River" (vs. 6).

Such confession and baptism must have been some of the " 'fruit in keeping with repentance' " (vs. 8). In light of the rapidly approaching coming of the kingdom, John is calling for Israelite believers to turn from their old ways of thinking and acting to a new way of life.

The subject of baptism brings us to John's climactic theme—Jesus. According to John, his water baptism is only a symbolic foreshadowing of the more important baptism that will be administered by the One who is to come after him. The coming One will not baptize merely with water but with "the Holy Spirit and with fire" (vs. 11). While it is not crystal clear as to how Jesus will baptize with the Holy Spirit and fire, the most likely suggestion is that "he will baptize the truly penitent in the grace of the Holy Spirit, and that he will baptize the impenitent in the fire of judgment" (Bruner, 1:80). That suggestion certainly fits into both the general context of Matthew 3 and the specific context of verse 12, which pictures Jesus in the last judgment wielding a winnowing fork and "gathering the wheat into his barn [i.e., heaven] and burning up the chaff with unquenchable fire [hell]" (see also Rev. 14:14-20).

The King's Anointing

One of the most shocking things in Matthew 3 is that Jesus comes to be baptized by John. After all, hasn't John already publicly announced Jesus as the One who will baptize with a baptism that is superior to his own (vs. 11)? And now Jesus shows up as a recipient of baptism as His first adult action in the Gospel story. No wonder John is shocked.

And then consider the meaning of John's baptism. It is the baptism of repentance, accompanied by confession, and here is One presenting Himself for baptism who needs neither repentance nor confession. Given the facts, it is little wonder that John remonstrates with Jesus, claiming that he has need of being baptized by Him rather than vice versa (vs. 14).

But Jesus won't take No for an answer. He tells John to "let it be so *now*," thereby implying that their relationship will change in the future as Jesus' Lordship comes more into the open. In the meantime, He tells the Baptist, "It is proper for us to do this to fulfill all righteousness" (vs. 15). These words, included only by Matthew among the Gospel writers, have given rise to much discussion concerning their exact meaning.

The meaning of Jesus' words here need to be viewed in the context of John's entire message in Matthew 3. Thus Jesus' use of *righteousness* appears to refer to the quality of life that John has demanded of his baptismal candidates. "By submitting to baptism," suggests Michael Green, "Jesus acknowledged God's claim on him as on others for total consecration of life and holiness of character" (M. Green, 61).

John's baptism is a symbol of that total dedication. Under these circumstances, John "consents" to baptize his acknowledged superior.

There were undoubtedly other reasons for Jesus' baptism. One was that by the end of His own ministry, He would be urging baptism upon His followers (28:19). From that perspective, Christ's baptism can be seen as providing an example for others to emulate. Thus Ellen White can claim that "Jesus did not receive baptism as a confession of guilt on His own account. He identified Himself with sinners, taking the steps that we are to take, and doing the work that we must do" (White, *The Desire of Ages*, 111).

It should never be forgotten that though He was personally sinless, Jesus identified with sinners throughout His life. Not only did He end His ministry on a cross between two thieves, but He began His public work in a river among penitent sinners. Matthew consistently pictures Jesus as " 'God with us.' "

Jesus' baptism should also be seen as the public announcement of the Messiah's arrival and the beginning of His ministry. Not only did it give John the opportunity to publicly announce Jesus as Messiah and Saviour (John 1:29-34), but it also provided God the Father with the opportunity for a public validation, even though it is impossible to gauge how many of those present understood what took place after Jesus' baptism.

At the very least, John and Jesus must have caught the significance of the events of Matthew 3:16, 17, but one can only speculate that those who were spiritually in tune with God must have had some inkling of the mysteries that took place as Jesus came out of the water. Of course, by the time the Gospels were penned, God had revealed the import of the postbaptismal events for posterity.

Those events, as set forth by Matthew, were three in number. First, the heavens opened, symbolizing that communication between heaven and earth was being restored (compare Ezek. 1:1). Since the death of the last of the Hebrew prophets (Haggai, Zechariah, and Malachi) some four hundred years before, there had been no direct visions from the Holy Spirit in Israel. The opening of heaven symbolized that the period of prophetic barrenness was over.

Beyond that, the opening of heaven prepared the way for the second postbaptismal event—"the Spirit of God descending like a dove and lighting on him" (vs. 16). That event should not be taken to imply that Jesus did not have the Holy Spirit before His baptism. After all, He was the Son of Mary "through the Holy Spirit" (1:18). Rather, it "marks a turning point in salvation-history, for only after the Spirit comes does the Messiah's ministry begin (cf. Acts 10.38); and it sets Jesus in line with certain national leaders of the OT—Gideon (Judg 6.34), Samson (15.14), Saul (1 Sam 10.6)—upon whom the Spirit came and with the prophets" (Davies and Allison, 1:335). Time after time in the Old Testament, individuals began their work for God *after* the Spirit rested upon them. So it was with Jesus (see also Isa. 11:1, 2).

The third postbaptismal event was the voice from heaven saying, " 'This is my Son, whom I love; with him I am well pleased' " (vs. 17). Those words demonstrated that truly heaven had been opened.

But more astounding than the event was the content of the message. The words from heaven were a fusion of two Old Testament verses—Psalm 2:7 and Isaiah 42:1. All Jews accepted Psalm 2 as a description of the Messiah, the King of God, who was to come. The quotation from Isaiah 42 ("with him I am well pleased" [3:17]) begins a passage on the Servant of Yahweh, whose destiny is to suffer abuse or opposition. With these facts in mind, William Barclay concludes that "in the baptism there came to Jesus two certainties—the certainty that He was indeed the chosen One of God, and the certainty that the way in front of Him was the way of the Cross. In that moment He knew that He was chosen to be King, but He also knew that His throne must be a Cross" (Barclay, 1:53).

Thus Jesus was to be both Messianic Son and suffering Servant. The descent of the Spirit, however, not only set Jesus apart for ministry, but it equipped Him for His task. Beyond that, it was the Spirit who led Jesus into the next step in His earthly experience.

■ Getting Into the Word

Matthew 4:1-16

Read Matthew 4:1-16 through at least two times. On your final reading, begin to examine the following questions and issues.

1. **List the common elements between 3:16, 17 and 4:1, 2. How do these common elements demonstrate the linkage between the story of the baptism in chapter 3 and that of the temptations in chapter 4?**

2. **List the common elements in the three temptations. Along that line, note the differences in the manner that the devil addresses Jesus in the third temptation, as opposed to the first two. In a paragraph or two, put down your thoughts regarding the impact of the common elements. In like manner, set forth your thoughts regarding the difference of approach in the third temptation.**
3. **Do you find any elements of progression in the three temptations? If so, what are they?**
4. **What is the overall significance of the story of the temptations to the development of Matthew's presentation? Note what you believe to be the essence or central implication of each temptation. Does the Holy Spirit ever lead anyone into temptation?**

■ Exploring the Word

The King's Test

All three Synoptic Gospels place the temptations of Jesus immediately after His baptism and the divine manifestation of His Sonship. Jesus is now ready to enter publicly into His work of introducing people to the kingdom of God. The crucial question facing Him is *how* He should fulfill His task. He left His baptism, as we saw in our previous section, with parts of Psalm 2:7 ("this is my Son") and Isaiah 42:1 ("with him I am well pleased") ringing in His ears (3:17). The first of these passages alludes to a possible role as a conquering King, the second to that of suffering Servant. The most important choice facing Christ at the beginning of His ministry is the very nature of that ministry. Will He adopt the path of the conquering King or of the suffering Servant? Will He opt for a throne or a cross? The temptations of Jesus must be seen in terms of their Messianic import.

The great temptation of Christ throughout His earthly life was to avoid the cross of the suffering Servant. That temptation stands at the core of Matthew 4. Additionally, as Matthew makes clear, that temptation will continue to be seen at the great crisis points in Christ's life right up through Gethsemane, as He wrestles with doing God's will (see, for example, 16:21-24; 26:36-44).

In chapter 4 Matthew introduces us to Christ's major antagonist in the great controversy between good and evil. He is called "the devil" in verse 1 and "the tempter" in verse 3, and in verse 10 Christ calls him Satan (adversary)—his proper name since his fall. Prior to chapter 4, the devil has been active behind the scenes, as with Herod, but now he comes to the forefront.

It should be noted that neither God nor the Holy Spirit is the active agent in Christ's temptation. Matthew is quite careful in his wording: "Then Jesus was led by the Spirit into the desert to be tempted *by the devil*" (vs. 1). James plainly tells us that God tempts no one (James 1:13). But God does allow His followers to be tempted for the development of their characters. Christians should not feel they are out of harmony with God when they come to straight places. After all, Christ's temptations came right after His spiritual high at His baptism. God's followers are not exempt from the pressures of the world. Rather, they are given strength to resist those pressures (1 Cor. 10:13). So it was with Jesus. He was faced with the common temptations of all humankind, yet, He found victory (Heb. 4:15).

The devil first approaches Jesus at the point of His greatest immediate need—food. Christ, in the tradition of Moses (Exod. 34:28) and Elijah (1 Kings 19:8), has been without food for forty days, and, as Matthew puts it, "he was hungry" (vs. 2). Satan, as he does with all of us, latches onto Jesus' immediate need as a possible entering wedge into the citadel of His soul.

Here is a genuine need, and Jesus can fill it for Himself if He chooses to. With that in mind, the devil picks up on the very words that Christ has heard the Father speak at His baptism. "This is my Son," God has affirmed (3:17). Satan puts his own twist on these words: " '*If* you are the Son of God,' " he challenges, " 'tell these stones to become bread' " (vs. 3). As with Eve in the Garden of Eden, the adversary's first point of attack is to create doubt and distrust in God and the truthfulness of His Word (Gen. 3:1). Thus the " '*if* you are.' "

It should be recognized at the outset that the temptation to make bread out of stones is a Messianic temptation, aimed at One who not only has the power to carry out the act but knows that He has it.

The temptation to make bread out of stones is no temptation at all to you and me. We could spend the next three years in the rock garden behind the church parking lot commanding stones to become bread and never have a loaf to show for it. But—and this is the point—Jesus, as the agent of all creation (John 1:3), could make bread out of stones, or even out of nothing.

Some Christians engage in endless discussion of what it meant for Jesus to be tempted "in every respect . . . as we are, yet without sin" (Heb. 4:15, RSV). It seems from a simple reading of the Bible that irrespective of the constitution of His human nature, Jesus was tempted far beyond what any other person can ever be tempted. Most of His temptations are not even temptations to us, because we lack the ability to respond to them successfully.

While Jesus was undoubtedly hungry, and while the suggestion to make bread out of stones must have been attractive, we miss the point if we see the first temptation as merely a temptation to satisfy His appetite. At the core, it was a temptation for Jesus to use His divine power to satisfy His own needs. To do so would have meant that He had opted not to live like every other child of Adam. To take such a course would have been fatal to the plan of redemption, since Jesus would at that point have reneged on His plan to come to earth to live as a human being. Using His own power to help Himself would have indicated that Jesus had opted to become a political King rather than God's suffering Servant.

Even more central to the bread temptation was its implications for avoiding the all-important cross. By creating bread out of stones, Jesus could have set up an immediate economic/political kingdom, and the Jews would have followed Him gladly. That is clear from John 6, where Jesus fed the five thousand. In that miracle the Jews saw the predicted prophet who would be like Moses (Deut. 18:18). After all, hadn't Jesus performed an equivalent to the manna miracle? John writes: "After the people saw the miraculous sign that Jesus did, they began to say, 'Surely this is the Prophet who is to come into the world.' " Their intention was to "make him king by force" (6:14, 15). Even the disciples got caught up in the move to make Jesus into a political Messiah at that time (Matt. 14:22).

At the heart of the bread temptation is the temptation for Jesus to establish His kingdom without a cross, the temptation for Him to become the political/economic/military Messiah that the Jews expected. In responding to Satan, Jesus rejects the road of grandeur for the road of the cross. He chooses, rather, to become God's suffering Servant, in whom God can be well pleased.

It should be noted that in all three temptations Jesus responds to the devil with words from the Bible. " 'It is written,' " is His consistent reply. His three responses come from Deuteronomy 8:3, 6:16, and 6:13. Jesus was a student of Scripture.

In spite of their differences, the second and third temptations need to be viewed in the same light as the first. If Jesus' first temptation came at His greatest point of immediate weakness (hunger), the second is aimed at His greatest point of strength—His familiarity with the Bible and God's promises. Quoting from Psalm 91:11, 12, Satan suggests that Jesus should jump to fame (vss. 5-7). Taking Jesus to the pinnacle of the Jerusalem temple, Satan, quoting Scripture, suggests that Jesus can prove His divinity by jumping into the milling throng below.

Absurd as it may seem to us, that wasn't a bad idea. After all, weren't the Jews always looking for a "sign" (12:38; 1 Cor. 1:22) by which to identify the Messiah when He came? Here is the perfect sign. A jump from the top of the temple, towering more than four hundred feet above the Valley of Hinnom below, would be impressive indeed! Malachi had predicted that " 'the Lord whom you seek will suddenly come to his temple' " (Mal. 3:1, RSV), and certain rabbis had predicted that "when the king Messiah appears, he will come stand on the roof of the Temple" (*Pesikta Rabbati*, 36).

For the Jews, there was nothing like fulfilling a Bible prophecy. The people would easily line up behind that type of Messiah. They wanted a spectacular Messiah. The public temple jump was a temptation precisely because it would be a more popular and painless way to win a following than a crucifixion. And its results would have been immediate.

But Jesus once again answers Satan from the Bible. This time, He pits Scripture against Scripture (" 'It is *also* written' "—vs. 7), which is particularly appropriate in this instance, since Satan has misapplied his passage from Psalm 91. In His answer, Jesus teaches us that mere quotations from inspired writings are not enough. Those quotations must be accurately interpreted for meaning within their specific context and within the overall context of the character of God. To run with quotations out of context may make a person into a fanatic, but such a practice cannot make individuals into followers of Matthew's Jesus.

The third temptation is aimed at the very purpose for which Jesus has come to the earth. He can become World Ruler (and presumably in the process rescue His people from their sin [1:21]) *if* He will only bow down and worship Satan (vs. 9). The point of the third temptation is that the Jews rightly perceived world dominion to be a Messianic function (Isa. 2:2; Jer. 3:17). The people of Israel were ready for a political Messiah who would overthrow hated Rome.

But Jesus will have nothing to do with the devil or his methods. He has gone into the temptations with the tension between the modes of conquering King and suffering Servant ringing in His ears. He will come out of the experience with His mind made up. He will follow God's way of suffering Servant, the way that will eventually lead to a distasteful cross. In the long run, that is the only valid way to the goal of conquering King (see Rev. 19).

The temptation is over. Jesus has chosen God's way rather than the route of convenience and least resistance. He has opted for the way of the cross—the cross that will climax Matthew's Gospel.

Matthew tells us that at this point, "the devil left him, and angels came and attended him" (vs. 11). Jesus has passed the test. He is now prepared to enter His formal ministry.

■ Applying the Word

Matthew 3:1–4:16

1. What are the implications for my personal life in John the Baptist's call for repentance in the face of the soon arrival of God's kingdom? In what ways is my life producing "fruit in keeping with repentance"?
2. Is my primary relationship to my church or to God? How much reliance do I put on my religious pedigree? Have I, like the Jews of old, come to the conclusion that God is somehow dependent upon my particular denomination for ushering in His kingdom? What are the implications of my position; of the position that I perceive to be that of my denomination?
3. What do I need to learn from the humility of John the Baptist? (Compare Matthew's treatment of the Baptist with John 3:30.)
4. How familiar am I with my Bible? Can I, like Jesus, reply to Satan with an *accurate*, "It is written"? What can I do to improve my knowledge of God's Word and the proper way to understand it?
5. What lesson can I glean from Christ's temptations for my life? Does my daily life give evidence that I seek to emulate the kingly way or the way of the cross? In what ways?

■ Researching the Word

1. Look up the word *baptize* and related words (e.g., *baptism* and *baptizing*) in a concordance. Examine each reference, and make a list of texts that help you understand (1) the meaning of New Testament baptism, (2) the method of biblical baptism, (3) the conditions for receiving baptism. *After* thoroughly studying the topic from the Bible alone, you may want to examine the topic from the perspective of a Bible dictionary or some similar reference work.

2. John the Baptist in 3:2 tells us that the kingdom of heaven is "near." Use a concordance (for this exercise, either Strong's, Young's, or the *NIV Exhaustive Concordance* is much easier to use than Cruden's, but Cruden's will still do) to discover the temporal nature of the kingdom. Did it come at Christ's first advent, or will it come at the second? List your evidence. What difference do your conclusions make? What is the kingdom of heaven? Compare your findings with those in a Bible dictionary.

■ Further Study of the Word

1. For general insight, see E. G. White, *The Desire of Ages*, 97-131.
2. For extensive treatment of John's baptism and the baptism of Jesus, see G. R. Beasley-Murray, *Baptism in the New Testament*, 31-67.
3. For treatment on questions related to the temptations of Jesus, see J. B. Green and S. McKnight, eds., *Dictionary of Jesus and the Gospels*, 821-827.
4. For discussion of the theological nature of temptation, see G. R. Knight, *My Gripe With God*, 78-99; G. R. Knight, *The Pharisee's Guide to Perfect Holiness*, 138-144.

PART TWO

The Proclamation of the King

Matthew 4:17–16:20

CHAPTER THREE

Principles of the Kingdom—Part 1

Matthew 4:17–5:48

Matthew's first four chapters have brought us all the way from the birth of Jesus to the beginning of His ministry in "Galilee of the Gentiles" (4:15). Matthew 4:17 is one of the great pivotal verses in the first Gospel. The phrase "from that time on Jesus began to" is a literary device that Matthew uses here and at 16:21 to divide his Gospel into its three main sections.

The first four chapters have dealt with the person of the King. The next twelve deal with the proclamation of the King. Matthew 4:17 is Jesus' announcement of the kingdom; 4:18-25 treats the beginning of Christ's ministry and the early progress of the kingdom; then chapters 5 through 7 present the principles of the kingdom in the impressive Sermon on the Mount.

There is a logic in Matthew's placement of the sermon. Jesus has had a rapidly expanding ministry, and people need to know what is involved—what it means to be a follower of Jesus. The Sermon on the Mount is the explanation. At the very outset of Jesus' work, Matthew has Him laying the principles of the new age on the line for all to see.

Jesus's sermon has proven to be one of the great documents of world history. In it He deals with a Christian's character, influence, righteousness, piety, goals and priorities, relationships, and commitment.

The sermon ends by noting that Jesus was unlike the Jewish teachers, because He taught with "authority" (7:29). The nature of that authority will be the topic of Matthew 8 to 10.

■ Getting Into the Word

Matthew 4:16–5:12

In order to get a feel for the entire Sermon on the Mount and its context, read 4:17 to 7:29 through once or twice.

1. Note the progression of the material. Note also the major differences in content between chapters 5, 6, and 7. Your Bible has a list of subheadings for the sermon. They are helpful, but see if you can *outline* the sermon in your notebook on Matthew in a way that captures its inner logic.
2. Now that you have examined the sermon as a whole, take time to read its context in 4:17 to 5:1 and its first major division in 5:2-12. After your second reading, begin to deal with the following items.
3. Matthew 4:23 (see also 9:35) indicates the three aspects of Jesus' ministry. List them. Use a Bible dictionary or commentary to discover the exact meaning of each of those aspects. How do they relate to each other in the total context of Christ's ministry?
4. Begin to analyze the eight beatitudes (count 5:10-12 as one double beatitude) by creating four columns on a blank piece of paper. In the first column, list the human characteristics for each beatitude; in the second, the implications of each characteristic; in the third, the blessing; and in the fourth, when the blessing is bestowed.
5. A few years ago, Donald Kraybill wrote a book based upon the principles of 5:3-12 entitled *The Upside-Down Kingdom.* As you look at the eight beatitudes, write a short paragraph for each, demonstrating how the principles of God's kingdom differ from the principles of this world.
6. As you examine the beatitudes, do you see any way to categorize them or outline them? Do you see any line of progression in them, or is their order random? Enter your thoughts and/or outline in your Matthew notebook.

■ Exploring the Word

The King's Early Ministry

Perhaps the first thing one notices upon reading 4:17 to 5:2 is that Jesus' message is identical with that of John the Baptist: " 'Repent, for the kingdom of heaven is near' " (4:17; 3:2). Jesus' ministry should be seen as a continuation of His forerunner's. Like John, He urges that people need to turn away from their sins and turn toward God, that is, repent, *because* the kingdom of heaven is coming. It is important to note that Jesus is not calling for repentance *so that* the kingdom can come, but *because* it is near.

But just how near is near? After all, Jesus and John spoke their words nearly two thousand years ago, and still the world awaits the second coming of Jesus.

That thought brings us to the meaning of the kingdom of heaven. The phrase "the kingdom of heaven" is one emphasized by Matthew, who uses the phrase some thirty-two times. By way of contrast, Luke and Mark prefer to refer to "the kingdom of God." In essence the two terms mean the same thing, and Matthew equates them in 19:23, 24. Yet there is a good reason why he generally uses *heaven* rather than *God* when describing the kingdom. Out of reverence for the divine name, the Jews avoided pronouncing it. Matthew, who is writing for Jews, respects that cultural sensitivity and deliberately uses "kingdom of heaven," whereas Luke and Mark feel free to use "kingdom of God" for their Gentile readers.

Moving beyond the terminology, it is obvious that the basis for urgency in both John's and Jesus' preaching is the nearness of the kingdom. Whether God's kingdom is present or future has been a topic of debate since the time of Christ. The biblical answer appears to be that it is both. There is a sense in which the arrival of King Jesus on earth ushered in the kingdom, but there is another sense in which its consummation is still future. As a result, Jesus can say that " 'the kingdom of heaven *has been* forcefully advancing' " " 'from the days of John the Baptist until now' " (11:12) and that " 'the kingdom of God *has come* upon you' " (12:28) while still asking His disciples to pray for the future coming of the kingdom (6:10). The fullness of the kingdom will arrive at the second coming of Christ (chaps. 24, 25).

Thus the inauguration of the kingdom took place at the first coming, but it does not exist in its completeness until the second. There is a sense in which the kingdom is wherever the King rules or has dominion. As a result, even today, the King can rule in human hearts, even though His assertion of authority over all the earth awaits the end of the present age.

The important point to note at this juncture is that individuals can enter the kingdom when they accept Jesus' lordship in their lives. Matthew's next few verses describe some of the initial citizens of Jesus' new kingdom. First, Matthew tells us of the calling of four of the earliest disciples (4:18-22); then he goes on to narrate the acquisition of some of the kingdom's early lay citizens (vss. 23-25).

The cryptic recounting of the calling of Peter, Andrew, James, and John should not be seen as a full account of the calling of those disciples but rather as a sample account. Nor does the text rule out previous contact with Jesus. It is the positive aspects that are emphasized in the double telling of essentially the same story. Two points are highlighted by the text. First, both sets of brothers turned from their previous way of life "immediately." They did not take Jesus' call lightly. Not only did they leave their previous occupation, but they "followed" Jesus (vss. 20, 22). Second, they were to become "fishers of men" rather than fishers of fish (vs. 19).

These earliest calls illustrate the radical nature of Christian discipleship. The New Testament pictures the Christian way as a break with the values and goals of the old life rather than a gradual growth or continuation of the old ways. In another connection Jesus called it a new birth (John 3:3, 5), while Paul described entrance into the Christian life (kingdom) as a death of the old way and a resurrection to a new way of life (Rom. 6:1-11). The first disciples are a good example of turning from the old ways made explicit in John's and Jesus' core message (3:2; 4:17).

With the calling of the first disciples, we have the foundation of the church. Beyond that, we have the first hint at the missionary nature of that church. After all, its first members were to be fishers of men.

Matthew rapidly moves from the calling of the disciples to Jesus' early success among the people. In the process, he sets forth the threefold methodology of the King—teaching, preaching, and healing (4:23). That description of Jesus' work is so central to Matthew's understanding that he repeats it in 9:35. A well-balanced kingdom ministry consists of all three activities.

The Greek word used for *preaching* describes the work of a herald in a Greek city. It indicates a weighty announcement from an authority that should be heeded. Jesus' announcement is described as the "good news [gospel] of the kingdom" (4:23). Jesus was heralding the arrival of the kingdom of heaven.

"Teaching" generally took place in the Jewish synagogue. In a sense, it was an explaining of God's will. Closely related to His preaching, Jesus' teaching clears up questions raised by His preaching. The Sermon on the Mount is an example of Jesus' teaching.

"Healing" prepared the way for Jesus' preaching and teaching. Thus in 4:24, 25 the people are the object of Jesus' compassion and healing before they hear His words. He heals the multitudes. Because of that, they follow Him and willingly hear His words. Grace comes before Jesus' commands, healing before the Sermon on the Mount.

Matthew 5:1 says that the "large crowds" (vs. 25) attracted by His compassion gather "on a mountainside" to hear Jesus. Many scholars have seen a parallel between the mountain here and Sinai in the Old Testament. Thus, for example, W. D. Davies and D. C. Allison see Matthew 1 to 5 as being built on an Exodus typology. "The gospel opens," they explain, "with events recalling the birth and childhood of Moses. Then there is Jesus' baptism, which parallels Israel's passing through the waters. There follows next the temptation, in which Jesus re-experiences the desert temptations recounted in Deuteronomy. Finally, there is 4.23–5.2, where Jesus, like Moses, sits on the mountain of revelation. In other words, every major event in Matthew 1–5 apparently has its counterpart in the events surrounding Israel's exodus from Egypt. Moreover, the order of events in Matthew—childhood of Jesus, temptation, mount of revelation—lines up with the chronological order of events in the Pentateuch—childhood of Moses, exodus from Egypt, entry into the wilderness, Sinai. The typology is thus extensive and consistently thought through. *So when Jesus goes up on the mountain to utter the sermon on the mount, he is speaking as the mosaic Messiah and delivering messianic Torah*" (Davies and Allison, 1:427, emphasis supplied).

Such a parallel typology, presented in a carefully crafted book, would not be lost on Matthew's Jewish readers. If God through Moses set forth the principles of the Old Testament on Mount Sinai, so He is presenting the principles of the New Testament kingdom through Jesus on the unspecified mount of Matthew 5:1.

Jesus presents His kingdom principles in seven parts. The first deals with a Christian's character.

A Christian's Character

The beatitudes of Matthew 5:3-12 describe the ideal characteristics of Christ's followers. Unlike the gifts of the Spirit, of which some are given to one person and others to another, all eight characteristics must characterize each Christian. Thus a Christian is not a person who is either meek *or* pure in heart, but one who is both meek *and* pure in heart. The same can be said for the other six characteristics. The eight characteristics are to form the moral profile of every follower of Jesus. They are the principles of His kingdom, essential characteristics of its citizens.

Of course, the principles for which people are rewarded or blessed in Christ's kingdom are not the same as those generally rewarded in the world at large. For example, the wisdom of the present world order has it that the aggressive (rather than the meek) possess most of the earth. Likewise, the kingdoms of this earth belong to the proud and haughty rather than to those poor in spirit. Similar remarks can be made for the rest of the beatitudes. The point is that the principles of God's kingdom are at odds with the principles of the kingdoms of this world. Those two sets of opposing principles are at the heart of the great controversy between Christ and Satan.

Furthermore, the eight characteristics are not the characteristics of what the Bible refers to as the natural person. To the contrary, they are the fruit of God's transforming and empowering grace. They represent the opposite of the world's ideal of the natural person. They represent the fruit of those who have repented of their old ways for the kingdom's sake (3:2; 4:17). They are a part of the "fruit in keeping with repentance" (3:8). They represent the ideal of those who have forsaken their old ways and have "followed him" (4:22, 25).

Each of Jesus' eight beatitudes (verses 10 to 12 should be viewed as one double beatitude) begins with the Greek word *makarios*. That word can be translated in many ways, including "blessed" (NIV, KJV, RSV, and others) and "happy" (Phillips, the Living Bible, and others). But it seems to be a misreading of Jesus' intention to translate *makarios* as "happy" in Matthew 5:3-12. After all, Jesus is not speaking of a subjective state. Rather, He is making an objective judgment about such people. They are "blessed" of God because of what they are. That is a far cry from whether they feel happy.

The second half of each beatitude describes the eight blessings. And just as the eight characteristics of Christians represent the ideal for each believer, so do all eight of the blessings belong to each believer. Like the kingdom itself, the blessings are partly a present experience and partly future. The present foretaste will be brought to fullness with the consummation of the kingdom at the second advent of Christ. Thus while Christian mourners have some comfort in the present, they will be *fully* comforted at that time, and so on.

The simplest division of the beatitudes is to divide them in the same manner as the two tables of the law. Thus the first four can be seen as describing a Christian's relationship to God, while the second four focus on a person's relationships to other people. It should also be noted that they are arranged in a progressive order so that each characteristic leads to the next.

At the very beginning of Christ's classification of Christian characteristics is poverty of spirit (vs. 3). In the Old Testament, poverty came to have spiritual overtones that were identified with humble dependence on God. Whereas the rich and self-sufficient tended to rely on their own strength, the poor could only look to God for salvation and help in time of trouble. God came to the rescue of the "contrite and lowly in spirit" (Isa. 57:15; see also 41:17, 18; Ps. 34:6). It was to such "poor" that Jesus was sent to preach the good news of the kingdom (Isa. 61:1, 2; Luke 4:18; Matt. 11:5).

It is the "poor in spirit" who stand with the publican in Jesus' parable, crying, in their humbleness, " 'God, have mercy on me, a sinner' " (Luke 18:13). The Greek text actually says "*the* sinner," not "a sinner." The publican felt the unbearable poverty of what he had to offer God. Significantly, Jesus notes that it is this humble-in-spirit tax collector who had entered the kingdom, rather than the Pharisee who was so proud of his good works (Luke 18:9-14). As John R. W. Stott puts it, it was the "publicans and prostitutes, the rejects of human society, who knew they were so poor they could offer nothing and achieve nothing," who received the kingdom in the Gospel story. "All they could do was to cry to God for mercy; and he heard their cry" (Stott, *Christian Counter-Culture*, 40). "Theirs is the kingdom of heaven" (5:3).

After recognizing one's helplessness and spiritual poverty, the next step is the sorrow of repentance (vs. 4). It is one thing to acknowledge our spiritual poverty; it is another to mourn over it. "The mourning here brought to view," suggests Ellen White, "is true heart sorrow for sin" (White, *Thoughts From the Mount of Blessing*, 9).

Thus the Christian life is not one of constant lighthearted joy and laughter, as some would have us believe. The Christian weeps over his or her shortcomings, shortcomings that put Christ on the cross.

Such mourners, Jesus tells us, will be comforted. They will be comforted by the only comfort that can alleviate their distress—the forgiveness of God.

The third quality in Christ's progressive list is meekness (vs. 5). The Greek word for *meek* may also be translated as "gentle," "humble," "considerate," and "unassuming." Those who are truly poor in spirit and who mourn over their poverty will also be meek or humble.

Meekness should not be confused with weakness. The meek may have great authority and strength, but they choose not to use it for their own ends. The strength of the meek is accompanied by humility and a genuine dependence on God. Leon Morris suggests that "the strong who qualify for this blessing are the strong who decline to domineer" (Morris, *Matthew*, 98). Jesus describes Himself as meek in Matthew 11:29. He is the perfect illustration of the virtue. Although He had all power, He entered Jerusalem and went to the cross peacefully. That was the opposite of the program of the Zealot party, who expected the Messiah to overthrow the Romans by force.

Whether strong or weak, the meek are those who exhibit the virtues of humility and gentleness. For sinful humans, meekness flows out of their sense of helplessness and sin when they seek to live apart from the grace of God. Such people, rather than the assertive power brokers, will eventually inherit the earth. Of course, the blessing in the third beatitude has quite a definite eschatological (end-time) focus. Its fulfillment, more than the blessings connected with the other beatitudes, awaits the second coming of Jesus.

Hungering and thirsting after righteousness is the fourth characteristic of Christian character that is highlighted by Jesus. We have now come to a major turning point in the beatitudes. The first two exemplified a *turning away from* our human weakness and sin, while the third expressed the Christian's humility in light of that weakness. The fourth, by way of contrast, is a *turning toward* the positive aspect of Christianity. It is a hungering and thirsting to be like God.

Thus the Christian life is more than a mourning over past sin.

It is also a hungering for future righteousness. It is the desire to be holy as God is holy, to be like Jesus. As D. Martyn Lloyd-Jones puts it, hungering and thirsting after righteousness "means that one's supreme desire in life is to know God and to be in fellowship with Him, to walk with God the Father, the Son and the Holy Spirit" (Lloyd-Jones, 1:79). Such individuals will not be disappointed. They will be progressively filled.

The fourth beatitude forms a natural bridge between the first four and the second four. After all, the righteousness of character that Christians hunger after is connected to their fellow humans as well as to God. Thus it is not surprising to find that the fifth beatitude focuses on the merciful (vs. 7).

Mercy is compassion for people in need. It is rooted in the mercy that God has already shown Christians in forgiving their sins and lifting them out of the pit of hopelessness. One of the great teachings of Matthew's Gospel is the necessity for God's children to pass on to others the mercy that He has already shown to them. Perhaps Jesus' greatest illustration of this principle is the parable of the unmerciful servant (18:21-35; see also 6:12, 14).

The sixth beatitude is purity of heart (vs. 8). In the Greek original, the "pure" heart is the "clean" heart. We might think of it as the sincere heart, the heart that is free from falsehood and guile.

In the Bible the heart stands for a person's whole inner state. The natural heart is self-centered and unclean, but Jesus calls for a transformed heart. That transformation is crucial to Christian living, for, as He will later tell us, " 'out of the heart come evil thoughts, murder, adultery, sexual immorality, theft, false testimony, slander' " (15:19). Purity of heart is crucial, because the heart is the wellspring of life. Those with a pure heart will not only see God in a fuller way here on earth, but they will meet Him face to face in the hereafter.

The seventh beatitude is peacemaking (vs. 9). Peacemaking is the natural outcome of a pure heart, since the most frequent cause of conflict is intrigue and selfishness. Making peace is a divine act, because it is an act of reconciliation. Christ is the great Peacemaker. "Through Him," God worked "to reconcile to himself all things, whether things on earth or things in heaven, by making peace through his blood, shed on the cross" (Col. 1:20; see also Isa. 9:6).

God is the great Peacemaker in Scripture, while the devil is the great troublemaker. Unfortunately, the Christian peacemaker, from time to time, has to work for peace through confrontation. It was so in Jesus' life, and it will be so in ours. The aim of Christians is not peace at any price, but peace based upon Christian principles. Such peace is a motivating force in the Christian life.

It is not surprising that such people are blessed as the "sons of God." After all, they are merely acting like their Father.

It is paradoxical that the eighth and final beatitude appears to contradict the seventh. The peacemakers are rewarded with persecution (vss. 10-12). That state of affairs comes about because some people refuse peace. The natural heart is against God's ideals and rebels against them. Thus the persecution of 5:10-12 is not persecution in the abstract. God's children are persecuted "because of righteousness" (vs. 10) and "because of me [Jesus]" (vs. 11).

Realistic Christianity takes into account the conflict between the principles of this world and the principles of the kingdom of heaven. The two sets of principles are diametrically opposed. The basis of one is pride and selfishness. The foundation of the other is humility and service to others. The great controversy between Christ and Satan over these basic sets of principles is one of the ultimate realities in both the Bible and daily life.

The end result is that the humble peacemakers will be persecuted because of their principles and allegiances. But all is not lost. To all such, Christ says, "Great is your reward in heaven" (vs. 12). That promise is the reason Christians can "leap for joy" in the face of trouble here on earth (Luke 6:23). While they have not been promised total bliss in this life, they have been assured of final and ultimate victory.

In these ten terse verses, Christ sets forth His profile of the Christian's character. He will next turn to the Christian's influence.

■ Getting Into the Word

Matthew 5:13-48

Read 5:13-48 two times. On the second reading, begin to give attention to the following items:

1. Verses 13 to 16 refer to Christians as the salt of the earth and the light of the world. In what ways is that true? How can salt lose its saltiness? Compare 5:14 with John 8:12 and 9:5. How is it that both Christ and Christians can be called the light of the world?
2. What does 5:17 mean by "the Law or the Prophets"? You may want to compare that verse with Luke 24:44 as you think about your answer. How did Jesus "fulfill" the law and the prophets? Look up *law* in a Bible dictionary, and outline its many New Testament uses. List the evidences you find in 5:17-48 that Jesus did not abolish the Ten Commandment law.
3. The Pharisees spent their entire lives trying to keep the law perfectly. Yet Jesus said in 5:20 that unless the righteousness of Christians surpasses that of the Pharisees, they would " 'certainly not enter the kingdom of heaven.' " *Righteousness* has several meanings in the New Testament. Use a concordance to look up every mention of righteousness in Matthew. Write out your thoughts on what you believe Matthew means by righteousness in 5:20. Examine 5:21-48, and list what you discover to be wrong with the righteousness of the Pharisees. Again, list those ways in which a Christian's righteousness must surpass that of the Pharisees and teachers of the law (scribes). Is Matthew here teaching some kind of righteousness by works? If not, what part does grace have in 5:21-48?
4. One of the Sermon on the Mount's most debated statements is found in Matthew 5:48, where Jesus tells Christians to be perfect, even as God is perfect. In a paragraph

or two, discuss what Jesus means by that command. Before giving your answer, be sure to study the immediate context in 5:43-48 and the parallel passage in Luke 6:32-36. List the ways in which the immediate context in 5:43-48 sheds light on God's actions that Christians are called upon to emulate. How does Luke's parallel passage also help our understanding? What light, if any, does Christ's definition of the greatest commandment in the law (22:37-40) shed on the possible meaning of 5:48?

■ Exploring the Word

A Christian's Influence

Jesus' proclamation of a Christian's influence through the salt and light metaphors of verses 13 to 16 is closely related to His description of the Christian's character in verses 3 to 12. After all, a Christian's influence depends on his or her character. Without a "Christian" character, there can be no "Christian" influence. The salt must be salty to be effective, and the light must be shining.

Salt has many functions. In societies without refrigeration, it is used as a preservative. It is rubbed into meat to prevent decay. Another positive function of salt is flavoring. Many foods taste better when salt is added. But in order to achieve its purpose, salt must penetrate food. Salt left a fraction of an inch away from food can neither preserve nor flavor.

Jesus describes Christians as the " 'salt of the earth' " (vs. 13). He has not commanded us to *become* salt, but has stated a fact— " 'You *are* the salt.' " Christians function as salt by intermingling with the surrounding culture. Only in this way can they carry out their God-given role of preserving and flavoring their society. Although Christians often don't realize it, their daily lives moderate the people and society around them as they live out the Beatitudes. Their daily lives "flavor" the society through the little kindnesses they show, the humility they demonstrate, and so on. Even proud and hardened people often find it difficult not to respect true Christians, although they may not choose to emulate them. Thus one effect of Christian influence is to slow down the personal and social degeneracy so aptly described by Paul in Romans 1:18-32.

Christians have no choice about whether they will be salt. If they are truly Christians, they will mix with the world in a way that makes the world a better place.

Whereas Christians cannot avoid being salt, they can choose not to function as salt. They can withhold their saltiness through failing to share it. Jesus describes such people as having lost their saltiness. In effect, He is saying that they have lost their Christianity. After all, it is impossible for salt not to be salty. Such Christianity is " 'no longer good for anything, except to be thrown out and trampled by men' " (vs. 13).

With that last statement, we have the first hint in the Sermon on the Mount of divine punishment for the unfaithful. Thus verse 13 not only highlights the world-saving mission of Christians, but it also points to possible disaster for them. "What a downcome," exclaims A. B. Bruce, "from being saviours of society to supplying materials for footpaths!" (A. B. Bruce, 102).

Matthew 5:14-16 presents light as a parallel metaphor to salt. Once again, Jesus highlights the worldwide mission of the church as He labels Christians " 'the light of the world.' " And once again, Jesus implies that Christians, if they are Christians, have no choice. They are either light, or they are not Christians. They have the same function as Christ, who in another connection referred to Himself as " 'the light of the world' " (John 8:12; 9:5; see also Matt. 4:16). Christians are like Jesus in letting their "good works" (5:16, KJV) shine forth to their neighbors. Yet they don't do it for their own glory (6:1), but that people might praise their "Father in heaven."

As with saltiness, Christians have no choice about being light. However, they can choose not to be functional as light. The implication is the same as for the saltless ones: In the end, Christians who fail to share their light will be judged to be outside the Christian fold (see also 10:32, 33).

In summary, Jesus has given two illustrations to help us understand a Christian's influence. They are alike, suggests Helmut Thielicke, in that "they give and expend themselves—and thus are the opposite of any and every kind of self-centered religiosity." Yet they differ in their modes of operation. "Salt works and expends itself in secret, and you cannot see it operating. One thinks of the quiet, unobtrusive influence of a Christian upon his environment, his family, his associates, which he exerts just by being what he is, by being there in prayer and in love. . . . Light, on the other hand, can be seen; it works openly and visibly. And here one thinks of the church's task of witnessing publicly to the gospel and of sending men and women into all branches of public life" (Thielicke, 33).

Thus far in His great sermon, Jesus has spoken about a Christian's character and influence. He now turns to a Christian's righteousness.

A Christian's Righteousness

Christ talked about Christian character in the Beatitudes. He now returns to character in the rest of Matthew 5, but this time He deliberately treats it in the context of the Old Testament and the Jewish legal code.

One thing that Jesus wants His followers to be clear on is His relationship to the Old Testament (the only Scriptures of the time). In the plainest words possible, He tells His hearers that He is in harmony with the Jewish Scriptures (the law and the prophets). He has not come to change or abolish any part of them, but to fulfill them (vss. 17, 18).

The word *fulfill* has been understood in at least three ways: (1) Jesus accomplished or obeyed the requirements of the Old Testament through His obedient life, (2) He brought out the full meaning of the Scriptures through His teachings, and (3) He fulfilled the predictive elements of the Old Testament, as such elements were included in both prophecy and the sacrificial service.

In a sense, Jesus fulfilled the Old Testament in all three ways, but it is the second that forms the immediate context to His teaching in verses 17 and 18. In verses 21 to 48, Jesus brings out the full meaning of certain ideas set forth in the Old Testament.

Whereas verses 17 and 18 speak of Jesus' relationship to the law, verses 19 and 20 treat the issue of the Christian and the law. Jesus is adamant that Christians will not only be personally faithful to God's commands, but that they will teach others to do likewise.

He then goes on to make one of the most astounding statements recorded in Matthew's Gospel: A Christian's righteousness must surpass that of the Pharisees and scribes (" 'teachers of the law' ") if they are to have a place in the kingdom (vs. 20). What makes that statement absolutely astounding is that the scribes and Pharisees spent their entire lives meditating upon the law and seeking to live up to its demands. They were totally dedicated religionists. Not only did they discover 613 commandments in the books of Moses (248 positive and 365 negative), but they also built up a massive array of oral traditions (or oral law) to support them. For example, they developed some 1,521 rules for keeping Sabbath alone! Their oral tradition covered every aspect of life. An individual had to be zealously sincere to live the pharisaic life.

Jesus' hearers must have wondered how anybody could be more righteous than the scribes and Pharisees. The same thing has troubled many Christians. Some have even gone so far as to say that Jesus couldn't possibly have taught the ideas in verse 20—that this text must have been a later addition of some pharisaic Christian who desired to impose a new legalism on the church.

A more common way of escape from the implications of verse 20 has been to suggest that the righteousness urged upon Christians is not really their own righteousness but the righteousness of Christ accepted by faith. Such an interpretation may be praiseworthy as an attempt to preserve the gospel of free grace through faith, but it utterly fails when one considers the meaning of Matthew 5 as a whole. Verse 20 explicitly states, "Unless *your* righteousness exceeds" (RSV). And verses 21 to 48 tell *how* Christian righteousness can and will exceed pharisaic righteousness.

It is crucial not to confuse Matthew's presentation of Jesus' teaching with Paul's presentation of the gospel. Like James, Matthew is writing primarily to Jews, and thus he emphasizes their concerns with law and works. This does not mean that Matthew (or James) believes in a way of being saved that differs from Paul, but rather that Matthew has his own way of approaching the truth of salvation as he presents Jesus' teachings. F. D. Bruner appears to be on track when he writes: "If we will be patient with Matthew and not try too quickly to baptize him in Paul, we will find him teaching a gospel. Right now Matthew's Jesus is urging on us a real personal righteousness." In fact, Bruner goes on to note, the first Gospel's emphasis on greater righteousness will eventually drive Christians to prayer for divine help (Bruner 1:172).

In verses 21 to 48, Jesus illustrates some of the ways a Christian's righteousness must exceed that of the Pharisees. His focus is not on a greater number of commands and prohibitions but on the issue of quality.

The scribes and Pharisees, in order to make obedience more attainable, toyed with the demands of the law. Thus, as John Stott points out, *they restricted the commandments and extended the permissions of the law* (Stott, *Christian Counter-Culture*, 79, 80). For example, the scribes and Pharisees apparently restricted the biblical prohibitions of murder and adultery to the act alone. Jesus, on the other hand, extended (or fulfilled) them to include angry thoughts, insulting words, and lustful looks (vss. 21-30).

Not content to restrict the implications of the law to their convenience, the scribes and Pharisees also widened its permissions. Thus some of them sought to extend the permission of divorce beyond the single, biblical ground of "something indecent" (Deut. 24:1) to include almost any displeasure a man might find in his wife. Jesus stood against such extensions by noting that there was only one ground for divorce (vss. 31, 32).

In essence, Jesus was reversing the Jewish tendency to restrict the demands of the commandments and to extend their permissions. The law under the interpretation of Jesus was infinitely more difficult to keep than under its trivialization by the Jews. They emphasized keeping certain aspects of the letter of the law. Jesus said that it must also be kept in spirit.

In verses 21 to 48 Jesus provides us with six illustrations on the law's depth. That very depth points to heart righteousness, the need of forgiving grace when it is not kept in spirit, and the need of empowering grace if the law is really to be lived out in daily life. This heart righteousness was the very righteousness predicted of the Messianic age. Jeremiah wrote, " 'I will put my law in their minds and write it on their hearts' " (Jer. 31:33), and Ezekiel penned, " 'I will give you a new heart and put a new spirit in you. . . . And I will put my Spirit in you and move you to follow my decrees' " (Eze. 36:26, 27).

Whereas the Pharisees taught that external conformity to the law would be righteousness enough, Jesus calls for a deeper and fuller righteousness. He preaches a righteousness that keeps the spirit as well as the letter of the law, a righteousness that is deeper and greater than that of the Pharisees. This spiritual keeping of the law can only be accomplished by those who, having been born from above of the empowering Spirit, can call God their "Father" (5:16, 45, 48; 6:9; John 3:3, 5). After all, while it is possible to avoid the very act of adultery and to love one's neighbor *some* of the time, it takes an act of transforming grace to love one's enemies *all* the time (vss. 43-48).

So Jesus provides His listeners with six examples that illustrate the spirit of the law lying at the heart of the righteousness which surpasses that of the Pharisees and scribes (vs. 20). In the process He sets Himself forth as an authority in a way that no teacher of the law would have dared to do. " 'Truly, *I* say to you' " (vs. 18, RSV) and " 'You have heard that it was said. . . . But *I* say to you' " (vss. 27, 28, RSV). This was Jesus' approach. Truly "he taught as one who had authority, and not as their teachers of the law" (7:29). It should be noted in passing that in His six examples, Jesus was not challenging the Old Testament but the human traditions that had grown up around Old Testament law. He was not out to destroy the Old Testament but to fill up (fulfill) its meaning (vs. 17).

Before moving away from verses 21 to 48, we should briefly look at verse 48: "Be perfect, therefore, as your heavenly Father is perfect." That text should be linked to verse 20, which calls for greater righteousness than the scribes and Pharisees. These two texts bracket Jesus' six examples regarding the depth of the law. They present God's ideal before and after those illustrations.

Thus there is a sense in which being perfect like the Father is equated with keeping the spirit of the law, as opposed to its legalistic letter. As Davies and Allison point out, "Each of the six paragraphs in the section [vss. 21-48] calls for 'perfection,' that is, each makes an absolute demand which cannot be surpassed. What more, for example, can be done about lust than to drive it out of the heart (5.27-30)? And who else is left to love after one has loved the enemy (5.43-48)?" (Davies and Allison, 1:560).

But in an even more specific way, verse 48 belongs to the paragraph beginning in verse 43. This is demonstrated by a comparison of verse 45 with verse 48. Both call for Christians to be like their Father in heaven. Verses 43 to 47 make explicit what that likeness is like. Christ is not dealing in abstractions here. Being like the Father means loving one's enemies, just as God loves His enemies. After all, doesn't He provide sunshine and rain for evil people, just as He does for the good? Anybody, even a tax collector, can love his or her friends. God demands supernatural love for *all* people. Just as the Father so loved the world that He gave His Son to die for people who were ungodly and His enemies (John 3:16; Rom. 5:6-10), so are Christians to love even those who despitefully use them. This is the ultimate in God-likeness.

The idea that in verse 48 God is calling for perfect love from His children is strengthened by the parallel passage in Luke 6. In verses 32 to 35 Jesus discusses enemy love in Luke's equivalent to the Sermon on the Mount. Then in verse 36 He says that Christians are to "be merciful, just as your Father is merciful." Thus Luke and Matthew equate perfect love with showing mercy. To show mercy even to one's enemies is to emulate the essence of God's perfect character.

And the essence of God's character as a character of love

(1 John 4:8) lines up with the heart of the law as Jesus saw it—love to God and one's neighbor (Matt. 22:37-40). And, it is important to remember, Jesus interpreted *neighbor* in such a way as to include enemies (Luke 10:29-37).

Thus the heart of the God-like character, the perfect character, is letting God fill lives with His love through the indwelling of the Spirit. Such persons keep the spirit of the law. They have a quality of righteousness surpassing that of the scribes and Pharisees.

This ideal is about as high as human thought can imagine. Falling short of it will, of necessity, drive a sincere Christian to his or her knees for God's forgiving grace. Jesus promises that very grace in the next section of His sermon, when, in the Lord's Prayer, He asks us to pray for forgiveness.

At this point we have reached the end of Jesus' discussion of a Christian's righteousness. In the first half of Matthew 6, He will expound upon a Christian's piety.

■ Applying the Word

Matthew 4:17–5:48

1. **How does repentance provide me an entrance into God's kingdom (4:17)? What does repentance mean to me in terms of my experience? How am I different when I repent from when I do not? Is repentance an occasional act or attitude for me, or is it a way of life? What is implied by each of these ideas?**
2. **In what ways does my life measure up to each of the first seven beatitudes (5:3-9)? For which of the beatitudes do I need to pray for an extra measure of God's grace?**
3. **In what ways have I experienced "persecution" in the past few months? Looking back, can I say that I rejoice over those experiences? If not, what practical steps can I take right now to fulfill Jesus' promise to believers that they *will* rejoice in persecutions?**

4. **How have I been salt (silently permeating) and light (openly witnessing) to the world in the last few days? In what ways might I have been even more so? What can I do in the next few days to increase my saltiness and light to the world?**
5. **As I reflect on my thoughts and attitudes of the past few days, have I kept the law in its most spiritual sense? Have I felt hatred or lust or some other spiritual problem? If so, when? Have I experienced victory over these spiritual problems? If so, when? How did I achieve that victory? What can I do to ensure future victories?**
6. **How "perfect" am I in emulating the love of Jesus in my relationship with my friendly and not-so-friendly neighbors? In what ways could I improve *today* through God's grace?**

■ Researching the Word

1. **Using an exhaustive concordance (*Strong's*, Young's, or the *NIV Exhaustive*), find all the references to *righteousness* in Matthew 1 to 5 and Romans 3 to 5. (The same task can be accomplished by reading these chapters if you do not have an exhaustive concordance.) Compare and contrast the ways our two authors use the word *righteousness* in their passages. Now look up the words *justify* and *justified* in your concordance for Romans 3 to 5. (The verb for *being justified* in Greek has the same root as the word for *righteousness*.) In what ways does Paul's use of the verb *justify* add to your understanding of the differences between our two authors in the passage under consideration? Does Paul always use the words for *righteousness* and *justify* in the same way? Use your concordance (or read your Bible) for Romans 2 (note especially vs. 13) and 6 as you think about that last question. What has this exercise taught you about automatically applying the meaning of a word used in one passage to various other parts of the Bible or even to other**

parts of the same book? How can Paul's and Matthew's theology be harmonized? For further study, you may want to consult a Bible dictionary on the words being studied in this exercise.

2. Compare Matthew's Sermon on the Mount (5:1–7:27) with Luke's "Sermon on the Plain" (Luke 6:17-49). In two columns, outline the content of each. How are they similar? How are they different? Do you think the two accounts are two separate sermons or the same sermon preached on two occasions? What reason can you give for your answer?

■ Further Study of the Word

See at the end of chapter 4.

CHAPTER FOUR

Principles of the Kingdom—Part 2

Matthew 6, 7

In Matthew 5 Jesus set forth the principles of a Christian's character, influence, and righteousness. In chapter 6 He will discuss a Christian's piety, goals, and priorities, while in chapter 7 He will focus on a Christian's relationships and commitments. In its totality, the Sermon on the Mount is a broad-based document that states principles that apply to every sector of a person's life.

■ Getting Into the Word

Matthew 6

Rapidly read through Matthew 6 a couple of times in a single sitting. As you read, look for answers to the following items. Writing out your answers in a notebook will help you remember your conclusions.

1. **Compare 6:1 with 5:16. Can these texts be harmonized? If so, how?**
2. **Matthew's counsel on almsgiving, prayer, and fasting (vss. 2-6, 16-18) is built on a threefold repetition of the same pattern. Analyze that pattern, and list its basic components.**
3. **Look up the word *hypocrite* in a Bible dictionary. In what**

ways does the meaning of the Greek word illuminate the nuances of the word in English?

4. **Some have held that Jesus is arguing against public prayer in verse 6. List the hints in both verses 5 and 6 and in the Lord's Prayer (vss. 9-13) that may help resolve that issue.**
5. **Some people have suggested that the Lord's Prayer is an ideal prayer. List the prayer's basic elements in the order that Jesus gives them (for example, the first element is adoration of God). Discuss the logic in the order of these elements.**
6. **Each paragraph in verses 19 to 34 contains a powerful principle-based sentence that is outstanding for its counsel to Christians. Underline what you consider to be the most important sentence in each paragraph. Then in a few lines discuss the way that the sentence you underlined illuminates the meaning of the paragraph in which it is found.**
7. **List the arguments that Jesus puts forth against worry in verses 19 to 34. In one sentence, give what you believe to be the essence of His argument against worry.**

■ Exploring the Word

A Christian's Piety

In chapter 6 Jesus moves from the moral righteousness of 5:21-48 to what might be called "religious" righteousness. The first part of the chapter deals with three areas of personal piety—almsgiving, prayer, and fasting. Because they were common acts of Jewish piety, Jesus uses these areas to illustrate principles that can be applied to other acts of religious piety. In other words, these are samples of piety rather than an exhaustive listing of Christian practice.

Note that Jesus does not command these activities. Rather, He expects them to be practiced by citizens of the kingdom of heaven. That fact is interesting in itself, since one of the three (fasting) has fallen into disuse by evangelical Christians and is even viewed by some as a Christian perversion of the Middle Ages.

Matthew 6:1 plainly states that Christians should not let their "acts of righteousness" be seen by other people. Doing so would negate any reward from the Father. Yet we saw in 5:16 that Christians should let their "good deeds" be evident to other people. While on the surface these two verses seem to contradict each other, in actuality, they are complementary teachings. The topic in 5:16 is public witness, while the subject matter of the three illustrations in chapter 6 is personal devotions. But more important, the goal in 5:16 is the glory of God, whereas the false practices of piety in chapter 6 aim at glorifying their practitioners. In that light they are condemned, since all worship and every act in a Christian's life should be directed at honoring God, the Source of all our possessions and blessings.

Jesus' three illustrations of personal piety basically repeat the same pattern. First comes a description of the false way of piety, which focuses on public display of the practitioner's "holiness." Because of insincere motivation, such play actors (the Greek idea underlying *hypocrite*) are told that their ego trip is the only reward they will get for their activities. In other words, God does not recognize their piety as genuine.

The second half of each illustration suggests a proper way to fulfill the obligation. In each case, the central idea of these suggestions is that personal piety is between the individual and God. That is, the motivation for personal devotion should be grounded in a person's relationship with the Father, rather than in his or her sinful desire for self-exaltation. All three illustrations close with the statement that faithful worshipers will receive their reward from God.

Some readers have found the idea of rewards for personal piety distasteful, since, as they see it, it seems to express salvation by merit. But such reasoning fails to take into consideration that the Sermon on the Mount is addressed to those already saved, who can address God as their "Father." Thus their acts of devotion are not meritorious acts to *get into* the kingdom but a response of love and adoration from those *already on the inside*.

One of the general thrusts of the New Testament, and of Matthew in particular, is that people's actions will be rewarded (see, for example, 16:27; 25:14-46). Actions, of course, do not stand alone. They are an outgrowth of an individual's relationship to the Father. In short, personal piety and other Christian activities are not ways to get into the kingdom but the fruit of those who are members of the family of God.

Just as Jesus' treatment of almsgiving, prayer, and fasting are examples of personal piety, so the Lord's Prayer is an illustration of public piety. The public nature of the Lord's Prayer is signaled by the use of "*Our* Father" in verse 9 and the plural pronouns throughout.

Jesus is saying that it is not the length of our prayers which makes them effective (vss. 7, 8), but their sincerity. His great sample prayer is composed of several elements that demonstrate an inbuilt logic. The most basic division in Jesus' prayer is between the "you" and "us" petitions. Ideal prayer starts with adoration of God and only then moves to human need. Thus Jesus' prayer, after addressing God as "Our Father," hallows His name, requests completion of the plan of salvation through the coming of His kingdom in its fullness, and pleads that His will be done on earth (vss. 9, 10).

Only after addressing God and His concerns does the prayer move into petitions regarding human need, such as daily sustenance, forgiveness of sin, protection, and deliverance (vss. 11-13). Through His sample prayer, Jesus has put the focus of prayer back on God, where it should be, since He is the source of all that is. Christians find it all too easy for their prayers drift quickly away from God and the broader concerns of the kingdom and into the "gimme" mode that centers prayer on human beings and their wants and needs.

It is not that these needs and desires are unimportant. But they should be put in their proper perspective. It is to the topic of proper perspective that Jesus now turns in the second half of chapter 6.

A Christian's Goals and Priorities

While the first half of Matthew 6 deals largely with the Christian's private life in the "secret" place, the second half deals with material concerns. Jesus summons His followers to be different from popular culture—different from the hypocrisy of the religious in personal piety (vss. 1-18) and different from the materialism of the irreligious (vss. 19-34). Although the Pharisees were largely on Jesus' mind at the beginning of the chapter, He bids us renounce the value system of the Gentiles in the latter part (vs. 32).

In verses 19 to 24 Jesus presents His hearers with three sets of antitheses: earth versus heaven (vss. 19-21), darkness versus light (vss. 22, 23), and money versus God (vs. 24). The first antithesis presents us with two treasures, the second with two eyes, and the third with two lords. All three deal with a person's goals and priorities. The point of the three "Devotions" of verses 1 to 18, suggests F. D. Bruner, "was that we seek the Father's praise rather than the world's. The three Devotions gave us examples of *how* to do this. The Goals now finesse the Devotions by teaching us *where* to aim our life goals" (Bruner, 1:259).

The first antithesis (vss. 19-21) suggests a value reorientation. Human beings are born collectors. Some collect dollars, while others collect cattle, precious stones, and so on. But in all societies, the ones with the largest collections of those things considered valuable are deemed to be great and important. Jesus here commands His followers to get their ideas about values and goals converted. They need to set their ambitions and goals on building up treasure in the currency of heaven. In the context of the Sermon on the Mount, such treasures are the human and spiritual values that Jesus has been discussing. Such values are permanent and indestructible.

The second antithesis likens the human eye (vss. 22, 23) to our goals and ambitions, which color and shape the way we perceive everything else in our surroundings. And, as the health of the physical eye determines whether we live in physical light or darkness, so the condition of our spiritual eye determines whether we dwell in spiritual light or darkness. Thus it is crucial that we have a correct view of our priorities and values.

In the third antithesis (vs. 24), Jesus puts the point He has been driving at in the first two on the line for all to plainly see. Either we will serve God or the present world. We are faced with a blatant choice as to the motivating basis of our lives, our goals, and our priorities. "No one can serve two masters. . . . You cannot serve both God and Money."

We are each forced to choose the Lord of our life. Bruner sums up the intent of the three antitheses by suggesting that "the Old Testament's 'Thou shalt have no other gods before me' is paralleled now by the New Testament's more subtle 'Thou shalt have no other goals before me,' for 'where your goal is there will your heart be also' " (Bruner, 1:261).

Jesus' teaching on worry is the climax to His teaching on priorities, goals, and true wealth. The point of His counsel is found in verses 32 and 33. Here He tells His followers that they should not act like the pagan Gentiles who don't know the Father, and, as a result, spend their lives running after material goods—only to worry about them once they have been acquired. Rather than acting like money-worshiping pagans, Christians are to seek *first* God's kingdom and His righteousness, and in the end, "all these [other] things" will be given to them as well. That promise lines up with the promise in the Beatitudes, in which Jesus said that the meek will "inherit the earth" (5:5). In short, Christians' goals are kingdom-of-heaven goals rather than earthly goals.

In the process of reaching His conclusions regarding goals and priorities, Jesus gives some helpful counsel related to worry that enables Christians to navigate through the trials of daily existence. On the one hand, Jesus provides at least three arguments against worry. First, worry is useless. He illustrates the uselessness of worry by pointing out that people cannot add a single hour to their lives through worry (vs. 27), nor can worry add to their height (vs. 27, margin).

Second, life itself is based on trust in and dependence on God for its most essential properties (vs. 25). After all, our lives and bodies are gifts of a loving Creator. They never came through worry. He who provided the greater gift—life itself—is certainly capable and willing to supply the lesser—material necessities—without our constant fretting. The birds and plants in nature don't worry, and people are far more valuable than plants and animals. He who takes care of the less valuable will care even more for the more valuable.

Third, to worry is pagan, if not atheistic (vss. 31, 32). To worry is to act like those who have no faith or trust. Worry is essentially distrust in God. The worried Christian is a contradiction. Citizens of the kingdom cannot be overcome by worry, because they know and believe in the God of love—a God who cares about all their needs.

Jesus not only provides us with arguments against worry in our daily lives, but He also puts forth two strategies for overcoming it. First, we need to get our priorities straight—"seek first his kingdom and his righteousness" (vs. 33). Too many of our worries stem from the fact that we are trying to live in two kingdoms at the same time—an impossible task (vs. 24). We are too often worried about the perishable, when all the while, Jesus says that if we are to be concerned about anything, it should be our relation to God and His kingdom. When we focus on one goal instead of two, we will be less burdened. Beyond that, in God's time and place, "all these [other] things will be given to [us] as well" (vs. 33).

Jesus' second strategy for overcoming worry is to live one day at a time, since "each day has enough trouble of its own" (vs. 34). Why burden ourselves with tomorrow's supposed problems when we can do nothing about them today? Faith and trust involve a day-by-day, moment-by-moment relationship with God. Kingdom living is living in constant connection with the God who cares for His children. God's answer to worry can be summed up as *trust* in "Our Father." And this trust must be renewed every day, for we can only live one day at a time.

■ Getting Into the Word

Matthew 7

Read Matthew 7 meditatively two or three times. After you have the flow of the chapter in mind, work on the following issues and questions. Keep your Matthew notebook close by for jotting down important thoughts.

1. Matthew 7:1 commands us not to judge. From the context in verses 1 to 6, develop a list of reasons why we should not judge. Then add to your list other reasons from Scripture or elsewhere as to why we should not judge others. What personality traits are evident in persons who feel free to set themselves up as judges of others? Is there a "contradiction" between verses 1 and 6? If so, what do you find problematic?
2. Do verses 7 to 11 imply that anything Christians ask God for will be given them if they ask persistently enough? Explain how you would relate such texts as 2 Corinthians 12:8, 9 and Matthew 26:39-46 to verse 7. What implications does verse 7 have in the context of the entire Sermon on the Mount?
3. What is the function of verse 12 in the sermon? Is there any connection between that verse and 5:17-20? If so, explain what it is.
4. Verses 13 to 27 present three swiftly moving word pictures that come to similar conclusions. Study these three pictures carefully, and list their common points. Then, in a paragraph or two, write the overall impression that these verses leave you with. How is this passage linked to the overall message of the Sermon on the Mount?
5. As we come to the conclusion of the sermon, read it through one last time, and make a list (with references) of the ways in which Jesus taught with "authority" (vs. 29).

■ Exploring the Word

A Christian's Relationships

Matthew 7 treats every Christian's two major relationships—their relationship to other people (vss. 1-6, 12) and their relationship to God (vss. 7-12).

It is all too easy for people who are serious about religion to judge their friends, relatives, and fellow church members who seem not to be quite as serious or zealous in their walk with God as they perceive themselves to be. That was the disease of the Pharisees, and the problem is certainly alive in the modern church. Unfortunately, such an attitude is deadly for vital religion. Ellen White points out that people's satisfaction with their own religious accomplishments creates an "atmosphere of selfish and narrow criticism [which] stifles the noble and generous emotions, and causes [them] to become self-centered judges and petty spies" (White, *Thoughts From the Mount of Blessing*, 123). Judgmentalism, claims Douglas Hare, is "a disease of the spirit" in which "the critic arrogantly assumes a superiority that entitles him or her to assess the failings of others" (Hare, 76).

Jesus condemns such an attitude on the grounds that arrogant people have no insight into themselves. Despite His injunction *to be* perfect (5:48), no one *is* perfect. Thus people need to work on cleaning up their own act (vss. 3, 4) before they can be in a position to give kindly advice to their neighbors (vs. 5). And that kindly advice will always be given within the context of the gentle mercy that God has given us (18:23-35; 6:14). Such individuals will continue to be judged by the Father with kindness (7:2; 18:33, 35). In the light of Jesus' words, I am always wary of preachers and members who major on being critical of other people and the church, especially when the critic's attitude is arrogant and sarcastic.

The attitude of the Pharisees lives on in those self-righteous individuals who have, in their *own* eyes, tried harder and gone farther than others in their Christian walk. Such an attitude, says Jesus, is a fatal delusion. It overlooks both the weakness of human nature and the abundant mercy of God. *All* humans, due to their failings, have a great deal of room for humility. Fortunately, humble Christians who have, through God's grace, dealt honestly with themselves are in a position to humbly help their neighbors (vs. 5).

The injunction not to judge one another does not imply that Christians cannot discriminate. After all, we are told not to cast our pearls before swine or give the sacred to dogs (vs. 6). The implication is that Christians must make judgments of blatant and open sin. Thus Paul counseled the Corinthians not to tolerate the cohabitation of a man with his stepmother (1 Cor. 5:1-5), and Jesus taught that we should not force the gospel on those who openly despise it (Matt. 7:6).

At first glance it appears that verses 7 to 11 unconditionally promise that we can get anything we pray for if we do so with sufficient tenacity. But experience shows that to be false. Thus it was in the case of Paul, who repeatedly prayed for healing, only to be told that God's grace would sustain him in his weakness (2 Cor. 12:8, 9). And so it was in the case of Jesus, who thrice prayed for the cup of His crucifixion to be removed from Him, but was crucified anyway (Matt. 26:39-46).

Far from being an unconditional promise of answered prayer for anything and everything, Jesus' command for His followers to ask, knock, and seek must be interpreted within the context of the Sermon on the Mount. After reading the sermon, the sensitive Christian will be overwhelmed by Jesus' demand for His followers to exhibit righteousness that exceeds that of the scribes and Pharisees (5:20).

Christ's imperatives are humanly impossible to fulfill. Thus they drive us to God's forgiving and enabling grace. And only by prayer do we find the grace that enables us to fulfill God's ideal as set forth in the Sermon on the Mount. As Hare puts it, "To take seriously the terrifying demands of the Sermon on the Mount is to take still more seriously God's readiness to assist us in fulfilling them" (Hare, 79). Those who ask, seek, and knock for such assistance will not be turned away.

The golden rule ("In everything, do to others what you would have them do to you" [vs. 12]) must also be understood in the context of the sermon. Jesus said that the rule "sums up the Law and the Prophets" (vs. 12). And mention of the law and the prophets takes us back to 5:17. Thus 5:17 and 7:12 bracket the central core of the Sermon on the Mount. As a result, the golden rule must be viewed as a summary of Christ's interpretation of the law and the prophets, with 5:21–7:11 being His expansion of several principles inherent in that summary.

A Christian's Commitment

Jesus concludes His sermon with three forceful eschatological (end-time) illustrations related to Christian commitment: the two ways (vss. 13, 14), the two trees (vss. 15-20), and the two builders (vss. 24-27). Matthew will repeat this pattern of three units having to do with eschatological rewards and punishments in four of his five major discourses. Thus the three final units of chapter 10's missionary discourse (vss. 32, 33; 34-39; 40-42) have to do with eschatological rewards and punishments. The same is true of the last three units in chapter 13's parables of the kingdom (vss. 44; 45, 46; 47-50) and the final three parables at the end of Jesus' great end-time sermon in Matthew 24 and 25 (25:1-13, 14-30, 31-46). The one major teaching discourse of Jesus in Matthew that does not follow the triadic pattern of three eschatological warnings really breaks only from the threefold aspect of the pattern, not from the eschatological (end-time) reward-and-punishment element. Thus Matthew 18 (the sermon on greatness and forgiveness) closes with a parable of the punishment of those who refuse to forgive their neighbor from the heart.

We see, then, that both eschatology and ethical action relating to that end-time reality stand at the center of Matthew's portrayal of Jesus the teacher. Matthew knows his message, and, under divine guidance he arranges Jesus' teachings in a skillful manner that drives home his emphases.

The common element in the three units making up Matthew

7:13-27 is *doing*, just as it was in the golden rule of verse 12. In the unit on the two gates (vss. 13, 14), the doing emphasis is not explicit. In fact, in a different context, it might be possible to interpret the gates as true and false theology (or belief). But the context of the gates makes it clear that doing the right thing, rather than believing the right doctrine, is the crucial element. Thus in verse 12 Matthew emphasizes *doing* the golden rule and in verses 15 to 23 (especially verse 21), he has *doing* God's will. Thus the two gates have to do with ethics (conduct), not theology (belief). The person who does Christ's injunction in the body of the sermon (5:21–7:12) will have greater righteousness than the scribes and Pharisees (5:20).

At first glance, verses 15 to 20 (the two trees) seem to be more concerned with false prophets than with ethical doing. But note once again in the illustration of verses 16 to 20 that Jesus makes no reference to their teaching. Rather, He focuses on their behavior; that is, false prophets act like "ferocious wolves" (vs. 15). Thus they are bad models for ordinary Christians.

The behavioral aspect is especially clear in the last three verses of the unit that runs from verses 15 to 23. Christ explicitly says that it is not what people believe but what they do that provides entrance to the kingdom (vs. 21). The righteousness that exceeds that of the scribes and Pharisees consists not only in possessing the teachings of Jesus but in acting on them. The final judgment scene of the sheep and goats in Matthew 25:31-46 and the great commission of 28:18-20 reinforce that conclusion. Many will claim to have prophesied, to have had other charismatic gifts, and to have held to a belief in Jesus, but if they have not practiced the *agapē* love that undergirds the Sermon on the Mount, they will be rejected by King Jesus in the final judgment (vs. 21; see also 1 Cor. 13:1-3).

Jesus closes His sermon with the illustration of the two builders. Both are doers, but both do not do the right thing. The wise builder builds on the rock of Jesus and His teachings in the Sermon on the Mount, while the foolish builder "does not put . . . into practice" Jesus' "words" in the sermon (vs. 26). In the judgment, the foolish man is found wanting (vs. 27).

The sermon's epilogue points out two things: First, the crowds were "amazed" at Jesus' teaching, and second, they were amazed "because he taught as one who had authority, and not as their teachers of the law" (vss. 28, 29).

The theme of Jesus' authority first arose in the sermon when Jesus placed Himself in an authoritative position in regard to the law and Jewish tradition (e.g., "I tell you" [5:18, 20]; "You have heard. . . . But I tell you" [5:27, 28]). The theme of Jesus' authority will appear periodically throughout the rest of Matthew, climaxing in His great commission to His disciples in Matthew's last three verses—"All authority in heaven and on earth has been given to me" (28:18).

Matthew 7 closes with the crowds being amazed at Jesus' teaching authority. Chapters 8 to 10 pick up the theme of His authority and apply it to the everyday world.

■ Applying the Word

Matthew 6, 7

1. **As I examine my prayer life (or other aspects of my devotional practice) in the light of Matthew 6, in what ways can I improve it and make it richer?**
2. **In the light of 6:19-34, where is my treasure? In what ways, according to Matthew 6, can I determine where it is?**
3. **How do I relate to the temptation to be critical of others? What does it tell me about other people when they seem to always have critical or judgmental remarks about other individuals or when their critical remarks greatly outweigh their positive remarks?**
4. **Do I really believe the golden rule? In what specific ways can I ask God today to help me with the rule in my daily life?**
5. **What lessons can I learn for my life from the two gates, the two trees, and the two builders?**

■ Researching the Word

1. Using a concordance, look up all the references to *pray*, *prayed*, *prayer(s)*, *praying*, and similar terms in Matthew. Summarize what you learn from that study.
2. Matthew 6:14 deals with forgiveness. Using an exhaustive concordance, examine every reference to *forgive*, *forgiven*, *forgiveness*, and similar terms in Matthew. List the conclusions that can be drawn from your findings. What does a study of these words in the rest of the New Testament add to your knowledge? If you are feeling ambitious, you may want to pursue your study in the same manner in the Old Testament.

■ Further Study of the Word

1. For a general overview of issues related to the Sermon on the Mount, see G. W. Bromiley, ed., *International Standard Bible Encyclopedia*, 4:411-417.
2. For insightful treatment of the Sermon on the Mount, see R. Guelich, *The Sermon on the Mount*; J. R. W. Stott, *Christian Counter-Culture*; E. G. White, *Thoughts From the Mount of Blessing*.

CHAPTER FIVE

The King's Authority

Matthew 8:1–10:42

A reading of Matthew 4:23 and 9:35 indicates that they are almost identical. It seems obvious that Matthew has a reason for doing this. He is a very organized writer, and he uses such repetitions to set apart major sections in his Gospel.

The section beginning in 4:23 and ending in 9:35 has an introduction to Jesus' earliest ministry (4:23-25). Then follow two subdivisions of the passage that center upon Jesus' authority.

The first subdivision is the Sermon on the Mount (chaps. 5–7). In these chapters, Matthew presents Jesus as the authoritative teacher.

The second subdivision is chapters 8 and 9, which present Jesus as an authoritative actor in the real world as He performs miracle after miracle.

The two subdivisions of the five chapters are tied together by 7:29, which notes that the crowds were amazed because Jesus taught as one with authority. In the overall scheme of Matthew, chapters 5 to 9 present Jesus as the Messiah of authoritative word, while 8 and 9 present Him as the Messiah of authoritative deed.

Chapter 10 is a continuation of the authority theme raised in 5 to 9. In 10:1 Matthew tells us that Jesus gave His authority to His disciples. The chapter continues with Jesus instructing the disciples on their healing and preaching/teaching mission. Thus while 5 to 7 present the words of Jesus and 8 and 9 present the deeds of Jesus, chapter 10 finds Jesus commissioning His disciples to preach His words and to do His deeds.

■ Getting Into the Word

Matthew 8, 9

Read Matthew 8 and 9 through two times. Then consider the following issues and questions.

1. Chapter 8:2-15 tells us about three of Jesus' miracles. List the common factors in all three miracles and in any two of them. Discuss the social standing in Jewish culture of the three recipients of Jesus' ministry. What do you think Matthew is trying to teach us in these verses?
2. Matthew 8:23 to 9:8 contains a second trio of miracles. Each pictures Jesus exercising authority over something. List that "something" in each case. What has the second trio added to the first in terms of our understanding of Jesus' authority?
3. Read about the call of Matthew in 9:9-13. Using the comparative references found in your Bible, read also the accounts in Mark and Luke. (If your Bible does not have comparative references, use a concordance to find the parallel accounts by looking up *Matthew* and *Levi*—his other name.) Using all three accounts, make a composite list of what we know about Matthew from the Gospels. Compare your findings with the discussion found in a Bible dictionary.
4. Discuss, in a paragraph or two, what we can learn about 9:13 in its context from a study of the text's Old Testament marginal references in their contexts.
5. Describe the role of faith in the third miracle trio (9:18-33).
6. Compare 9:33 with 7:28, 29. List the similarities. In the context of Matthew's developing theme, what do those similarities mean for his story? What is the real point of contention in 9:34? What do you think the function of 9:34 is in Matthew's developing story?

■ Exploring the Word

The King's Authority Recognized

Matthew 8:2 to 9:33 contains nine miracle stories. Matthew carefully brackets these miracles with allusions to crowds. In 8:1 we read that "large crowds followed him" as Jesus descended from the mountainside. And in 9:33 we read that "the crowd was amazed and said, 'Nothing like this has ever been seen in Israel.' " Note that 9:33 not only serves as the ending bracket for the miracles, but it also parallels the ending of the Sermon on the Mount. Thus at both the end of Jesus' words and at the end of His deeds, the crowds are amazed at His authority and the uniqueness of His ministry (see also 7:28, 29).

Between 8:1 and 9:33, Matthew has carefully crafted his presentation. Continuing his use of triads (groups of three) as a teaching device, the passage has three sets of three miracles each. Between each triad we find an interlude of two units of material each. We can diagram it like this:

First triad of miracles
Interlude
Second triad of miracles
Interlude
Third triad of miracles

We will now examine each of these triads of miracles and the interludes between them.

The first triad of miracles. The first triad (8:2-15) contains three healing miracles. Jesus heals a leper, the servant of a Gentile officer in the Roman army, and Peter's mother-in-law. In addition to all being healing miracles, these three all focus on people excluded from full participation in Israel's religion.

Leprosy was the most dreaded disease in the ancient world. Beyond the slow physical deterioration of the leper was the social ostracism that put such persons away from the comfort of home and community. Immediately upon diagnosis, the leper was completely banished from human society. Moses wrote: "As long as he has the infection he remains unclean. He must live alone; he must live outside the camp" (Lev. 13:46). In the time of Jesus, lepers were barred from all walled cities, including Jerusalem. Thus they were obviously excluded from the temple worship. According to the Levitical regulations, those infected with leprosy had to wear torn clothes, avoid combing their hair, cover the lower part of their face, and cry, "Unclean! Unclean!" (Lev. 13:45) so that no healthy humans would ever jeopardize their own health by coming into contact with them.

Yet Jesus healed a leper! He not only healed the leper, but He "reached out his hand" and did the unthinkable—He "touched the man" before he was healed (8:3). The lesson is clear: Jesus has authority over the most dreaded of diseases; Jesus has authority over leprosy.

The second miracle is healing the servant of a Gentile (vss. 5-13). To the Jewish way of thinking, only a leper was more unclean than a Gentile. While lepers couldn't enter Jerusalem at all, Gentiles could not fully worship in the Jewish temple, since they could go no farther into the temple complex than the outermost court of the Gentiles.

The centurion, recognizing his unworthiness in the eyes of a Jew, exemplifies remarkable faith. Comparing Jesus to himself as a military commander, the centurion says that Jesus does not need to go to his home to perform the miracle. All He needs to do is issue a command, and the healing will take place. The centurion is the first person in Matthew's Gospel to understand the scope of Jesus' authority—that Jesus doesn't even need to be present for His word to be carried out. Thus Jesus had authority, not only over disease, but also over distance.

Jesus not only commends the centurion for his faith, but He also takes the occasion to present a picture close to the Jewish heart. The Jews expected that at the coming of the Messiah a great banquet would be held, in which all Jews would sit down to feast. Gentiles would not be present.

But Jesus puts a new twist on the story. According to Him, many Gentiles (those "from the east and the west") will be at the feast, but many of the Jews ("the subjects of the kingdom") will be "thrown outside, into the darkness, where there will be weeping and gnashing of teeth" (vss. 11, 12).

Thus with one stroke Jesus set forth two themes that run throughout Matthew's Gospel. The first is the salvation of the Gentiles. This theme begins with Jesus' female, Gentile ancestors in the genealogy of chapter 1. It continues with the favorable response of the Magi (also Gentiles) in chapter 2. The climax comes with the gospel commission at the end of Matthew, with its command to preach the gospel to all nations (28:18-20).

The second theme is the precarious situation of the Jews if they reject the Messiah. Once again, that theme runs throughout Matthew's Gospel, beginning with the Jewish leaders' rejection of the Baby Jesus as the Messiah and extending through Jesus' crucifixion and the Jewish authorities' rejection of His resurrection. In Matthew's Gospel, the dual theme of Gentile acceptance and Jewish rejection at the Messianic feast functions as a double spur to awaken his fellow Jews.

The third miracle in the first triad (8:14, 15), while hammering home the point that Jesus has authority over disease, also demonstrates His compassion for women—another group who did not have full temple privileges. Even if they were both healthy and Jewish, women could not proceed beyond the court of the women in the temple area.

Thus the first triad of miracles demonstrates two things: Jesus' authority over disease and the inclusive nature of citizenship in His kingdom. As D. Hare points out, "Jesus is the Messiah by whose power and authority the excluded are included" (Hare, 90).

The interlude between the first and second triads. Between the first and second miracle triads in Matthew 8 and 9, we find an interlude on discipleship—a topic that Matthew is building toward as he approaches chapter 10. The subject of this interlude (8:19-22) is two would-be disciples. The first one is a learned but overeager scribe who wants to follow Jesus. Jesus tells him that he needs to count the cost of discipleship. The second would-be disciple is a less-than-eager follower who, in line with the custom of the day, claims he will become a disciple as soon as his father dies and is buried. That, of course, could take years. Jesus impresses upon him the urgency of making a decision now (vss. 21, 22). A decision to follow Jesus cannot be postponed indefinitely. Kingdom business is urgent, and one's response to the King is of utmost importance. Matthew will continue to highlight possible responses to Jesus in 8:23–9:8.

The second triad of miracles. In the second triad, Matthew focuses on the power of Jesus: His power over nature in calming the storm (8:23-27), His power over demons in healing the two demon-possessed men (vss. 28-34), and His power over sin in forgiving and healing the paralytic (9:1-8).

Jesus' power over sin in forgiving the paralytic makes explicit what the miracles dealing with nature and the demonic imply: in these three stories, Jesus of Nazareth is laying claim to divine authority. In Jewish thought it was the prerogative of God alone to rule over all three areas in the second triad, and Jesus demonstrates that He has the power of that rulership. Thus we see a progression from the amazement of the people who ask what kind of man Jesus is (8:27) to the demoniacs' identification of Jesus as the Son of God (vs. 29) to Jesus' openly claiming for Himself the prerogative of God to forgive sin (9:2-6). Matthew is setting Jesus forth not only as having the power of God, but as being the very Son of God.

The miracles of the second triad are also closely related in that they emphasize the reaction of the onlookers. After the calming of the storm, the result is wonder and questioning: "What kind of man is this? Even the winds and the waves obey him!" (8:27). The answer to the query is left open. After the healing of the demon-possessed men, the response is negative. "The whole town . . . pleaded with him to leave their region" (vs. 34). And after the healing of the paralytic, the response is positive. The crowd was "filled with awe; and they praised God, who had given such authority to men" (9:8).

Thus the second miracle triad brings us back to one of the main issues of Matthew 2—the necessity of responding to Jesus, the Messianic Son of God. That, of course, is also the topic of the stories of the two would-be disciples in the first interlude of 8:19-22.

The interlude between the second and third triads. Response to Jesus is also the topic of the two disciple stories that form the second interlude. The first story pictures two responses to Jesus (9:9-13). One is that of Matthew, who gladly gives up his lucrative tax collection business to become a disciple of Jesus (vs.9). He has learned the lessons of sacrifice and immediate response illustrated in the disciple stories of 8:19-22.

Another response in this first story is that of the Pharisees, who become upset with Jesus because He eats with tax collectors and other social outcasts at a "great banquet" that Matthew puts on to celebrate his conversion and calling (Luke 5:29; see also 15:1, 2). In His reply to the Pharisees, Jesus makes it plain that they lack spiritual insight into their true condition. In quoting from Hosea 6:6 in verse 13, Jesus explicitly points out the Pharisees' lack of spiritual understanding in light of the Old Testament (see also Micah 6:6-8). They are very good at external law keeping, but they totally fail in the spirit of the Jewish religion (see also Matt. 23:23, 24). They are spiritually lost but don't know it. They need to see themselves as being among the sinners that Jesus came to save (9:13; see also 1:21). They need a physician but know it not (9:12).

The final disciple story in the second interlude deals with the disciples of John the Baptist (9:14-17), who apparently have been influenced by the Pharisees to think critically of Jesus. The question of John's disciples is not why Jesus celebrates with sinners (as in the preceding disciple story) but why He celebrates at all.

In replying, Jesus not only applies the God-like Old Testament imagery of the bridegroom (Hos. 2:16-23) to Himself, but refers in an indirect manner to His death (9:15). Jesus completes the dialogue with John's disciples with an illustration of old wineskins and old garments. His point is the radical new mold into which

Jewish religious thinking and life will have to be cast. The radical principles of the Sermon on the Mount are undoubtedly implied in the "new" that Jesus speaks of (vss. 16, 17).

The third triad of miracles. Newness is also a dominant theme in the third triad of miracles in Matthew 8 and 9. In them Jesus heals two women (9:18-26), two blind men (vss. 27-31), and a speech-impaired man (vss. 32-34). All these people are underprivileged outcasts. The woman with the continuous menstrual flow (vs. 20) and the dead girl (vs. 18) are unclean, while the blind (vs. 27) and the speech impaired (vs. 32) are blemished outsiders. By rabbinic definition, they cannot be holy. But Jesus turns this pervasive Jewish thinking on its head as He opts for mercy rather than sacrifice (see vs. 13). Jesus cares for despised outsiders. He provides, Michael Green points out, "new sight for the blind, new speech for the dumb, new health for the sick, new life for the dead. That is what the newness of Jesus means! And that is what these three miracles are intended to teach" (M. Green, 106).

But they also teach a second lesson: faith makes Jesus' power accessible. In these miracle stories, it is faith that allows the recipients to grasp the new thing presented by Jesus. Thus Jesus can say to the woman with the uncontrollable menstrual flow, " 'Your faith has healed you' " (vs. 22) and to the blind man, " 'According to your faith will it be done to you' " (vs. 29). Their faith may not have been perfect, but it has been placed in Jesus and is thus honored. Faith, notes Green, is what "binds the sinner and the Saviour together" (M. Green, 107).

On the other hand, it is possible to be near Jesus and receive no benefit. Thus the crowd surrounding the woman was also close to Jesus but received no blessing, because the people did not believe. In a similar manner, the professional mourners surrounding the dead girl were sent away empty. The same can even be said about the Pharisees. According to them, " 'It is by the prince of demons that [Jesus] drives out demons' " (vs. 34). They do not deny Jesus' mighty works, but rather what those works mean. To the Pharisees, the miracles of Jesus demonstrate that He is of the devil rather than of God.

Thus in chapters 8 and 9 Matthew sets up his readers for chapters 10 to 13. Chapter 10 will continue on the themes of authority and discipleship, while chapters 11 to 13 will focus more fully on responses to Jesus.

■ Getting Into the Word

Matthew 9:35-10:42

Read 9:35 to 10:42 at least two times. Then turn to the following exercises.

1. **What is the function of 9:35-38 in the plan of Matthew's presentation? Not only does the overall passage have a function, but so does each verse. Briefly describe these functions. What light do the marginal references shed on verse 36? Note especially the first half of the chapter in the Ezekiel reference. Also use a concordance to find Matthew's understanding of Jesus as shepherd.**
2. **Outline the main steps in Jesus' presentation in chapter 10.**
3. **In Matthew's list of disciples, we find a "tax collector" ("publican," KJV) and a "Zealot" (10:3, 4). Look up both terms in a Bible dictionary. How do you think these disciples, coming from such opposite political poles, got along with one another?**
4. **List the parallels between the ministry of the disciples in 10:5-25 and that of Christ. Supply references for the parallels in Jesus' ministry when you can locate them. In a paragraph, describe what you perceive to be the meaning of the parallelism.**
5. **How do you harmonize 10:34 with the fact that Jesus is the "Prince of Peace" (Isa. 9:6)? Explain from the immediate context of 10:34 and the more general context of the Christian faith why the peaceful message of Jesus brings conflict.**

■ Exploring the Word

The King's Authority Delegated

Chapter 10 is the second great teaching sermon in Matthew. The first one (the Sermon on the Mount) was preceded by a narrative section (1:18–4:22) that concluded with a note that Jesus taught in the Jewish synagogues, preached the good news of the kingdom, and healed every disease and sickness (4:23). It is no accident that Matthew, who is a very careful writer, does the same thing with the second sermon. The narrative section preceding it (the three triads of miracles we have just looked at) ends with a note that Jesus taught in the Jewish synagogues, preached the good news of the kingdom, and healed every disease and sickness (9:35).

Three transition paragraphs. Jesus' second sermon is about mission, and it is prefaced by three transition paragraphs. The first transition paragraph (9:35-38) prepares the way for chapter 10 by indicating that Jesus has compassion on the people because they are like sheep without a shepherd (9:36). That was a familiar Old Testament picture. The Old Testament Jewish leaders had failed. But in the Old Testament it was God Himself who would become their Shepherd (Ezek. 34:1-16; Zech. 10:2, 3). That teaching has not been lost on Matthew, and it probably was not lost on his audience. Christ the divine Shepherd is a theme that runs throughout Matthew (see 2:6; 25:31-46). The predicted great Shepherd of Israel has come in the person of Jesus of Nazareth.

Not only has the divine Shepherd come, but He will send out disciples to extend His work and teachings. Thus the purpose 9:37, 38 is to call for workers to gather in the ripening harvest. That thought brings us to the second transition paragraph (10:1), which announces the calling of the twelve disciples and provides the theme verse for chapter 10—Jesus' delegation of His authority to His followers. This is followed by the third transition paragraph (vss. 2-4), in which Jesus identifies His disciples by name.

It should be noted that the twelve represent the full political spectrum among the Jews in their relation to the Romans. At one extreme, we find the traitor Matthew, who as a tax collector had served as a Jewish puppet for the Roman government. At the other extreme is Simon the Zealot. The Zealots stood against Rome as terrorists in an effort to overthrow Israel's hated rulers. It was a good day for a Zealot when he could slip into a crowd and leave his dagger in a Roman or a Roman collaborator, such as Matthew. The miracle is that Jesus' small group contained both a Zealot and a publican. And the four Gospels record no contention between them, as they do among Peter, John, and some of the others. Throughout history it has been demonstrated that the Christian message can truly change people's hearts and lives. Genuine repentance brings conversion and a new life in Jesus, even among deadly enemies.

Section 1 of Jesus' sermon. Jesus' sermon on mission is divided into three major sections. The first is directed specifically at the twelve disciples (10:5-25), who in a sense will be taking the place of the Jewish leaders in God's neglected flock (9:36-38). Note that chapter 10 gives no information concerning the disciples' first mission, but rather provides us with Christ's instruction to them about the mission. This instruction is specifically directed to the twelve. It is important to understand that some of the specifics of this counsel are for them in their unique cultural setting and may not have universal application to all times and places. On the other hand, Jesus' instruction certainly contains principles that can and should be applied to other cultural settings and other historic periods.

Of particular importance in 10:5-25 is the parallelism between the ministry of Jesus and that of the disciples that runs throughout the passage. Thus the disciples, like their Lord, are to go only to the lost sheep of the house of Israel (10:5, 6; 15:24). That command, of course, is bound by chronology. After His resurrection, Christ commanded the disciples to go to all the world (28:18-20). Apparently, Jesus is setting forth the missionary principle, later made explicit by Paul, of presenting the message first to the Jews and later to the Gentiles (see, for example, Rom. 1:16; Acts 1:8, and Paul's method of labor in the book of Acts).

The disciples are also to preach the same message that Jesus preached—" 'The kingdom of heaven is near' " (10:7; 4:17; see also 3:2 for John the Baptist). Like Christ, they are to heal the sick, raise the dead, cleanse lepers, and cast out demons (10:8; 8:2-4, 14-17, 28-34; 9:18-26). They are also to wander from town to town and, like Jesus, stay in the homes of others (10:11; 4:23-25; 8:20). In addition, they will eventually suffer like Jesus. They will be arrested, brought before governors and kings, and flogged (10:17-19; 26:57–27:31). Also like Jesus, they will be betrayed by those closest to them (10:21; 26:47-56). Matthew is obviously conscious of these parallels, because the concluding verse of this section says that a student will be like his teacher and a servant like his master (10:25).

One verse in 10:5-25 that has greatly troubled Bible students is verse 23, which says that the disciples will "not finish going through the cities of Israel before the Son of Man comes." At first glance this passage appears to refer to Christ's second advent. But that interpretation is obviously in error, since Matthew penned his Gospel several decades after Christ sent out His disciples, and he obviously knew that the second advent had not yet taken place. Robert Mounce points to the most satisfactory interpretation of the verse when, following the lead of R. V. G. Tasker, he suggests that "the verse is best understood 'with reference to the coming of the Son of Man in triumph after His resurrection' " (Mounce, 95). That suggestion also lines up with the progressive interpretation of 10:5 and 28:18-20 presented above.

Section 2 of Jesus' sermon. The second section in Jesus' sermon on mission runs from 10:26 through 10:31. That paragraph functions much as 6:25-34 and 7:7-11 did in the Sermon on the Mount. Just as those passages encouraged listeners or readers overwhelmed by the demands of the sermon, so 10:26-31 encourages missionaries under the persecution of 10:17-25.

The command not to be afraid is repeated three times in our paragraph, giving three reasons why the followers of Jesus are not to be afraid. The first reason is that truth will eventually triumph (10:26, 27). One day God will make known His power and glory for all to see. The disciples and all Christians down through history will be vindicated, and God's kingdom will be fully established. This promise is directly related to the great eschatological (end-time) promises of the third and eighth beatitudes (5:5, 10-12). Because of the certainty of the kingdom, Christ's followers need not fear.

The second reason Jesus' followers should not be afraid is that, while the forces of evil can kill the body, they cannot take away a Christian's eternal life (that is, destroy the soul—10:28). Only God the Creator can do that. And He will eventually destroy those persons (souls) who deliberately choose to reject King Jesus and continue to rebel against His kingdom. That destruction will be complete and eternal. After being "devoured" and burned up in the fire that cleanses the earth after the millennium of Revelation 20, the wicked will be as if they had never been (Rev. 20:9, 11-15; see also 2 Pet. 3:11-13; Mal. 4:1-3).

The third reason Jesus' followers should not be afraid is that God loves the humblest of His creatures. If He cares for lowly sparrows, certainly He cares for citizens of the kingdom (10:29-31). These three arguments are aimed at dispelling fear and making the followers of Jesus into fearless advocates of the principles and deeds of His kingdom.

Section 3 of Jesus' sermon. The last major section of Jesus' sermon on mission (10:32-42) is also made up of three central thoughts. Before examining those thoughts, it should be noted that 10:32-42 duplicates some of the themes of verses 5 to 25. Both highlight such issues as persecution by authorities, ridicule by friends, and disapproval by family. But the duplication is not merely repetition for the sake of learning. While 10:5-25 is aimed at the mission of the disciples themselves, verses 32 to 42 are aimed at both the disciples and all believers across time. The change is signaled by such words as *whoever* (vss. 32, 33, 39) and *anyone* (vss. 37, 38, 41, 42). And whereas verses 5 to 25 have many cultural aspects aimed specifically at the disciples' own first mission to the Jews, verses 32 to 42 deal in principles without the cultural baggage of the first part of the chapter.

As in the Sermon on the Mount, the mission sermon closes with three sayings related to final rewards and punishments. The first saying promises that those who confess Jesus publicly will be acknowledged by the Father (vss. 32, 33). The second saying promises that anyone who puts Jesus first—even above his or her family—will certainly find life, with eternal life being implied (vss. 34-39). The third saying promises that the reward of the kingdom will be given to those who show kindness to Jesus' followers (10:40-42). That theme is implied in the Sermon on the Mount (7:12; 5:7, 43-48) and is made quite explicit in Matthew's judgment-day parable of the sheep and goats (25:31-46).

One of the great paradoxes of Christ's life is that even though He is the "Prince of Peace" (Isa. 9:6), accepting Him brings a sword that cuts so deeply that converts often find their closest relationships disrupted. That paradox finds its basis in the fact that the principles of Christ's kingdom as stated in the Sermon on the Mount (chaps. 5–7) are diametrically opposed to those of the kingdoms of this earth. When some members of a family or community operate on one set of principles, while others operate on another, animosity, and persecution are the inevitable result. Christ argues that a Christian's greatest loyalty must be to Him and His principles, even though such a position will bring trouble.

While Christians often have heart peace in this life, for them the fullness of external peace will not be realized until the "Prince of Peace" brings the kingdom to fullness at the second advent. Until that time, God's children are obligated to exist in the kingdoms of this earth while seeking to live according to the principles of the kingdom of heaven. Their dual citizenship brings its own tensions. Thus Christians have reason to look forward to Christ's return in the clouds of heaven.

Christ's second sermon in Matthew closes in the same way the first one did (and as the other three will)—with the words "After Jesus had finished instructing His twelve disciples" (11:1; see also 7:28; 13:53; 19:1; 26:1). As in the other sermons, Matthew's text in 11:1 shifts away from Jesus' teaching to a narrative account that focuses on His actions.

■ Applying the Word

Matthew 8:1–10:42

1. **What does it mean to experience the authority of Christ in my life? In what specific ways have I experienced His authority?**
2. **In what ways have I been close to Jesus? Has my faith grasped Jesus' power and applied it to my daily life, or have I been like the faithless crowd who touched Jesus without receiving either faith or blessing? How can I strengthen my faith in Jesus?**
3. **Am I afraid of bearing my testimony for my Lord in my community and in my family? What evidence can I provide for my answer? What insights can I gain from Matthew 10 to strengthen my courage for witness?**
4. **Am I kind to other Christians in my church and community? What evidence do I have for my answer? In what specific ways can I improve?**

■ Researching the Word

1. **Using an exhaustive concordance, study the word *faith* in Matthew. Describe what he means by faith. Does the word always have the same meaning for him? Do other Bible writers always use the word with the same meaning as Matthew? On that last question, compare Matthew's use of the word with that found in the Epistles to Timothy. What nuances of faith do those epistles add to Matthew's usage? Check your findings against those presented in a Bible dictionary.**
2. **A similar exercise can be carried out profitably for the word *soul* in 10:28. For this word, however, your study should include Old Testament usage also.**

■ Further Study of the Word

1. **For general insight, see E. G. White, *The Desire of Ages*, 262-280, 290-297, 315-320, 333-358.**
2. **For an overview of Gospel miracles and their significance, see J. B. Green and S. McKnight, eds., *Dictionary of Jesus and the Gospels*, 549-560.**
3. **For an overview of discipleship in the Gospels, see ibid., 182-189.**

CHAPTER SIX

Responses to the King

Matthew 11:1–13:58

In his first ten chapters, Matthew sets forth Jesus as King of the Jews (1–4), as the proclaimer of the new law and the higher righteousness (5–7), and as an individual of personal and delegated authority (8–10). Thus Matthew 1 to 10 sets forth the offer of Jesus the Messiah to the Jewish people.

Beginning with chapter 11, the first Gospel takes a radical shift in direction. It moves from the offer of the Messiah to Israel's refusal of that offer—a refusal that, as we will see, climaxes in chapter 27 with the crucifixion.

Thus Matthew 11 to 13 plays a crucial part in Matthew's story. Chapters 11 and 12 emphasize Jewish rejection of Jesus in a way that has only been hinted at in previous chapters. Chapter 13—the third great teaching discourse (sermon) in Matthew—continues the response-to-Jesus theme by setting forth acceptance and rejection of Him and His kingdom in the form of parables.

■ Getting Into the Word

Matthew 11, 12

Read Matthew 11 and 12 through two times. Then work out the following exercises, making a note of the results in your Matthew notebook.

1. **Why, according to the marginal reference, was John in prison (11:2)? Again, why was he discouraged about Jesus in 11:2, 3? Use your marginal reference for 11:2 to compare John's original expectations of Jesus with His actual ministry. How did Jesus' work differ from what John had suggested? What is the significance of Jesus' reply in 11:4-6? Once again, the marginal references will help you unlock the answer. What do you think Jesus meant when He claimed that John was both the greatest and the least (vs. 11)? What do you think Jesus was saying about *Himself* when He referred to John as Elijah in 11:14? Your marginal reference to the Old Testament will help you here.**
2. **What is the significance of Jesus' comparison of the Jewish cities of Korazin and Bethsaida to Tyre, Sidon, and Sodom? Use a Bible dictionary, a concordance, and/or marginal references to help you understand the symbolism of each of the Old Testament cities mentioned. Summarize your conclusions in a short paragraph.**
3. **Outline the confrontation of Jesus with the Pharisees regarding the Sabbath in 12:1-14. List what we can learn from that study. In a short paragraph, summarize the principles that undergird Jesus' approach to the events described. In comparing 12:14 with 12:2, what do you find of special interest in the mentality of the Pharisees? By using the aids in your Bible, discover what Mark adds to our understanding of principles in his parallel treatment of the confrontation over the Sabbath.**
4. **One could get the impression from 12:38 that the scribes and Pharisees had not seen Jesus perform any miracles. Is that true? Where were these Jewish leaders in chapters 8 and 9, and what was their response? What is the significance of their request in 12:38 in the flow of Matthew's Gospel? What is the significance of Jesus' answer (vss. 39, 40) in the Gospel's movement to its climax in chapters 27 and 28?**

■ Exploring the Word

Rejection, Judgment, and Rest

Matthew 11:2, 3 signals a turning point in Matthew's story. John the Baptist had heard about what "Christ was doing," and his mind was filled with doubts as to whether this could truly be the Messiah. " 'Are you the one who was to come,' " John asks in despair through his disciples, " 'or should we expect someone else?' "

At first glance, a reader might surmise that John was discouraged because of his physical circumstances. After all, he had had a run-in with Herod Antipas because of his criticism of Herod's illicit relationship with his sister-in-law (14:3-5). As a result, the Baptist had been imprisoned in the fortress of Machaerus, situated east of the Dead Sea (Josephus, *Antiquities*, 18.5.1,2). And yet Jesus had done nothing to release him. John could very easily have felt discouraged because of his circumstances.

While that problem may have bothered him, another issue lay behind his doubt. As he saw it, *Jesus wasn't acting like the predicted Messiah*.

Beyond the Jewish understanding of a conquering Messiah, John himself had implied that Jesus would bring the ax down on the root of the trees (3: 10), that He would be a "powerful" Messiah who would baptize with "fire" (vs.11), that He would be a judgmental Messiah of Israel's enemies—a Messiah who would appear on the "threshing floor" with a "winnowing fork . . . in his hand" to gather God's wheat into the barn and burn up "the chaff with unquenchable fire" (vs. 12).

In his frustration, John questioned his own experience of certainty at Jesus' baptism. Jesus just didn't act like the expected Jewish Messiah, not even like the Messiah he had announced to the crowds at the Jordan.

Jesus' reply to John's disciples is of crucial importance in our understanding of the kingdom of heaven. Jesus doesn't come out with a direct reply to John's representatives. He merely tells them to go back to John and tell him that they have seen " 'the blind receive sight, the lame walk, those who have leprosy . . . cured, the deaf hear, the dead . . . raised, and the good news . . . preached to the poor' " (11:5).

While that might not seem like much of an answer to us regarding John's specific doubts, to a Jew steeped in Old Testament prophecy, it was tantamount to claiming to be the Messiah. Jesus based His reply on Isaiah 35:5, 6 and 61:1, texts widely accepted at the time as Messianic, which predicted that the Messiah would do the very works Jesus had demonstrated.

Slowly but surely, Matthew is unfolding the complexity of the kingdom—a kingdom of grace established at Christ's first advent that will be followed by a judgment phase at the second advent. John was correct, but he had failed to realize the unfolding nature of the kingdom and the unfolding role of the Messiah. Matthew will show us more of that unfolding in his twenty-fourth and twenty-fifth chapters.

Meanwhile, the doomed John has had a satisfactory answer to his query. Jesus is indeed the Christ. But before Jesus is finished speaking about John to the crowd in 11:1-19, He will make a more explicit claim about His own exalted identity. That claim comes in 11:14, where Jesus notes that the Baptist " 'is the Elijah who was to come.' " In that saying Jesus is referring back to Malachi 4:5, in which God says that He will send " 'the prophet Elijah before that great and dreadful day of the LORD comes.' " When we examine this text in the sequence of Jesus' argument, He is saying that His forerunner (Matt. 3:11), John the Elijah, has come, which means that He Himself is the LORD who is to follow! Thus in 11:14 Jesus is claiming divinity. No wonder He says, " 'He who has ears, let him hear' " (vs. 15). Knowledgeable Jewish hearers would "hear" in this Elijah saying Jesus' claim to be " 'God with us' " (1:23).

In the process of making His own claim to identity, Jesus has some nice yet perplexing things to say about John. " 'I tell you the truth,' " Jesus tells the Jews. " 'Among those born of women there has not risen anyone greater than John the Baptist; yet he who is least in the kingdom of heaven is greater than he' " (11:11).

Alfred Plummer seems to have captured the essence of this paradoxical statement. "John's office and mission," Plummer asserts, "was higher than that of any of his predecessors. He not only prophesied of the Messiah, he was His Herald, and pointed Him out as come. But he was not within the Kingdom which he announced; and, in the Kingdom, the humblest members are higher than the greatest of those who are not members. In spiritual privileges and knowledge Christians are above John. He is the friend of the Bridegroom; they are His spouse" (Plummer, 162). Both John's doubt and his lack of understanding about the nature of the kingdom's principles demonstrate that he is still on the outside. For John, the kingdom is still only "near" (3:2).

In light of that fact, it is of interest that the leading Jews rejected both John and Jesus. They didn't like John's message of repentance any more than Jesus' declaration of the revolutionary principles of the kingdom (11:16-19).

It is in the context of Jewish rejection that the passage on the unrepentant cities of Korazin and Bethsaida has meaning. Three of Jesus' disciples came from Bethsaida; Jesus had given sight to a blind man there (Mark 8:22-26); and the five thousand were fed near there (Luke 9:10-17). Certainly Bethsaida and Korazin (which was close to Capernaum) and similar Jewish cities have had a chance to develop faith in Jesus. Yet they have not repented.

Jesus next contrasts their chances and choices with those of the heathen Gentile cities of Sidon and Tyre to the north of Israel. These cities were denounced in the Old Testament for their wickedness (see, for example, Isa. 23; Ezek. 26; Amos 1:9, 10). Yet, says Jesus, even they would have repented in "sackcloth and ashes" if they had had the same opportunities as Korazin and Bethsaida. Jesus takes the contrast a step further by comparing the probable response of Sodom to that of Capernaum. (Sodom was a city proverbial for its wickedness—a wickedness so terrible that it has contributed the word *sodomy* to the English language.) Capernaum was called Jesus' "own town" (9:1). It was the most favored city of His recorded ministry. But the comparison with Sodom is highly unfavorable. Why? Because the Jews are rejecting their Messiah, in spite of His many works. The result will be a worse judgment in the "day of judgment" for unresponsive Israel and its favored cities and people (vss. 24, 22) than for these heathen cities. Thus Matthew again hammers home his theme of the consequences of Jews rejecting their Messiah.

But all is not lost. Some Jews do respond to Jesus in a positive manner. That is the message of 11:25-30. Yet it is not generally the learned and privileged class who so respond, but the "little children"—the humble people (vs. 25). Knowing God in a saving way, Jesus says, does not depend upon human wisdom and education. Too often the privileged of this world conclude that their wisdom and position make them superior to others. Their self-sufficiency makes it difficult for them to trust in God. Such an attitude is death to knowing God in a saving way. Such individuals fail to enter God's rest.

But Jesus cries out to those, privileged or otherwise, who realize their need, who are burdened and weary. To all such, He offers "rest" (vss. 28, 29).

The word *rest* is the key to understanding this passage. The same root word in Greek is used in the Septuagint (Greek) translation of Exodus 33:14 to signify the rest that God was to give Israel through Moses' leadership. All along, Matthew has been comparing Jesus to Moses, and, as we noted earlier, the development of the first Gospel runs parallel to the Exodus experience. Jesus, in Matthew's eyes, is the prophet like Moses whom God said He would raise up (Deut. 18:15, 18).

However, the second Moses will succeed where the first failed. The second will give the rest that was promised through Moses, but was never achieved (11:28, 29; see also Heb. 4:1-11).

In a similar manner, Jesus promises an easier yoke (11:29, 30). The rabbis spoke of "the yoke of law" as a great blessing, but under their interpretation, the yoke of the law had become a burden rather than a blessing. Jesus later accused the scribes and Pharisees of making the people carry "heavy loads" by their legalistic demands (23:4). They had perverted God's intention in the law given through Moses. But Christ, in Matthew's Gospel, seeks to bring His followers back to God's original plan: that the law be a blessing as people focus on its spirit and not merely its letter. Thus R. T. France can write: "Jesus' yoke is *easy* . . . not because it makes lighter demands [its demands are actually heavier, according to 5:20], but because it represents entering into a disciple-relationship (*learn from me*) with one who is *gentle and lowly in heart*" (France, *The Gospel*, 201).

For those who have responded positively to Jesus the Messiah, the law still points to rest. But God's people must view the law properly and relate to it in a healthy way if it is to fulfill its purpose in their lives. With that idea in place, Matthew is ready to deal with the conflict over law between Jesus and the Pharisees. The point of conflict is the Sabbath.

Pharisaic Rejection Intensifies

In chapter 11 we saw the dark shadow of increasing opposition fall across Matthew's story. We saw John raise serious doubts about Jesus because his expectations were not fulfilled. We saw the crowd reject Jesus out of a lack of seriousness. And we saw certain favored Jewish cities reject Him. But in chapter 12 we find the most serious rejection of all—that of the Pharisees.

While Jesus had been widely accepted early in His ministry, over time the Jewish religious leaders came to see that His teachings and His deeds were incompatible with their basic position. They came to realize that if the people accepted and followed Jesus' teachings, their own leadership would be threatened. Thus the escalating conflict between Jesus and the Pharisees and other Jewish leaders. The principles of the kingdom of heaven were on a collision course with the principles of the kingdom of the Jewish church.

The first confrontation between Jesus and the Pharisees in Matthew 12 has to do with the Sabbath. Of all their religious practices, the Sabbath was the most important to the Jews. They took their Sabbath observance very seriously. For example, when enemy soldiers attacked them in the time of the Maccabees (second century B.C.), the Jewish soldiers allowed themselves and their families to be slaughtered rather than break the Sabbath by defending themselves (1 Macc. 2:31-38). The Jews eventually developed some 1,521 oral rules related to Sabbath observance (Moore, 2:28).

They were desperately in earnest to protect the Sabbath. They had a rule against almost every conceivable way to transgress the Sabbath law of the Ten Commandments. In this context, it is easy to see why Matthew places the conflict between Jesus and the Pharisees over the Sabbath immediately after Jesus' words about His yoke being easy and His burden being light (11:29, 30). He wants us to understand that Jesus is not against the Sabbath, but He does reject the multitude of manmade rules that keep it from being a blessing.

An occasion for conflict arose when Jesus' disciples plucked and ate grain as they walked to their destination on the Sabbath. The Pharisees accused them of Sabbath breaking rather than theft, because Deuteronomy permitted travelers to eat enough grain or other produce while walking through a field to stave off hunger (Deut. 23:25).

The problem was that Jesus' disciples were picking and eating the grain on the Sabbath. In the process, they broke several Jewish rules for the Sabbath. As the Pharisees understood it, picking grain was reaping, rubbing the grain from the husks (Luke 6:1) was threshing, blowing away the husks could be interpreted as winnowing, while the whole process was obviously the preparation of food—a task that should have been done on the sixth day. According to the Talmud, it was sinful to reap and grind grain that amounted to more than the bulk of a dried fig (Shab. 70b).

Given their regulations, it is not surprising that the Pharisees go to Jesus and accuse the disciples of Sabbath breaking (12:2). He answers them with two illustrations from the Old Testament. The first deals with David's unlawful eating of the consecrated shewbread (1 Sam. 21:1-6) and demonstrates that human need takes precedence over ritual precision. Jesus' second illustration is based upon Numbers 28:9, which indicates that God commanded the priests to offer a larger number of routine sacrifices on the Sabbath than on weekdays. Yet they were without guilt. Thus, Jesus says in effect, the worship of God takes precedence over the regulations of the day.

Jesus' argument climaxes in 12:6-8, where He claims to be greater than the temple and its services, and thus (as demonstrated in verses 3-5) greater than the Sabbath (vs. 6). In fact, He is the Lord of the Sabbath (vs. 8). The Sabbath is the Lord's Day, and He knows how it ought to be kept. In light of that knowledge, Jesus flatly claims that "mercy" (quoting Hosea 6:6) is better in the eyes of God than even the ritual exactness commanded by God in the Pentateuch—let alone the human rules developed by the scribes and Pharisees (12:7).

On the grounds that mercy is superior to ritual precision, the disciples' eating of grain is permissible. But to make His point crystal clear, Jesus *deliberately* heals a man with a crippled hand on the Sabbath day in the very presence of the accusing Jews (vs. 13). The rabbis permitted healing on the Sabbath if human life was in danger (Homa 8:6), but a crippled hand was hardly a life-threatening illness. Jesus' point is that " 'it is lawful to do good on the Sabbath' " (vs. 12). Mark puts the Sabbath and all other divine law in perspective when he quotes Jesus as saying that " 'the Sabbath was made for man, not man for the Sabbath' " (Mark 2:27).

It is a hallmark of all legalism that law is put above human considerations and mercy. But, as in the Sermon on the Mount, Jesus attempts to help the Jews see the spiritual nature of the law, that it must be rooted in *agapē* (love) if it is to be understood correctly.

Unfortunately, the Jews did not really understand the law. As a result, when Jesus pointed them to its foundation in *agapē*, they "plotted how they might kill" Him (12:14).

That is the paradox of legalism. Legalists, in their purported love for God and His law, become angry with those who disagree with them over their particular theological interpretations—so angry that they are willing to murder their opponents or destroy their reputation. Such anger, according to Jesus, is actually the equivalent of murder (see 5:21-26).

Anybody who has been a church member for very long knows that the spirit of Pharisaism is not dead. It is alive and well in the twentieth century among those who would attack and criticize others over differences of opinion. Indeed, most congregations have their contingent of Pharisees. Worse yet, there is a Pharisee within the skin of each of us that seeks to impose its spirit on an unsuspecting church and an undeserving world. Every Christian needs to remember daily that mercy is better than sacrifice and that *agapē* is the heart of God's law.

Matthew will return to Jesus' conflict with the Pharisees in the Beelzebub story of 12:22. But between the Sabbath conflict and the later conflicts of chapter 12, he inserts his longest quotation from the Old Testament—verses 18 to 21. He quotes Isaiah 42:1-4, which was seen by the Jews as a Messianic prophecy. Matthew accomplishes several things by quoting this passage from Isaiah. First, he identifies Jesus as the predicted Messianic Servant whom God loves (vs. 18). That expression of love to the Servant brings to the mind of Matthew's readers his use of " 'This is my Son, whom I love.' " Twice he repeats this phrase in his Gospel—once at Jesus' baptism (3:17) and once at His transfiguration (17:5). The unique identity of Jesus is never far from the surface in Matthew's Gospel.

A second major contribution of the Isaiah quotation is that it identifies Jesus as operating under the Spirit of God (vs. 18). This prepares us for the events of 12:22-37, in which Jesus is accused by the Pharisees of operating under the influence of the "prince of demons" (vs. 24).

Third, the Isaiah quotation twice reinforces the global aspect of the Messianic mission. "He will proclaim justice to the nations" (vs. 18), and "in his name the nations will put their hope" (vs. 21). Matthew loses few opportunities to pound home his themes. The tensions between Jewish rejection of the Messiah and Gentile acceptance runs throughout the first Gospel. Matthew loves his Jewish brothers and sisters, and he desperately wants them to respond positively to Jesus, but he repeatedly demonstrates from the Jews' own Scriptures that the Gentiles are not outside the pale of God's love, and that He is capable of raising up "children of Abraham" from outside the Jewish people (3:9).

In spite of Matthew's desire for the Jews to respond positively to Jesus, he is forced to report that the opposite is most often the case. In 12:24 he returns to the chapter's theme of Pharisaic rejection of Jesus.

The next rejection episode is the Beelzebub story (12:22-37). It begins when Jesus heals a blind mute. The frightening thing for the Jewish leaders is that the people are so enthused by the miracle that they begin to wonder out loud if Jesus might not be "the Son of David"—that is, the Messiah (vs. 23).

The frustrated Pharisees cannot deny the reality of the miracle, but they can deny that it came from God. Their solution is that Jesus is in league with the "prince of demons" (vs. 24).

Jesus immediately takes the offensive by telling them that if He were effecting cures through the agency of demons, then Satan's kingdom would be divided against itself and would be in ruins (vss. 25-28). To the contrary, argues Jesus, He is the devil's greatest enemy. He likens Himself to a thief who binds a strong man so he can plunder his house (vs. 29). In other words, Jesus the Christ (God with us) has invaded the territory of "the prince of this world" (John 12:31; 14:30; 16:11) to rescue God's children.

The climax of the confrontation in the Beelzebub story comes in 12:30-32. In this passage Jesus not only warns His hearers that there is no neutrality in the great struggle between good and evil, but He goes on to say that anyone who credits the work of God to the devil has committed the unpardonable sin (vs. 31). While it is technically true that people can speak against the Son and still be forgiven, they cannot do so and be forgiven if they are under the conviction of the Holy Spirit that Jesus is the Messiah. To do so would be to reject the prompting of the Holy Spirit in their heart and mind. The result is a hardened conscience (1 Tim. 4:2; Titus 1:15) that can no longer respond to the Spirit's work of leading people to repent of and confess their sin (John 16:8). Such rejecters are beyond the reach of God's Spirit, for they have tuned out the only channel through which God can reach them. When that is done, they are beyond hope. They have committed the unforgivable sin.

Many sensitive Christians worry that they have committed the unpardonable sin. The very fact that they are concerned is an indication that they are still listening for the Spirit and desire to respond to Him. Frederick Bruner is right on target when he writes that "the spirit of the sin against the Spirit is an unworried adamancy. It is impenitence, the unwillingness to repent. . . . It is not careless acts, it is a hardened state" (Bruner, 1:462).

Jesus goes on to claim that the true state of people can be told by the words that come out of their mouths (12:33-37). Such a truth does not bode well for the Pharisees, whose mouths have recently set forth the view that Jesus' actions were inspired by the devil rather than God. If they continue in that line, 12:22-37 implies, they will eventually commit the unpardonable sin.

The Beelzebub confrontation between Jesus and the Pharisees is immediately followed by one in which they ask for "a miraculous sign" (vs. 38). Read out of its context, a reader could easily get the impression that this was a sincere request. But chapters 8 to 12 indicate that the Pharisees were far from sincere. They had seen many miracles, but had attributed them to Jesus' cooperation with the devil (12:24).

As a result, Jesus again takes the offensive by calling them "a wicked and adulterous generation" (vs. 39). They will get only one sign—the sign of Jonah, who spent three days in a fish. In the same way, Jesus will spend " 'three days and three nights in the heart of the earth' " (vs. 40). The point of this saying is that Jesus will spend *only* three days in the earth. The disciples will later recall such statements. This is Jesus' first prediction of His resurrection.

At this juncture in the confrontation, Jesus once again warns the Jews along two lines. First, reminiscent of 11:20-24, He notes that Nineveh and the Queen of Sheba learned the lesson God had for them, but the Jews are failing to learn (12:41, 42). Second, Jesus tells the Pharisees that a negative religion is not enough.

Staying away from all the evil they have identified in their approach to law will not help them unless, at the same time, they fill their lives with the positive principles of the kingdom. Beyond that, in the context of the passage, the Pharisees need to repent of their attitude toward Jesus and fill their lives with what He has to offer. Even Pharisees need a Saviour and a positive religion based on mercy (vss. 43-45).

But those who do accept Him and His kingdom principles, Jesus warns, as He shifts the ground a bit, will not have it easy. His own life has demonstrated that living and teaching the principles of the kingdom of heaven can lead to rejection. So it will be with those who follow Him.

That seems to be the point of Jesus' using His family illustration in 12:46-50. Families have taken a beating thus far in Matthew's Gospel. In 4:21, 22 James and John leave their father when Jesus calls them to follow Him. In 8:22 Jesus tells a follower that he can't really be a disciple if he puts his father above Jesus. And in 10:34-37 Jesus tells His hearers that those who choose to follow Him will find themselves rejected by their own families. Jesus leaves no doubt that following Him must be put above all else. As in the Decalogue, Christians are allowed to put nothing before God and service to Him (Ex. 20:3).

But those who do give up all for Jesus, He tells us in 12:48-50, will not be left alone. They will have many brothers, sisters, and mothers in the faith when they do the will of the Father in heaven (vs. 50). These faithful ones "become children of God" (John 1:12, 13) and are "adopted" into the heavenly family (Gal. 4:5; Eph. 1:5). As W. D. Davies and D. C. Allison put it, "Jesus' demand to forsake family is only made in view of the Christian family which awaits new members with open arms. It is not a call to a solitary existence" (Davies and Allison, 2:367). Thus Matthew builds toward his doctrine of the church, a teaching that will come to fruition in chapters 16 and 18.

Meanwhile, it should be noted, those who respond to Jesus in a positive manner will have their reward—not only here but in the hereafter. That thought will arise again in chapter 13.

■ Getting Into the Word

Matthew 13

Read chapter 13 through two times. Then examine the following questions and issues.

1. **There are seven parables in this chapter (eight, if verse 52 is viewed as a parable). Describe in a few short sentences the major lessons in each parable.**
2. **List the reasons given in chapter 13 for Jesus' teaching in parables. Given the problem in chapters 11 and 12, what other reason might be added to that list? Can you think of still other reasons?**
3. **In one or two paragraphs, discuss the significance of 13:53-58. The word *amazed* (*astonished and marvelled*, KJV) has been used twice by Matthew already. Use a concordance to find those occurrences. Then discuss the implications of the word's repeated use. Repeat the process to discover the other mentions of the leading phrase in 13:53. Again, what are the implications of its repeated use?**

■ Exploring the Word

Parables of the Kingdom

Chapter 13 stands out in the flow of Matthew's Gospel because it represents Jesus' first extensive use of parables. (A parable is most easily defined as "an earthly story with a heavenly meaning" [Barclay, 2:62].) Up to this time, Jesus' teaching has been fairly straightforward. In particular, His two teaching discourses—the Sermon on the Mount (chaps. 5–7) and the sermon on discipleship (chap. 10)—did not make extensive use of parables. But in chapter 13, Matthew's third teaching discourse, that all changes. This chapter contains seven parables (eight if 13:52 is viewed as a parable), and parables will be in frequent use from here up through to the end of chapter 25.

Why, we must ask, do we have this radical shift in Jesus' teaching methodology beginning in 13:1? The primary answer lies in chapters 11 and 12. Jesus has been rejected by the Jewish leaders. That rejection, however, does not mean that He has decided to stop preaching to the Jews. Far from it! Jesus will continue ministering "to the lost sheep of Israel" (15:24), but henceforth, He must be more careful. After all, we noted in chapter 12, the opposition of the Jewish leaders to Jesus has become so strong that they are plotting to kill Him (vs. 54). Thus it behooves Him to preach in a way that will not alienate His opponents or allow them to use His words about the kingdom against Him in a court of law, as though they were subversive. He still wants to reach the Jewish leaders. But how to do this is becoming a growing issue. Parables are part of the answer to the problem. Because they use figurative language, parables can convey a message in a manner that is "safe."

Beyond being safe, parables are also good teaching devices. First, parables are interest grabbers. People love stories, and the Jews of old were no exception. Jesus, who proved Himself to be one of the great storytellers of world history, capitalized on a significant psychological factor through His use of parables. His parables, which begin with items familiar in the lives of His hearers, helped keep their attention.

Second, parables make truth concrete. Jesus was not speaking in abstractions, but about things familiar in the people's daily lives. Parables moved Jesus' hearers from the world around them to spiritual realities beyond this world. It was their world He was talking about. They could see that His stories not only had earthly meaning but also had meaning beyond their earthly experience.

A third teaching value of parables is their ongoing dynamic teaching function. Because Jesus' parables utilized concrete things in the daily lives of His hearers, every time they saw these things, they remembered His lessons. Ellen White put it nicely when she wrote: "Afterward, as they looked upon the objects that illustrated His lessons, they recalled the words of the divine Teacher. To minds that were open to the Holy Spirit, the significance of the Saviour's teaching unfolded more and more. Mysteries grew clear, and that which had been hard to grasp became evident" (White, *Christ's Object Lessons*, 21).

A fourth teaching value in parables is that they compel individuals to discover truth for themselves. Reflection led Jesus' hearers to flesh out truth for themselves as their interest in the subject matter of the parable caused them to think through the truth in the stories. Conversely, as Barclay puts it, "the parable *conceals truth from those who are either too lazy to think or too blind through prejudice to see*" (Barclay, 2:62). It is the dual elements in value four that Jesus seemed to be driving at in 13:11-15.

A final value in Jesus' use of parables as a teaching device is that Matthew sees in that methodology the fulfillment of one more Old Testament prediction (vss. 34, 35).

The rejection of Jesus by so many of the Jews and their religious leaders in Matthew 11 and 12 not only led to a radical shift in Jesus' teaching methodology in chapter 13, but also dictated the content of the parables of that chapter. After all, Matthew is faced with a dilemma as he writes his Gospel for his Jewish neighbors several decades after Christ's death: How is it that the Messiah could be rejected by His own people? That rejection seems to go against Jewish eschatological expectation. Why do some respond to Jesus, while most reject Him?

Matthew's answer begins with the parable of the four types of soil and its explanation (vss. 1-9, 18-23). In essence, Jesus teaches Matthew's readers that the root of the trouble does not lie with God. After all, God has made provision for the gospel to be preached to all types of people (soils), but all do not respond in the same way. Some allow the evil one to snatch the seeds of truth out of their hearts (vs. 19), others receive it with joy but give it up when they see the cost (vs. 21), some hear receptively but let the cares of this life strangle their interest in the life to come (vs. 22), while still others receive the word and bear Christian fruit (vs. 23).

Readers are left with two impressions after reading this parable. First, those who receive the word and remain faithful are definitely in the minority. That insight lines up with the experience of Jesus' first hearers and with the reality of evangelism in the late twentieth century. Second, the parable leaves the impression that the mixed reception to the gospel is not God's fault. He may provide the opportunity for salvation, but fruition depends upon human response. God makes the offer, but it is people in their free will who do the responding. Unfortunately, the proclamation of the gospel does not eradicate human waywardness and sinful humanity's alienation from God and the principles of His kingdom.

The parable of the weeds (vss. 24-30, 36-42) carries the explanation of the rejection of Jesus a bit farther than the parable of the four soils. While the soils emphasize the perversity of human reaction, the weeds parable points beyond the human realm to the supernatural activity of the devil—to the cosmic conflict between Christ and Satan. Thus the rejection of the Messiah is due not only to human responsibility, but is also due to the work of the devil.

Jesus also gave the parable of the weeds to help the disciples and Christians down through the ages to understand that the church is not perfect. It is a mixture of weeds (apparent Christians) and wheat (genuine Christians), and this condition will continue to exist to the end of the age. That does not imply that some weeds will not be removed through excommunication (see 18:15-20), but rather that in most cases human discernment will not be adequate for the weeding process to be carried out. The lack of human discernment is made worse by the complexities of human relationships and the deceptiveness of sin. All of this makes it impossible at present to do a thorough work of weeding the church. But the wheat will be separated by the angels at the end of the age, and at that time everyone will receive his or her reward (vss. 40-43). Until then, God's garden will be quite a bit less than perfect.

Parables three (the mustard seed) and four (the yeast) are also tied to the problem of rejection of the Messiah (vss. 31-33). In essence, these parables taught the earliest disciples (and us, by extension) not to be discouraged by small beginnings. Jesus' ministry may have appeared to have failed, but time would eventually prove that observation to be false. Just as a tiny mustard seed or a pinch of yeast could expand its influence, so would the kingdom of God. It is the hidden presence of Jesus that generates success, not outward appearances. Once again, these two parables point to ultimate victory when Christ returns.

The fifth (the hidden treasure) and sixth (the pearl of great price) parables (vss. 44-46) bring us back to the human response factor in the rejection of Jesus that we glimpsed in the parable of the four soils. It is little wonder that Jesus' kingdom was not (and has never been) popular with the majority, including religious leaders. After all, the cost of accepting Jesus as Messiah and Lord is nothing less than all we have and all we are. He will later tell His disciples that the price of the kingdom is the crucifixion of their very selves (16:24, 25).

Thus Dietrich Bonhoeffer could say that "when Christ calls a man, he bids him come and die" (Bonhoeffer, 99). The very cost of discipleship—that is, *all*—goes a long way toward helping Matthew's Jewish readers and Christians down through the ages to understand why so many have rejected Jesus and why some weeds have masqueraded as wheat in the Lord's garden. To become "genuine wheat," a person must be willing to give up *all* for the kingdom.

In light of that fact, it is high time that the "Pharisees" and other legalists in today's church stop downplaying *agapē* (love) to one's neighbor as a "cheap" perversion of the gospel. Jesus' demand is infinitely higher than the little abstinences and rituals that those with a legalistic mind-set prescribe. And, unfortunately, those very abstinences and rituals can lead to renewed pride in one's accomplishments. The call of the gospel is total surrender of all a person has and is. When Luther entered the monastery, notes Bonhoeffer, "he had left everything behind except his pious self." But when he met Christ, "even that was taken from him" (Bonhoeffer, 51).

The final parable in Matthew 13 is that of the net (vss. 47-50). Here Jesus returns to a topic already explored in the parable of the tares (vss. 40-43). The main point of the net parable is quite straightforward: The wicked, at the end of the age (the second coming of Jesus), will be separated from the righteous and suffer due punishment. As in Matthew's first two teaching discourses, this one ends with an eschatological (end-time) judgment scene (7:24-27; 10:40-42). Needless to say, the parable of the net also implies that there will be some intermingling of the good and bad fish in the kingdom up until the second advent.

Matthew binds off the discourse on the parables of the kingdom by noting that since the disciples understand the words of Jesus, they qualify as scribes or teachers of the law. In that function, their approach should be to value the old truths of Judaism at its best as well as the principles of the kingdom of heaven recently set forth. Thus they will bring out of their "storeroom new treasures as well as old" (vs. 52). In fact, given Matthew's presentation thus far, it can be inferred that the new will shed light on the meaning of the old.

Matthew 13:53 brings us to a turning point in his Gospel. He uses a saying very similar to the formula he used at the end of the Sermon on the Mount and the sermon on discipleship (7:28; 11:1) to conclude his third teaching discourse: "When Jesus had finished these parables."

Matthew then gives a short overview of Jesus' visit to His hometown of Nazareth, where, in keeping with the theme of chapters 11 to 13, most "took offense at him," even though they were "amazed" at His wisdom and power (vss. 54, 57).

The citizens of Nazareth demonstrated the truth of the proverb that "familiarity breeds contempt." They just didn't see how this hometown boy could be who He claimed to be. Jesus' comment to them was that " 'only in his hometown and in his own house is a prophet without honor' " (vss. 55-57).

The rejection response to Jesus as the Messiah, highlighted in chapters 11 to 13, will continue to the climax of Matthew's Gospel at the crucifixion.

■ Applying the Word

Matthew 11–13

1. What is my relationship to God's Sabbath? Is it a burden or a blessed rest in my life? What positive things could I do to make the Sabbath a richer experience in my Christian walk? Discuss each item in that last question in a specific way that can be put into practice.
2. Do I ever get so angry with those who differ from me theologically that feelings of hate or unhealthy aggressive behavior begin to surface? What do those feelings tell me about my walk with Jesus? In what ways can God help me with this problem?
3. What is my relationship to the family of God? In what ways can I enrich that relationship? In what ways can my local church improve its familylike atmosphere? How can my denomination do likewise?
4. Am I willing to sell all that I have for the kingdom? In what specific areas do I seem to be holding back sections of my life from Jesus' lordship?

■ Researching the Word

1. Using a concordance (preferably an exhaustive concordance), make a list of all the facts you can find about the Sabbath in the New Testament. What guidelines do you find for Sabbath observance? Do the same for the Old Testament. What indications do you find in both testaments that the Sabbath is special to the Lord?
2. The unpardonable sin of Matthew 12:30-32 has troubled many people. Hebrews 6:4-8 and 10:26-31 also speak of unpardonable sins. Study each passage in its context. How do the three passages differ from one another? How do they agree? What can be learned from a composite understanding of the three? You may want to use the *Seventh-day*

Adventist Bible Commentary and/or some other Bible commentary as an aid in gaining insight, but you will gain more from this study if you carefully study out each passage from your Bible *before* you seek the help of a commentary. Learn to wrestle with the Word, but, at the same time, learn to appreciate scholarly helps.

■ Further Study of the Word

1. For general insight into the reason Christ taught in parables and into the lessons of the parables in Matthew 13, see E. G. White, *Christ's Object Lessons*, 17-61, 70-134.
2. For more on the Pharisaic approach to sin and law, see G. R. Knight, *The Pharisee's Guide to Perfect Holiness*, 13-72.
3. For a sampling of Jewish regulations on Sabbath keeping, see D. F. Neufeld and J. Neuffer, eds., *Seventh-day Adventist Bible Students' Source Book*, 846-856.
4. For a relatively short but fairly comprehensive discussion of parables, see J. B. Green and S. McKnight, eds., *Dictionary of Jesus and the Gospels*, 591-601.

CHAPTER SEVEN

The King Withdraws

Matthew 14:1–16:20

In chapters 11 to 13 Matthew set the tone for the rest of his book: the escalating tension between Jesus and the Jewish leaders that will end with the Jews crucifying their own Messiah.

Matthew 14:1 to 16:20 starts with the beginning of the end—the death of Jesus' forerunner (John the Baptist) as a symbol of Jesus' own forthcoming death. The passage ends with Peter's straightforward proclamation that Jesus is " 'the Christ, the Son of the living God' " (16:16) and Jesus' explicit announcement of His death.

The theme of rejection by the Jews still is evident, and coupled with this theme is an increasing work by Jesus among the Gentiles. Throughout Matthew 14:13 to 16:20 is the repeated concept of withdrawal by Jesus, first into the hinterlands of Jewish territory and later into Gentile areas. At the close of the withdrawal interludes, Jesus sets His face toward Jerusalem and the accomplishment of His ultimate mission, as He is confronted by the kingdoms of this world.

■ Getting Into the Word

Matthew 14:1–15:20

Read 14:1 to 16:20 through one time, listing the evidence you can find of the withdrawal theme. Look up on the maps in your Bible the places to which Jesus travels. This will help

you trace that theme. After examining the entire passage, reread 14:1 to 15:20 twice. Then turn to the following exercises.

1. **What is the relationship between the withdrawing in 14:13 and the experience of John in 14:1-12?**
2. **In Matthew, Mark, and John, the feeding of the five thousand is followed by the story of Jesus walking on the water. Find these parallel passages through the study aids in your Bible (or through the use of a concordance), and read them carefully. Compare and contrast all three Gospels on the water-walking experience. How are they alike? How do they differ? In particular, look for hints through comparative study as to why Jesus "made" the disciples sail off without Him while He dismissed the crowd (14:22). What did the feeding of the five thousand have to do with the mass movement that Jesus had to dispel? (Note that you will need more than one Gospel account to answer that last question.)**
3. **In 15:1-20 Jesus talks to three distinct audiences. List these three groups and the inclusive passages that have to do with each. Then summarize in three paragraphs the message of Jesus to each audience. Finally, list the ways in which the three conversations reinforce one another.**

■ Exploring the Word

The Death of the Forerunner and the Threat of Herod

A new threat to Jesus arises in 14:1, this time in the person of Herod Antipas, the ruler of Galilee. Although Herod was quite familiar with John the Baptist's ministry, he seems to be relatively ignorant of that of Jesus. Thus, probably as a result of both superstition and an overwrought conscience, Herod confuses the two men and fears that perhaps Jesus is a resurrected John (vs. 2).

At this point in his story, Matthew lets us know why Herod's conscience is overwrought concerning John. Some time earlier, Herod had been confronted by the prophet of repentance regarding his unlawful liaison with his brother's wife. The upshot was that Herod had John arrested and would have put him to death had he not feared the people, who held John to be a prophet (vs. 5).

Herod's weakness shows through not only in his fear of the people but also in his relationship to his lover, who maneuvers him into beheading John against Herod's better judgment. Because Herod also fears the opinions of his guests, he lets himself be manipulated (vss. 6-11).

All in all, the story shows Herod Antipas to be a weak person who more than once in these few verses goes against his conscience. It is little wonder that his imagination gets the best of him when he learns about the powerful ministry of Jesus. Herod is hardly a man to be trusted. It is little wonder that Jesus "withdrew . . . to a solitary place" after John's disciples report his death to Jesus (vss. 13, 12).

At first glance it appears that the story of John's arrest and death is an aside to Matthew's ongoing narrative of Jesus. But a little reflection shows that conclusion to be hasty. To the contrary, Matthew's telling of John's end is integrally linked to Jesus' own forthcoming death. Matthew appears to be using the death of John to foreshadow Jesus' death. Just as John had been Jesus' forerunner in ministry (3:1-11), so will he be Jesus' forerunner in death (14:1-12). That parallelism is first indicated by the fact that just as Jesus calls Himself a prophet in 13:57, so is John identified as a prophet in 14:5. Not only is he a prophet, but he will soon receive a prophet's reward at the hands of Herod Antipas (vs. 10). Jesus will eventually follow His forerunner as the first Gospel moves toward Calvary.

W. D. Davies and D. C. Allison have argued persuasively that while the story of John is outwardly about him, in actuality it is a parable of Christ's death. They present evidence that Matthew's placement of the story about John at 14:1-12 is more than an interesting fact about John's death. Rather, it is a carefully crafted passage that foretells what is in store for Jesus. The chart below, which is quoted from their book, points out the following parallels:

John	Jesus
[1] Herod the tetrarch was responsible for John's death	Pilate the governor was responsible for Jesus' death
[2] John was seized (*krateō*, 14.3)	Jesus was seized (*krateō, 21.46, etc.)*
[3] John was bound (*deō*, 14.3)	Jesus was bound (*deō*, 27.2)
[4] Herod feared the crowds because they held John to be a prophet (14.5)	The chief priests and Pharisees feared the crowds because they held Jesus to be a prophet (21.46)
[5] Herod was asked by another to execute John and grieved so to do (14.6-11)	Pilate was asked by others to execute Jesus and was reluctant so to do (27.11-26)
[6] John was buried by his disciples (14.12)	Jesus was buried by a disciple (27.57-61)

Davies and Allison conclude that Matthew, writing after the fact of both deaths, was conscious of the parallelism in his treatment of the two deaths. Thus John's imprisonment and death are not an interesting aside but a part of the story of Jesus as He moves toward His own death (Davies and Allison, 2:475, 476).

In favor of their suggestion is the general fact, noticed earlier in our study of Matthew, that the first Gospel is indeed a carefully crafted literary piece. Also favorable to their suggestion is the placement of the story of John's death between the rejection stories of chapters 11 to 13 and Jesus' explicit announcement of His own death in 16:21.

While the validity of Davies and Allison's argument cannot be proven, it is evident from our passage that Jesus felt Himself to be in danger from Herod, and this led to His first withdrawal in chapters 14:1 to 16:20. Confrontation with the authorities would eventually have its time and place in the life of Jesus, but Galilee was not to be the place, and Jesus knew that His time had not yet come (see John 7:30; 17:1). For the present, it was best to avoid trouble.

The Feeding of the Five Thousand and the Attempt to Crown the King

Jesus' first withdrawal appears to be motivated by a desire to remove Himself from Herod's path. But the "solitary place" to which Jesus withdraws still seems to have been within the borders of Galilee. Not only does Luke 9:10 tell us that He fed the five thousand near Bethsaida, but from the way they reacted, those fed appear to have been mostly Jews.

The feeding of the five thousand demonstrates that although many, especially among the religious leaders, had rejected Jesus, the crowds still heard Him gladly. The picture is one of thousands following Him as they hang upon His words. The people even go so far as to make an educated guess as to where His boat may land on the shore of the Sea of Galilee so that they can be there when He arrives (14:13, 14).

Not only does the crowd respond positively to Jesus, but He responds in kind. He not only heals their sick, but He performs one of His great miracles in feeding five thousand people with just five loaves and two fish (vss. 14-21). In actuality, the miracle should be thought of as feeding twenty thousand rather than five, since according to Jewish reckoning, only adult males made up the count. The five thousand did not include women and children.

With this thought in mind, we can get a better idea of the word picture that Matthew has painted for us. It is one of dry hills in Galilee that are literally covered with a living stream of people, all eager to hear the words of Christ and to experience the power of His miraculous ministry. No wonder Herod Antipas has become concerned. Jesus is indeed a potential political threat.

And the reality of that threat takes a giant step forward with the feeding of the five thousand. It is no accident that right after Jesus' feeding of the five thousand Matthew records that "Jesus *made* the disciples get into the boat and go on ahead of him to the other side, while he dismissed the crowd" (vs. 22).

The reason Jesus has to *make* the disciples get in the boat and set sail by themselves is not evident in Matthew, but it becomes clear when we consider John's account. John tells us that when the people see the miracle of Jesus' feeding the five thousand, they begin to say, " 'Surely this is the Prophet who is to come into the world.' " Then follows a move on the part of the Jews to "make him king by force" (John 6:14, 15).

The people identify Jesus as "the Prophet who is to come" because of His powerful sign or miracle. Josephus tells us that in nearly every case, Jewish first-century political uprisings by would-be liberators were accompanied by themes of a prophet and the working of signs (see Brown, 1:249). Building on the Messianic promise that God would "raise up . . . a prophet" like Moses (Deut. 18:18, 15), the Jews at the feeding of the five thousand believed they were experiencing a fulfillment of prophecy.

The connection made is that Moses, the great deliverer, gave their "fathers . . . manna in the wilderness" (John 6:31, RSV). In Jesus they have someone who appears to be a second Moses, a second deliverer—another prophet, who like Moses can supply bread from heaven. This is the reason for the forcefulness that lies behind the drive to make Jesus king.

Even the disciples are carried away with the possibility. Matthew tells us that Jesus has to *make* them get into their boat and leave Him, while He dismisses the crowds alone (14:22). The disciples must have sensed the Messianic potential clearly. "Now," they must have thought, "is the time for Jesus to make His masterstroke. Now is the Messianic moment." With this thought in mind, it is easier to see why Jesus had to send the disciples away before He could handle the crowd.

The disciples' excitement and perhaps their knowledge of Jesus' "backwardness" in putting Himself forward as the Messiah undoubtedly caused some of them to consider it their job to push Jesus to the front in what they hoped would be the beginning of the Messianic kingdom of glory. After all, up through the resurrection of Jesus, they still perceived His kingdom to be a political kingdom that would overthrow the Roman oppressors.

We miss a major point of the story if we fail to see Jesus tempted to obtain the kingdom without a cross. Jesus is facing His ultimate temptation. This is a repetition of His first wilderness temptation (4:3, 4), but with greater forcefulness. He has demonstrated that He can indeed make bread out of "stones," and the people have been profoundly impressed—so impressed that they are ready to set up His kingdom on the spot. Even Jesus' "support group" (the twelve disciples) is behind the movement. Here is temptation of the first order: "Build the Kingdom on bread. Make it the first point of your programme to abolish hunger. Multiply loaves and fishes all the time," and the people will love You (Denney, 210).

Here is the old temptation to establish His kingdom without a cross, without having to follow the path of a rejected servant. The seriousness of the episode is reflected by the fact that immediately after dismissing the crowds, "he went up on a mountainside by himself to pray" (14:23; see also John 6:15). Jesus needs to commit Himself anew to the accomplishment of God's will and to pray especially for His disciples, who as yet desire a Messiah out of harmony with God's will. Doing God's will in the accomplishment of His mission must remain central in Jesus' life. That is always a matter of prayer.

Jesus is successful both in dispersing the crowd and in overcoming His normal human inclination to achieve the kingdom without a cross. Yet the episode has a lasting impact on His ministry. Matthew 15 and 16 find Jesus working outside the borders of Galilee among Gentile populations. Apparently His withdrawal to a "solitary place" in Jewish territory had not been sufficient, given the Messianic excitement of the crowds. His next step will be to withdraw beyond the reach of Jewish politics so that He can continue to instruct His disciples before taking decisive steps toward His final confrontation with the Jewish and Roman authorities in Jerusalem.

In the meantime, after being forced to leave the scene of the movement to make Jesus king, the troubled disciples are struggling with more than spiritual discouragement and disappointment. They are also being buffeted by physical waves. But at this point they spot Jesus walking on the water toward them (14:24-27).

The narrative then tells of Peter's failed attempt to walk on the water (vss. 28-31) and of the storm dying down after both Peter and Jesus get into the boat (vs. 32).

The climax of the story is not Peter's experience or Jesus stilling the storm but the worship and confession of the disciples. " 'Truly,' " they exclaim to Jesus, " 'you are the Son of God' " (vs. 33). It is impossible to tell exactly what they mean by that phrase, but as Jewish students of the Old Testament, they can hardly have failed to recognize that in walking on the waves and in subduing the storm, Jesus has exercised divine prerogatives assigned to Yahweh Himself (see, for example, Job 9:8; Ps. 77:19; Isa. 43:16; 51:9, 10; Hab. 3:15).

In spite of our uncertainty about the exact meaning of the disciples' words, it seems clear that in calling Jesus the Son of God they have taken a step forward in their understanding of Him. Matthew 14:33 is the first time the disciples give that title to Jesus, but it will not be the last. And with each repetition, the title will have greater meaning. In Matthew 14 their faith is still based upon His mighty acts rather than on an adequate understanding of His person and mission. Their understanding will be more complete in 16:16, though still nowhere close to adequate until after the resurrection. We need to remember that the Synoptic Gospels show that the faith of the disciples developed by degrees.

Matthew 14 closes with one of several passages throughout the first Gospel that show Jesus healing large numbers of unidentified individuals (vss. 34-36). The first part of chapter 15 brings the narrative back to Jesus' escalating conflict with the Pharisees.

The conflict between Jesus and the scribes and Pharisees in chapter 15 centers outwardly around ceremonial defilement, but at a more profound level, it is based on the very nature of religion and the depth of human sinfulness.

As in so many confrontations between Jesus and the scribes and Pharisees, they have gone out of their way to provoke an argument. Matthew tells us they have come "from Jerusalem." A glance at the map in the back of your Bible will show that, given the size of the Jewish homeland, they made quite a trip. Not only did they come from Jerusalem into rural and despised Galilee, but they came specifically "to Jesus" (15:1). Their journey was not just a pastoral tour. It had a definite purpose: to question Jesus about why His disciples broke the tradition of the elders.

Note that these Jewish leaders are not accusing Jesus of breaking the tradition. Rather, they are implying that He approves of His disciples doing so and that He must therefore have taught them to take the tradition lightly. Leon Morris points out that teaching others to disregard the tradition was probably worse than breaking it oneself from time to time, since the latter could be thought of as a thoughtless aberration in a moment of weakness, whereas "teaching people to act contrary to the tradition meant a systematic and thought-out practice. It meant breaking the tradition as a matter of principle" (Morris, *Matthew*, 389).

In the case at hand, Jesus does not disappoint the suspicions of His accusers. He has definitely taught a different position from theirs, and He does not deny it.

According to Matthew (Mark has more items of contention), the problem has to do with the washing of hands. It is important to understand that the issue was not washing for sanitary purposes, but to avoid ceremonial uncleanliness. In their genuine and sincere desire to honor God, the Pharisees had picked up on God's instruction through Moses on priestly washing in the sanctuary (Exod. 30:17-21), but then they expanded the idea to everyday life. In addition, they multiplied the number of things causing ceremonial defilement and ritualized the cleansing process. So important did ceremonial washing become to them that they eventually devoted an entire book of the Mishnah (the written version of the oral tradition) to it (called Yadaim or "Hands"). The faithful were required to wash their hands in the prescribed manner, or their food, and by extension their whole person, would be unclean. Thus they would be unfit for worshiping God.

As pointed out in our earlier discussion on the oral tradition surrounding the Sabbath (12:1-14), the Jews developed thousands of rules to protect people from breaking the Ten Commandments. By the time of Jesus, it was almost impossible to even know all the rules, let alone keep them. They had become a burden (see 11:28).

Before coming down too hard on the ancient Jews, we must realize that they did all this out of religious sincerity. Their sin was not willful rebellion or even carelessness, but rather "the sin of *devotion*" (Bruner, 2:543, emphasis supplied). *It was the sin of religious people trying hard to be religious.*

It is important to understand that the sin of devotion is not restricted to the Pharisaic party. It can be found in medieval Catholicism and even among Baptists, Adventists, Methodists, and other groups of our own day. The sin of devotion is very subtle, because it looks religious. But, as Jesus points out, it is not really religious. In reality, the sin of devotion destroys true religion, for it too often inspires its practitioners to hurt other people in the name of God. Thus the church is faced with the angry deacon, the Inquisition, and people who become "violent" when other church members differ from them on their definition of the human nature of Christ, perfection, or any other doctrinal point. The church still needs to hear the word from Jesus on the sin of devotion.

As in His confrontation with the Jews over proper Sabbath keeping, Jesus once again shows how their traditions actually undermine the very law they think they are keeping and protecting. In chapter 12, Matthew points out that Jesus' challenge to their tradition leads them to think of murder. Here, Jesus shows that the rule allowing adult children to neglect the physical needs of their aged parents (by devoting their material goods to God) is a violation of the fifth commandment. In so doing they are more faithful to their human rules than they are to God's Ten Commandments. Thus they nullify God's word for the sake of their tradition. It is little wonder that Jesus calls them religious hypocrites (play actors) and proclaims their religion to be in vain (15:3-9).

Their rules, made to protect God's law of love, have actually made them unloving—so unloving that their religion causes them to hurt other people (in this case, their parents). Such is the consistent fruit of the sin of devotion—even in the present day.

The second half of our passage finds Jesus turning His back on the Pharisees and speaking first to the crowd, who have apparently been standing back out of the line of fire, and then to the disciples. He tells the crowd that the Pharisees don't really understand true religion. They see sin as external defilement rather than as an internal problem (vss. 10, 11). Later Jesus will expand on this thought in His comments to the disciples as He sums up His teaching and ties the three parts of this episode together.

Apparently a period of time passes between Jesus' exchange with the Pharisees and the crowd and His talk with the disciples, because the Pharisees have had an opportunity to complain to the disciples about what Jesus said. Jesus' reply to the disciples regarding the complaint is short and to the point: the Pharisees, being spiritually blind, are unfit to be religious leaders. Following them can only lead to disaster (vss. 12-14).

But Peter, and probably the other disciples, isn't satisfied, so he presses Jesus for more explanation. Apparently the teaching on ceremonial uncleanness is so pervasive in Judaism that even the disciples are having a difficult time understanding Jesus' perspective. This explains His exasperated words to them in verses 16 and 17. In essence He says, "How can you be so dull? After all the time you have listened to me, can't you see what I mean?" He then goes on to explain that genuine defilement is not a matter of externals—what goes into a person. Rather, sin is rooted in the heart (a person's inner being), and it is out of a sinful heart that sinful acts proceed (vss. 17-20; see also 12:34, 35).

In short, true religion is not a matter of externals. Rather, it means an attitude of love toward both God and one's neighbors. That attitude will become the source for all a person's actions. Later Jesus became even more explicit on this point, noting that all of God's commands are built upon *agapē* (love) to God and other people (22:36-40). That theme runs through His teaching in Matthew, climaxing in the great judgment scene of 25:31-46.

Jesus has taught us several things in Matthew 15:1-20. First, religious tradition does not have the same authority as Scripture. As a result, the traditions of *all* religious groups must be evaluated in the light of Scripture and condemned where necessary. Second, Pharisees and other legalists should not be followed. Third, true religion is internal rather than external. Fourth, human sinfulness is rooted in sinful nature. It is not a surface matter dealing with what a person does, eats, or touches. These activities may be sinful, but they are not the root of the problem. Sinfulness is part of the natural person's inner being. It is a matter of the heart. Thus overcoming sin is more than merely stopping this action or that. It implies a change of heart (a conversion). It is heresy to suppose that people are basically good and will become better (or even perfect) if they avoid this or that behavior or if they try harder to overcome. All this is foreign to Jesus' thinking and that of the New Testament. For Jesus, sin is a matter of the heart, and a person must be born from above through the Holy Spirit in order to get the direction of his or her heart changed (John 3:3, 5; see also Rom. 12:2).

■ Getting Into the Word

Matthew 15:21–16:20

Read 15:21 to 16:20 two times before examining the following questions.

1. **Look up Tyre and Sidon (15:21) on a map in the back of your Bible. How do you explain Jesus' treatment of the Canaanite woman in 15:22-28? Write a paragraph putting the worst possible construction on His words. Do the same for the best possible construction. What do you see as the point to this episode?**
2. **Matthew 16:1, 6, 11, 12 each set forth a strange combination of Jewish parties. You should already be familiar with the Pharisees and what they stand for, though if you are not, go to a Bible dictionary and refresh your mind on the topic. Also use a concordance to discover what you can about the Sadducees from the New Testament. List your conclusions. Then go to a Bible dictionary to fill in your**

understanding. Explain in a paragraph or so the significance of Matthew's coupling of these two Jewish parties.

3. **Look up the location of Caesarea Philippi on a Bible map. Examine the phrase *Son of Man* (16:13) in a Bible dictionary to get some background for an essential understanding in this chapter. What do you see as the significance of Peter's declaration in 16:16? In a sentence or two, describe what the church is built upon, according to 16:16-18. How does that understanding line up with such texts as 1 Corinthians 10:11; Ephesians 2:20; Acts 4:11; and 1 Peter 2:4-8? Verse 19 talks about the "keys of the kingdom." Write out your impression of the implications of that gift as you study 16:19, 20. Does Luke 11:52 have any connection to Matthew 16:19, 20? If so, what is it?**

■ Exploring the Word

Withdrawal to Gentile Territory

While chapter 14 saw Jesus withdraw to a "solitary place" in Galilee, the second half of chapter 15 and most of 16 find Him north of Galilee in such places as Tyre, Sidon, and Caesarea Philippi (15:21; 16:13). Because of Herod Antipas, Jesus no longer feels safe in Galilee, and He certainly doesn't see any safety in Judea. This explains the excursion into Gentile territory. He is seeking to buy time for further instruction of His followers before they and He must face their ultimate crisis.

The most crucial understanding they still need to gain is a firm sense of Jesus' identity and mission. Only after they gain this more complete insight will they be prepared for Jesus to carry out the rest of His mission. Yet even then, their understanding will barely be enough to carry them through the crisis. Like most Jews, they still see Messiahship in terms of a conquering king rather than a suffering servant.

Verses 21 to 28 present the first of two episodes in chapter 15 in which Jesus deals directly with the Gentile population of the regions He visits. The first of these episodes is Jesus' perplexing conversation with the Canaanite woman.

The woman comes to Jesus begging for mercy for her suffering daughter. Jesus does something that seems offensive to readers, but which is certainly expected by His Jewish disciples. He ignores the woman. The disciples, sensing what they perceive to be Jesus' attitude, ask Him to send her away. Jesus responds by telling the woman that He has been sent to the Jews, but undeterred, she keeps imploring Him for help. Jesus then tells her that it is not right to toss the children's food to the dogs. At this point, she sees a glimmer of hope. She presses her claim by admitting she is willing to be a dog if she can only receive the blessings of the kingdom.

Jesus rewards her profusely. Not only does He commend her faith, but He heals her daughter. This unnamed Canaanite woman has grasped what the disciples have failed to understand—a person must be willing to become nothing in order to enter the kingdom (see also 10:38, 39; 20:24-28).

Jesus performed only two healings for specific individual Gentiles in Matthew—this woman and the centurion of 8:5-13. Both were willing to admit their unworthiness, both showed extraordinary faith, and both had the subject of their request healed at a distance. Certainly the disciples were learning lessons that would later be meaningful to them as they extended their work to non-Jews!

But while all this may be true, modern readers still feel perplexed—almost offended—by Jesus' apparent harshness to this woman. Why would He turn her down, going so far as to refer to her and her people as "dogs"? We need to remember that Jesus' words were accompanied by facial expressions and body language. Floyd Filson is probably correct when he states that the effect of Jesus' words on the woman "would depend much on the speaker's tone and facial expression. The woman senses that his word is not final, and she is quick to show him that he can help her without giving up his concentrated mission to fellow-Jews" (Filson, 180). While the disciples, like other Jews, saw only the hardness in Jesus' treatment of the woman, she saw only hope. As Ellen White puts it, "Beneath the apparent refusal of Jesus, she saw a compassion that He could not hide" (White, *The Desire of Ages*, 401). No wonder He commends her for her faith!

In the process of dealing with the woman, Jesus reasserts that in the order of heaven the Jews were to receive the gospel of the Messiah before it went to the Gentiles (15:24; 10:6; Rom. 1:16; Acts 1:8). One lesson of this story is that Jesus remained faithful to God's covenant with the Jews, even though they rejected Him. They were still God's chosen people, even as they were in the process of rejecting the heaven-sent Messiah. The covenant-keeping God has not changed. The assurance of the Christian faith is firmly founded on our God's faithfulness to His covenant. He will not let His people down—in either the first century or the twentieth.

Jesus' second experience with Gentiles in chapter 15 is found in verses 29 to 39. All Matthew tells us is that the feeding of the four thousand took place near the Sea of Galilee, but Mark adds that the events surrounding the miracle took place on the Gentile side of the sea in the region of Decapolis (Mark 7:31).

There is nothing especially different about this feeding from the feeding of the five thousand (14:13-21) except the conclusion. This time, after Jesus "had sent the crowd away, *he got into the boat*" and departed with the disciples (15:39). Apparently the four thousand, being a largely Gentile audience, did not seek to turn this "bread-from-heaven" miracle into a Messianic event by attempting to crown Jesus king (compare with 14:22; John 6:14, 15).

At the beginning of chapter 16, Matthew inserts a Jewish conflict story that finds Jesus briefly back in Galilee (vss. 1-4). That conflict is followed by Jesus recrossing the Sea of Galilee (vs. 5) and reentering Gentile territory. During the trip, Jesus again warns the disciples against "the teaching of the Pharisees and Sadducees" (16:6-12).

Perhaps the most significant thing about this passage is that Jesus links the Pharisees and Sadducees together in their testing of Him. The significance lies in the fact that these two groups were opponents in Jewish religious and political life. The wealthy Sadducees were of the priestly class and usually accommodated to Greco-Roman culture. They were also liberal in their religion and denied the resurrection (22:23), the ministry of angels (Acts 23:8), and the validity of the Jewish Scriptures, except for the Pentateuch. By contrast, the Pharisees (the "separated ones") accepted all of these beliefs and were anti-Roman in their politics and culture.

Yet 16:1-12 finds these two opposing parties working together. This is significant. Jesus proves to be a serious threat to the Jewish status quo. Only this could unite these two groups. They now have a common enemy. That tenuous unity will last through the crucifixion.

The King Recognized by Peter

Matthew 16:13 indicates that after arriving on the eastern side of Galilee, Jesus went north to the region of Caesarea Philippi. Here, He puts a crucial question to His disciples: " 'Who,' " He asks, " 'do people say the Son of Man is?' " They reply by naming several Jewish heroes. Jesus then gets down to the question He really needs to ask during this time apart from the Jewish crowds, who generally make quiet reflection an impossibility. " 'Who,' " He asks, " 'do *you* say I am?' " (vss. 13-15). Jesus is not nearly as concerned about who people in general think He is as in who His disciples and soon-to-be successors in mission think He is. It is absolutely crucial that they have a clear understanding of both His true identity and the implications of that identity.

Peter's answer, " 'You are the Christ [Messiah], the Son of the living God' " (vs. 16), gives Jesus an opportunity to present the disciples with a two-part lesson that is of utmost importance. The first part deals with both the founding of the church that will continue His work and the prerogatives of that church (vss. 17-20). The second part has to do with Jesus' explanation to the disciples of what it means to be Messiah as suffering Servant rather than

Messiah as conquering King. It also touches on the implication of His suffering Servant role for the disciples (vss. 21-27). While the disciples undoubtedly found the first part of the lesson to be agreeable in the extreme (vss. 17-20), they found the second part of the lesson to be distasteful and, initially, at least, unacceptable (vss. 21-23).

Verse 17 finds Jesus pronouncing a blessing on Peter for his answer and telling him that the answer came as a divine revelation from the Father. But His next statement provided the basis for a debate that has raged over the course of church history: " 'I tell you that you are Peter, and on this rock I will build my church' " (vs. 18).

The point of contention is the meaning of "this rock" upon which the church is founded. Does it mean Peter, or does it refer to Peter's confession that Jesus is "the Christ, the Son of the living God"? In favor of the former position is the fact that Peter's name means "rock" (*petros*). Thus some have interpreted Peter (*petros*) as the rock (*petra*) upon which Christ built His church. Many, taking that view, have seen Peter as the first pope.

However, this interpretation of Jesus' words flies in the face of other New Testament passages, which teach that Jesus is the foundation upon which the church is built. Thus Paul wrote that "no one can lay any foundation [for the church] other than the one already laid, which is Jesus Christ" (1 Cor. 3:11) and that "Christ Jesus himself" is "the chief cornerstone" of the church (Eph. 2:20). Peter himself set forth Jesus as "the living Stone," "a chosen and precious cornerstone," upon which the church is built (1 Pet. 2:4-7; see also Acts 4:11). In addition, earlier in Matthew we found Jesus claiming that His teachings were the rock (7:24).

Given those facts, it seems safest to conclude that it was Peter's confession of Jesus as Messiah and Son of God which formed the bedrock foundation upon which a healthy church could be established and built up. The Christian church has always been strong when it has kept Christ at its center. And whenever the church has kept Jesus at its center, "the gates of Hades" have not been able to prevail against it.

Even though Peter was not "the rock" upon which the church was founded, it is important to recognize that he did have preeminence among the disciples in the Gospels and early in the book of Acts. Yet that preeminence was far from undisputed. For example, even after Christ blessed Peter, the disciples continued to argue over who was the greatest (18:1; 20:20-27; Mark 9:34; Luke 9:46; 22:24). Many years later the Corinthian church was far from clear on the matter (1 Cor. 1:12), and we find James as president at the first church council (Acts 15).

Part of the blessing tied to Peter's confession of Jesus in Matthew 16 was Jesus' gift of the keys of the kingdom and the promise that whatever he bound on earth would be "bound in heaven," and whatever he loosed on earth would be "loosed in heaven" (vs. 19). Note, however, that in Matthew 18:18 Jesus bestows the latter part of this blessing on all the disciples. This is further evidence that the blessing of chapter 16 was tied to Peter's confession rather than to his person.

Just as the interpretation of the rock upon which the church is built has been debated down through church history, so has the interpretation of the "keys of the kingdom." The key is an obvious metaphor for admitting people through a door. A lead in understanding the "key" symbol is found in Luke 11:52, where Jesus condemns the scribes for misusing "the key to knowledge" and thus hindering people from "entering" the kingdom. And later in Matthew we find Jesus berating the scribes and Pharisees because they " 'shut the kingdom of heaven in men's faces' " and refuse to " 'let those enter who are trying to' " (23:13). These texts need to be coupled with Jesus' saying in John 17:3 that to know Him is eternal life (see also John 6:68).

In their work, the scribes and Pharisees have been misusing the key and blocking people from a knowledge of Jesus. Peter, by contrast, is to open the way. That is exactly what we find in Acts 2 and 3, where his preaching brings many Jews into the kingdom, and in Acts 10, where he opens the door for Gentiles to enter. That role, of course, is not restricted to Peter. In Matthew 28:18-20, we find Jesus commanding all His disciples "to the very end of the age" to use the teaching key, so that many can come to a knowledge of Him and be baptized.

Peter's blessing also includes binding and loosing—a responsibility that is extended to all the disciples in 18:18. Alfred Plummer notes that "the two words are technical expressions, the meaning of which was well understood" by the Jewish community. Thus "to 'bind' is to forbid, to 'loose' is to permit" (Plummer, 231). That idea is reflected in the New English Bible's translation of 16:19: " 'What you forbid on earth shall be forbidden in heaven, and what you allow on earth shall be allowed in heaven' " (see also Phillips). The idea underlying the passage, therefore, is not excluding from or admitting into the kingdom or forgiving or not forgiving sins, as it is in John 20:23, but the regulation of conduct and the setting of acceptable standards. The keys imply admission and exclusion, not the loosing and binding. Again, the passage says "*what*ever you bind," not "*whom*ever."

That function became essential in the Christian movement as it separated from Judaism and its way of life. The Christian community needed to set its own standards. As it turned out, that proved to be no easy task, as Jews and Gentiles confronted each other in the church. The church council in Acts 15 gives us an example of church leaders undertaking their binding and loosing function as they determine standards of conduct for Gentile converts. Like the function of the evangelistic keys, setting standards of conduct is an ongoing responsibility of Christian leadership.

Jesus closes off the conversation with the disciples by warning them "not to tell anyone that he was the Christ" (vs. 20). Why the secrecy? There were excellent reasons. The term could too easily be understood politically and misinterpreted in terms of the conquering Messiah who was so dear to Jewish hopes. As Morris points out, "To know that Jesus was the Messiah was one thing; to understand what messiahship meant was quite another" (Morris, *Matthew*, 427). And that meaning was not even clear in the disciples' minds, as the rest of Matthew 16 demonstrates.

Davies and Allison help us grasp the significance of Matthew 16:13-20 in the development of the first Gospel. They see this passage as the high point in Matthew's fourth narrative section. The first narrative section (1:1–4:23) introduced us to Jesus; the second (8:1–9:38) recounted His mighty acts and witness to Israel; and the third (11:1–12:50) recorded the negative response of corporate Israel to the Messiah's activities. "What we have then in the next narrative section, 13. 53-17. 27, is the consequence of the rejection of the Messiah: the people of God are founded anew. In other words, the birth of the ecclesia [church]—of Jew and Gentile—is traced directly to the failure of Israel to live up to her eschatological calling" (Davies and Allison, 2:642). Thus in 16:13-20 we have the beginning of the doctrine of the Christian church.

■ Applying the Word

Matthew 14:1–16:20

1. **How can one know when to withdraw and when to move forward in Christian living? What can I learn from Christ about the times and seasons for confrontation and peaceful coexistence?**
2. **The disciples were carried away with the crowd after the feeding of the five thousand because they had not listened carefully to what Jesus was trying to tell them. How carefully do I listen as I read? What evidence do I have that I am or am not reading my prejudices and desires into His words? Can I list some ways that all of us can get around that all-too-human danger?**
3. **In what ways has Christianity made me more loving? In what ways can I improve? What does it mean when I find myself becoming angry when someone disagrees with me over some lifestyle issue or doctrine? Who is in the greatest need of change in such a circumstance?**
4. **Who is Jesus to me? What impact has that reality had on my life? Have I been a faithful steward in my use of the keys? In what ways can I improve?**

■ Researching the Word

1. In 16:1 we find the Pharisees and Sadducees asking Christ for a "sign." That is not the first time they have done so in the first Gospel. Using your concordance (exhaustive concordance, preferably), see what you can discover about signs or miracles in the New Testament. Summarize your main findings by category in your Matthew notebook. Now examine the Old Testament. In what ways does a study of the use of signs in the Old Testament better help you to understand the Jews whom Jesus had to confront?
2. Reread 15:1-16. Compare the parallel passage in Mark. What significant additions does Mark make to the passage? What is the significance of the use of parentheses in Mark 7:3, 4, 11, 19? What do you think Jesus meant by foods in Mark 7:19? Explain the difference, in the context of Matthew 15 and Mark 7, between declaring all foods clean and declaring all foods healthy. Given the context, do you believe all foods are "clean"? If so, does that make them healthy and good to eat? Explain your answer in a paragraph or so.

■ Further Study of the Word

1. For general insight, see E. G. White, *The Desire of Ages*, 214-225, 364-382, 395-418.
2. For a more detailed examination of Peter's confession and Christ's response, see L. Morris, *The Gospel According to Matthew*, 418-427.
3. For insight into the problem of ritual cleanliness and tradition, see F. D. Nichol, ed., *Seventh-day Adventist Bible Commentary*, 5:621-626.

PART THREE

The Suffering, Death, and Resurrection of the King

Matthew 16:21–28:20

CHAPTER EIGHT

Glimpses of Crosses and Kingdoms: The Shape of the Future

Matthew 16:21–17:27

Matthew 16:21 marks one of the great turning points in the first Gospel. "From that time on," the text reads, "Jesus began to explain to his disciples that he must go to Jerusalem and suffer." The first few words of the verse are reminiscent of 4:17, which says, "From that time on Jesus began to preach."

In a very conscious way, our author has marked out the great turning points of his Gospel. The two "from that time on" passages divide the book of Matthew into its three great sections: the first (1:1–4:16) dealing with the person of the King, the second (4:17–16:20) treating the proclamation of the King, and the third (16:21–28:20) presenting the suffering, death, and resurrection of the King. Thus, beginning with Jesus' announcement of His suffering, death, and resurrection in 16:21, the rest of the first Gospel moves Jesus and His disciples inexorably toward the cross and its aftermath. Of course, Jesus' movement toward the cross and His movement toward Jerusalem are one and the same thing. That movement sets us up for the Gospel's climax.

The passage under study in the present chapter (16:21–17:27) presents a foretaste of the future in three vivid word pictures. The first is a shocking glimpse of crosses for both Christ and us (16:21-28); the second is a gratifying glimpse of the future kingdom of glory (17:1-13); and the third consists of two frustrating glimpses of the disciples' unpreparedness (17:14-27).

■ Getting Into the Word

Matthew 16:21–17:27

Read through Matthew 16:21 to 17:27 twice. Then write a few sentences in your notebook about the theme, and respond to the following questions:

1. Matthew 16: 21 is the first of three predictions by Jesus in Matthew of His death and resurrection. Use your marginal references *and* a concordance to find the other two. Compare the three. List the distinct items that Christ specifies about His ordeal in 16:21. Then list the items of information added in the other two references.
2. From what you know about the Jewish concept of the Messiah and human psychology as it applies to Peter and the other disciples, write a paragraph or two highlighting the reasons for Peter's reaction to Jesus' announcement in 16:22. Then discuss why Jesus reacted so vigorously in verse 23. Using your marginal references (or a concordance), discover where else in Matthew Jesus made a similar "Satan" statement. What implications does that other passage have for 16:23?
3. What was a cross? What was its purpose? Write a summary of the meaning of 16:24 in light of that purpose and in light of the verses that follow. Find Luke's parallel passage to 16:21-28. What does Luke add to our understanding of 16:24?
4. Do your best to explain 16:28 as if it were an isolated text (that is, without any context). Then seek to explain it in light of 16:27. Also explain it in the light of 17:1-13. Now, after examining the contextual implications, write a summary of what you think the text means in its context.
5. List the basic elements involved in the Transfiguration. What is the meaning of that event for Jesus? For the disciples? Why do you think Jesus took only three of His

disciples with Him?

6. **Summarize in a few sentences the main point or lesson in 17:14-21. How does that lesson fit into the flow of Matthew's Gospel as Jesus and the disciples move toward the cross?**

■ Exploring the Word

Glimpses of Crosses

It is difficult to overemphasize the importance of 16:21. By chapter 16, it had become evident that Israel as a corporate body was not going to accept Jesus as the Messiah. That left two tasks for Jesus to accomplish in this pivotal chapter. First, He needed to establish a new community—the church—and provide it with instructions. He began that in 16:13-20. Second, He needed to begin preparing His disciples for His death.

Matthew 16:21 is the first explicit announcement related to that second task. Therefore, we should be aware of each element in it. According to Jesus, He

"*must go* to Jerusalem"
"*suffer* many things" at the hands of the Jewish leaders
"must *be killed*"
"and on the third day *be raised to life*."

Interestingly, most of those elements have already been alluded to in Matthew: the opposition of the Jewish leaders to the point where they wished to kill Jesus (2:1-6; 9:34; 12:1-8, 14); Jesus' self-perceived role as suffering Servant (12:15-21); His determination to die to redeem His people (1:21; 9:15); and His triumph over death (12:40; 16:4). These have all been set forth by Matthew. But nobody seems to have been listening—at least very carefully. So in 16:21 Jesus places His cards on the table in such an explicit manner that His meaning can no longer be ignored. He has reached a crisis point in His ministry. His disciples finally recognize Him to be the Messiah. Now He must begin to get across to them what being the Messiah means.

Note that Jesus says that He "*must*" go to Jerusalem to suffer and die. That trip was not an optional part of His ministry. *It was a necessity* for Him to go and die. In fact, that was the very purpose of His coming to earth. He came not only to live a good life, but "to give his life as a ransom for many" (20:28). " 'This is my blood of the covenant,' " He told His disciples at the Last Supper, " 'which is poured out for many for the forgiveness of sins' " (26:28). *Christ's death was not an optional part of the plan of salvation. Without that substitutionary death, there would be no plan of salvation.*

But that point was not intuitively obvious to the disciples. They had grown up with the view universal among the Jews that the Messiah would be a conquering king who would overthrow the nation's enemies. Besides that, the disciples had a great deal to gain from that type of Messiah, since they formed Jesus' "cabinet." They would be the twelve highest officials in the soon-coming kingdom.

With these points in mind, we should not be overly surprised when the man who a short time before (16:16-19) perceived himself to have been appointed the new kingdom's prime minister or senior vice-president should react rather strongly to Jesus' announcement. " '*Never*, Lord! . . . This shall *never* happen to you!' " (vs. 22). Peter could not have said it stronger.

But Jesus' response to Peter is even stronger. " 'Get behind me, Satan! You are a stumbling block to me; you do not have in mind the things of God, but the things of men' " (vs. 23). It is hard to believe that Jesus is talking to the same man He had blessed a short time before (vss. 17-19). Earlier Jesus had said that Peter was under inspiration from the Father, but now he is under the guidance of the devil. These have to be totally opposing positions in the struggle between good and evil.

The question naturally arises, Why such a vigorous response from Jesus? The answer lies in the fact that Jesus finds the thought of His death even more distasteful than does Peter. Jesus has seen crucifixions in His travels, and, like any normal human being, He has no desire to exit the world by the excruciating death of the cross. He would have found it much easier to become the political

Messiah the Jews (including the disciples) wanted. Beyond that, Jesus has no desire to bear the judgment of the world by becoming sin for all humanity in the great sacrifice on Calvary (John 12:31-33; 2 Cor. 5:21). The thought of separation from God while bearing the sins of the world on the cross is abhorrent to Him in the extreme.

The temptation to do His own will by avoiding the cross is *the great temptation* of Jesus' life. It will come to a head in Gethsemane, where Christ will repeatedly pray, " 'If this cannot pass unless I drink it, thy will be done' " (26:42, RSV).

As we saw in Matthew 4, the heart of the temptations in the wilderness was to establish His kingdom without a cross. At the conclusion of that experience, the Lord cried out, " 'Away from me, Satan!' " (vs. 10). Again in Matthew 16 we find very similar language, but this time directed at Peter: " 'Get behind me, Satan!' " There is no more forceful rebuke in the New Testament! But look at the cause. Peter, the leading disciple, has taken up the exact position that Satan adopted in the wilderness. The forcefulness of the rebuke implies the importance of the cross in Jesus' ministry. J. C. Ryle reasons from the strength of the language used in rebuking Peter that "there is no doctrine of Scripture so deeply important as the doctrine of Christ's atoning death" (see Morris, *Matthew*, 430, n. 48). Thus Peter has become a "stumbling block" or trap to Jesus, because Peter has in mind the "things of men" rather than the "things of God" (vs. 23).

Unfortunately, Christ's cross will not be the only cross. He goes on to say that each of His followers will have his or her own cross. " 'If anyone would come after me,' " Jesus tells His disciples, " 'he must deny himself and take up his cross and follow me' " (vs. 24).

To fully understand this statement, we need to put ourselves in the place of the disciples. The idea of being crucified does not do much to our twentieth-century imaginations. We have never seen a crucifixion. To us, *crucifixion* is a dead word. But this was not true for the disciples. When they saw a knot of Roman soldiers escorting a person through town carrying or dragging part of a cross, they knew it was a one-way trip. They knew the cross to be the cruelest and most humiliating of deaths. To Jesus and the disciples, the cross symbolized nothing but death.

But what needed to die in the disciples? The answer is found in 16:24-26. They needed to "deny" their "selves." They needed to give up their willful lives so they could gain eternal life. Jesus was to be crucified on a physical cross, but before He got to the wood of that cross, He first had to give over His will to the Father. No one could make Him get on the cross (or stay there, for that matter). The struggle in Gethsemane was a struggle to give over His will to the Father so that He could will to do the Father's will.

So it is with each of His followers. Most of us will never have to endure a physical cross, but each of us must crucify the willful nature that above all wants to do its own thing.

To understand Jesus' meaning in verse 24, we need to remember that sin, in its most basic sense, is putting our self and our will, rather than God and His will, at the center of our lives. Sin is rebellion against God in the sense that we choose to become the ruler of our own lives. Sin is saying No to God and Yes to self.

It is the self-centered life principle so natural to human beings that must die. Thus Bonhoeffer spoke to the heart of what it means to be a Christian when he wrote that "when Christ calls a man, he bids him come and die" (Bonhoeffer, 99).

Jesus pointed to the essential human problem when He claimed that " 'no one can serve two masters' " (6:24). The bottom line is: Who will I put on the throne of my life? My self or God? My will or God's? I cannot serve both at the same time. *When I come face to face with the claims of Christ, I must either crucify Him or let Him crucify me. There is no middle ground.*

Thus the cross is not some little abstinence in a Christian's life or a nagging husband or an unfaithful wife. The cross is the way of death to self-centered living. But, fortunately, after the cross in a person's life comes the new birth in Christ (John 3:3, 5; Rom. 6:1-11). Thus the paradox—we gain real life here and eternal life in the hereafter through the crucifixion of the self-life (16:25, 26). And just as the great temptation in Christ's life was to avoid the cross, so will it be in ours.

Unfortunately, the life of the cross is not a one-time experience. Luke's parallel passage says that Christians must take up their crosses "daily" (Luke 9:23). But the struggle will not be without benefits. Jesus not only claims that self-surrender is the way to life, but that when He comes again " 'in his Father's glory with his angels, . . . then he will reward each person according to what he has done' " (16:27).

The lesson of Jesus' death was one of the most difficult for the disciples to grasp. Twice more in the first Gospel, He will repeat the teaching of His death and resurrection (17:22, 23; 20:18, 19), and once more He will speak of His resurrection (17:9) and His crucifixion (26:2) separately. Yet the disciples, given their mind-set, were unprepared for both events. Such is the power of past experience and the pull of desired outcomes. It can blind the mind to even the most straightforward language.

Glimpses of Kingdoms

Peter and his fellow disciples were so shocked by Jesus' prediction of His death on the cross that they completely overlooked the prophecy that "on the third day" He would be "raised to life" (16:21). They were so disoriented by the catastrophe that they missed the promise. The grave would not be the end for Christ. He would rise again and ascend to the Father. His death would be the boundary line between the role of Messiah as suffering Servant and Messiah as Ruler.

The disciples were not altogether wrong in their expectation of the kingdom. But they, like other Jews, did not realize that the kingdom was to come in stages. On the other hand, had they been listening carefully to all Jesus was telling them in Matthew 16, they would have had a better understanding of the progress of the kingdom.

Not only does Jesus foretell His resurrection, but in verse 27 He plainly tells them of His second coming. In that coming, He will not be coming as a baby to a dirty manger in Bethlehem, but " 'in his Father's glory with his angels.' " Yes, the Messiah is to be a glorious conquering King, but only after He has died as a suffering Servant. The kingly Messianic picture is best viewed in Revelation 19:11-21, where Christ at the second advent is pictured as a conqueror riding a white horse.

Following Christ's promise of His second coming is one of those sayings that has perplexed readers who have wrestled with its meaning. " 'I tell you the truth,' " says Jesus, " 'some who are standing here will not taste death before they see the Son of Man coming in his kingdom' " (16:28).

The explanations for that passage have been many, and two are suggested by its immediate context. One is that it refers to the Transfiguration, which follows in the next thirteen verses. Another is that it refers to the second coming mentioned in 16:27. That latter explanation, however, forces one to see verse 28 as a failed prediction. Thus of the two contextual explanations, the Transfiguration as a foreshadowing of the kingdom of glory is the most satisfactory.

While the Transfiguration explanation is helpful, it may not uncover the full meaning of the prediction. Herman Ridderbos offers the insightful suggestion that prophecy "often compresses the distinct phases of the future into a unity" (Ridderbos, 314, 315). We have already seen that tendency in John's (3:2) and Jesus' (4:17) preaching of the nearness of the kingdom of heaven. Neither made clear the kingdom's progressive nature by explaining that the kingdom-of-grace aspect would precede the kingdom-of-glory aspect by at least two thousand years. In like manner, the aspects of Christ's exaltation are not differentiated in the preresurrection Gospel narrative.

Only after Jesus' resurrection did the disciples begin to realize that His exaltation would take place in stages. They would indeed live to see the beginning stages of His coming in glory in His resurrection and ascension, but would not live to see the later stages, such as the second advent. Thus it appears that a combination of Ridderbos's compression insight with the idea of the Transfiguration as a foretaste of the kingdom of glory offers the best solution to the meaning of 16:28.

The first thing that jumps off the page as we read about the Transfiguration in 17:1-13 is that Peter is there—the very same Peter who has recently been rebuked as Satan. As in the case of David and so many less-than-perfect biblical heroes, Peter's presence on the Mount of Transfiguration is an amazing statement of God's forgiving and compassionate grace.

The Transfiguration of Jesus (17:1-8) is found in all three Synoptic Gospels right after Peter's confession of Jesus and Jesus' announcement of His death and resurrection. Chapter 16 has carried the disciples from the heights of hope in Peter's confession to the depths of despair in Christ's announcement. The disciples have to be troubled. Who is this Jesus they are following? They think they know, but He doesn't seem to fit their expectations.

The Transfiguration is the answer to their question. Beyond that, it provides reassurance to Jesus Himself. Exactly "six days" after the events of chapter 16 He takes His three closest disciples up into a mountain by themselves. It should be noted that such exactness of time in the Synoptics is unusual. Dale Bruner suggests that the six days is significant, since "six days were considered the number of days necessary to prepare for a holy event in Israel: Creation had prepared six days for the institution of the sabbath, for example (Gen 1); Moses waited six days on Sinai for the glory of the Lord (Exod 24:16). And now after another six-day interval something special is given to God's people" (Bruner, 2:600). Such symbolism would be especially pertinent to Matthew, who wrote with a Jewish audience in mind. (Mark 9:2 also has six days, but Luke 9:28 has "about eight days.")

That special event is the glorification of Jesus, the appearance of Moses and Elijah, and the voice from heaven saying, " 'This is my Son, whom I love; with him I am well pleased. Listen to him!' " (17:2-5).

The Transfiguration plays an important role in Matthew's Gospel. First, the glorification of Jesus, in which His "face shone like the sun, and his clothes became as white as the light," takes the disciples' minds back to Exodus 34:29-35 and the glory that shone on Moses' face when he met God on Mount Sinai (see also 2 Cor.

3:7). Thus Jesus' experience is parallel to that of Moses, the great leader of God's people in Old Testament times; the man God used to establish the kingdom in Jewish history.

Second, Moses and Elijah appear. Those two individuals are important for several reasons. For one, they were recognized by the Jews as the supreme representatives of the law (Moses) and the prophets (Elijah). And here they are talking to Jesus, who came to fulfill what the law and the prophets had looked forward to (5:17). A second reason for their importance is that in Jewish thinking, both of these men were connected with the end of time. Elijah was to appear before the "great and dreadful day of the Lord" comes (Mal. 4:5), and all Israel expected the reappearance of Moses in some form (Deut. 18:15). But perhaps the most significant thing about Moses and Elijah is that Moses was raised from the dead (Jude 9), while Elijah was translated to heaven without ever experiencing death (2 Kings 2:11, 12). Thus Moses and Elijah serve as types of those who will be resurrected and translated when Jesus comes the second time to establish His kingdom of glory (1 Thes. 4:16, 17), and the Transfiguration itself is a type of that glorious kingdom. It is a foreshadowing in miniature of the coming kingdom.

The third significant aspect of the Transfiguration is the voice that sounded from heaven (17:5). This voice signifies that Jesus is not merely equal with the great heroes of the Jewish Bible, but that He is their Lord. Thus the revelation and person of Jesus are greater than that of Moses and Elijah, of the law and the prophets. Here is not merely another prophet but the very Son of God. But beyond recognizing Jesus as the Son of God, the voice also recognizes Him as the Messiah. That last thought comes from the last three words of 17:5. " 'Listen to him' " is a quotation from Deuteronomy 18:15, which identifies the Messiah as a prophet like Moses and ends in the words, "You must listen to him."

The Transfiguration makes both an immediate and a lasting impression on the three disciples. The immediate impression is signaled in 17:6 by the fact that "they fell facedown to the ground, terrified." Years later Peter expressed the lasting impression when he penned, "We did not follow cleverly invented stories when we told you about the power and coming of our Lord Jesus Christ, but we were eyewitnesses of his majesty. For he received honor and glory from God the Father when the voice came to him from the Majestic Glory, saying, 'This is my Son, whom I love; with him I am well pleased.' We ourselves heard this voice that came from heaven when we were with him on the sacred mountain" (2 Pet. 1:16-18).

Thus the three disciples have the assurance through the Transfiguration that they are not being misled. They are able for a short time to see beyond the suffering Servant of 16:21-23 to the coming King of 16:27.

But soon they must go back down the mountain to present reality, and it will be a dismal reality indeed. Yet no matter how dismal their immediate reality might be, Christ asserts ultimate victory in 17:9 as He once again tells them that He will be " 'raised from the dead.' " The Transfiguration stands as a pledge of that resurrection hope.

But between their mountaintop experience and the resurrection of Christ, the disciples are not to tell anyone what they have seen. It will all make sense to them after the resurrection, but not before. After the resurrection they will be able to preach Christ's victory over sin and death with both knowledge and enthusiasm. His resurrection will then join with the Transfiguration as a guarantee of the future kingdom and of the resurrection (like Moses) or the translation to glory (like Elijah) of all who have believed in His name.

But the whole event on the Mount of Transfiguration has raised a major question in the disciples' minds. How can Jesus be the end-time Messiah, since Elijah has not come to "restore all things" (vss. 10, 11)? Jesus' answer sets forth two truths. First, John the Baptist functioned as Elijah in the fulfillment of Malachi 4:5. Second, Jesus Himself will "suffer at their hands" in a manner similar to John. Thus, for those who are listening carefully, Jesus adds another warning of His coming death to the promise of His resurrection in verse 9 (vss. 12, 13).

Frustrating Glimpses of the Disciples' Unpreparedness

Matthew 17 closes with two stories that illustrate the unpreparedness of the disciples for the task ahead of them. The first of these stories begins with the failure of the disciples to heal a demon-possessed boy while Jesus was on the Mount of Transfiguration (vss. 14-21).

No sooner do Jesus and His three closest disciples come off the mountain than He is confronted with a curious crowd, a sick boy, a disappointed father, and, undoubtedly, nine red-faced disciples. After rebuking the crowd, Jesus heals the boy. This healing provides the focal point for Luke's telling of the story. Luke says that the crowd "were all amazed at the greatness of God" (Luke 9:43).

But Matthew—one of the nine embarrassed disciples—gets a different lesson from the event. For him, the real lesson is that the disciples failed because they lacked faith (17:20). That must have been fairly close to the ultimate frustration for Jesus. After all, while He was up on the mountain the nine disciples were provided with an opportunity to carry on His work without Him. The result: failure, abysmal failure!

And that failure has taken place, as Jesus sees it, just a short interval from the time that His personal presence will be taken from them on a permanent basis. The significance of the story is that the disciples are not yet ready to carry on without Jesus. It is little wonder that Jesus will spend much of His remaining time on earth teaching them. They need stronger faith if they are to succeed after His ascension. Without faith, they will be powerless to be effective in ministry. But with faith, they can "move mountains" (vs. 20).

Some may be asking at this point, Who would want to move a mountain, anyway? That would certainly be a useless exercise in sensationalism standing outside the model of Jesus' ministry. The answer seems to be that Jesus was speaking metaphorically in line with a phrase common among the rabbis. According to Michael Green, "To 'tear up' or 'remove' mountains was a way of saying 'remove difficulties' " (M. Green, 166). Thus faith in God was the key that could not only make the disciples effective in ministry, but could also help them face and/or solve the difficulties that loomed large for them. The same holds true in the twentieth century. A ministry or a witness without faith is powerless.

Mark adds to the story of the disciples' failure the idea that prayer is also a key element in successful Christian work (Mark 9:29; the same idea along with fasting is found in some ancient Matthew manuscripts also—see the marginal reading for 17:21). The lesson of the Gospel writers is that successful ministry is built upon both faith and sincere prayer. The two, of course, are integrally related. The sincere prayer is the prayer based on genuine faith, and genuine faith will certainly lead to a life informed by prayer. Jesus' disciples then and now need to continually learn the necessity of prayer and of spending time with God—a lesson the Gospels frequently report when they claim that Jesus went apart to pray.

The second passage illustrating the unpreparedness of the disciples is the story of Jesus and the temple tax (vss. 24-27). That event takes the form of an attempt by the Jewish leaders to trap Jesus by creating a situation in which either answer to their question can implicate Him.

The question is put to Peter: "Doesn't your teacher pay the temple tax?" A negative answer will provide a pretext for charging Jesus with overthrowing the temple service. Peter, wanting to avoid that horn of the dilemma, quickly answers that Jesus will pay the tax.

But that hasty reply merely lands Peter (and Jesus) on the other horn of the dilemma. After all, priests, and apparently others occupied solely in God's service (including prophets), could claim exemption from the temple tax (see Morris, *Matthew*, 452). Thus when Peter, without consulting Jesus, claims that Jesus will pay the tax, he is in effect disclaiming Jesus' role as a prophet and teacher in Israel. Thus the same apostle who a short time before had set forth Jesus as the Son of God and the Messiah (16:16) now stumbles over himself and sanctions the very conception of Jesus put forth by the Jewish leaders.

Jesus does His best to disarm the situation. After advising Peter that because of His Sonship He is exempt from the tax for His "Father's house" (Luke 2:49), He tells His chief disciple to go to the lake, throw out his fishing line, and remove the tax money from the first fish he catches. He is to pay the tax with that coin (17:27).

At first glance, this miracle seems out of character with what we read in the biblical Gospels. It is more in line with some of the stories in the apocryphal gospels, which have Jesus performing many exotic and wondrous miracles. But a moment's reflection shows that the miracle of the fish with a coin in its mouth fits the very need of Jesus at the time. For one thing, it definitely proves to the stumbling Peter that Jesus is a prophet, since Jesus knows which fish the coin will be in as well as the value of the coin. Second, it is almost impossible to believe that Peter could keep his mouth shut, perhaps even to the tax collectors, about how the tax money was raised. Thus the miracle made both horns of the dilemma disappear. Third, it can be argued that even though Jesus outwardly complied, technically, it was not His money that paid the tax.

And we should not miss the lesson that Jesus avoided useless confrontation whenever possible. Many Christians could learn from that object lesson today. There is a time for confrontation (see, for example, Matt. 23), but most of the time confrontation is both unnecessary and destructive to preaching the gospel.

In summary, in the last half of Matthew 17, we find two stories illustrating the unpreparedness of the disciples to take over from Jesus. The first story illustrates their lack of faith, while the second illustrates their lack of practical wisdom.

Given these deficiencies, it should come as little surprise that Jesus spends so much of His time after the trip to Caesarea Philippi directing His instruction specifically at the disciples. Not the least of that instruction will be repeated announcements of His death and resurrection. A second full announcement of these events is found tucked in between the two stories relating to the disciples' inadequacies (17:22, 23).

■ Applying the Word

Matthew 16:21–17:27

1. How is the cross in my life? Have I crucified Christ, or have I let Him crucify me? Am I really a Christian, or am I just "playing church"? What evidence can I list to support my answers?
2. If I am really honest with myself, what would I give my life for? What rewards do I really cherish in life? Are they honor, prestige, money, position, and the other perks of my daily existence, or are they more closely related to God's kingdom? How can I really tell what I value? In what specific ways can my values become more healthy and Christian?
3. In chapter 17 the disciples were found to be in need of both more faith and more wisdom. How is my supply of those commodities holding up? In what ways do they affect my daily life? How can I grow in both faith and wisdom?

■ Researching the Word

1. Compare the passages in Matthew, Mark, and Luke that deal with the healing of the boy with a demon. Make three columns on a blank page in your notebook. Outline in a rather detailed fashion the presentation in each Gospel. Then, at the bottom of your page, develop a summary. Begin with a list of all that Matthew contributes to our understanding of the story. Then summarize with a list of what Mark and Luke have added to Matthew's presentation. Can you think of any logical explanations for the different approaches?
2. Using a concordance (exhaustive, preferably), study Matthew's use of *cross*, *death*, *raised*, *resurrection*, and equivalent terms as they apply to Jesus and His followers.

(If you are using a concordance based on the KJV, you will have to check for the exact words used in that version.) What is the composite picture that you arrive at? What can be learned from that composite picture?

■ Further Study of the Word

1. For general insight, see E. G. White, *The Desire of Ages*, 410-434.
2. For a discussion of all sayings in the four Gospels dealing with Jesus' prediction of His passion and resurrection, see J. B. Green and S. McKnight, eds., *Dictionary of Jesus and the Gospels*, 630-633.
3. For a discussion of the Transfiguration and issues surrounding it, see ibid., 834-841.

CHAPTER NINE

The Life of the Cross: Qualifications for Citizenship in the Kingdom

Matthew 18:1–20:34

In chapter 16, we found Jesus' first explicit announcement of His coming death and resurrection and the disciples' reaction to that announcement. Chapter 17 featured the Transfiguration as a pledge and foretaste of ultimate victory, along with two glimpses of the unpreparedness of the disciples.

That unpreparedness sets the stage for 18:1 to 20:34, which has Jesus largely providing significant instruction to His disciples on humility and forgiveness (18:1-35), divorce (19:1-12), the inadequacy of self-sufficiency (19:16-27), the "unjust" nature of grace (19:28–20:16), and the fact that some people still don't understand the nature of the kingdom (20:17-34). The various teachings in 18:1–20:34 can be summed up as qualifications for citizenship in the kingdom, or, alternately, living the life of the cross.

A significant shift in the Gospel's narrative takes place in 19:1, where we are informed that Jesus leaves Galilee for Judea. That trip will be a one-way experience. Thus the importance of the teachings that Jesus wants to leave with His disciples in 18:1–20:34 (covered in this chapter) and in 21:1 to 25:46 (covered in the next two chapters).

Jesus knows their unpreparedness for what will prove to be the most traumatic event of their lives. And He needs to do all that He can to prepare them for both that event and the responsibilities that will follow on its heels. After all, in a few short weeks the disciples will be the leaders of His church.

■ Getting Into the Word

Matthew 18:1–19:15

Read 18:1 to 19:15 through at least two times. Then work out the following issues and questions in your Matthew notebook.

1. **Outline chapter 18. Then, in short paragraphs, summarize the major teaching in each section. Discuss the themes that hold this chapter together.**
2. **Explain the relationship between Peter's question in 18:21 and the parable that begins in 18:23. How many times should we forgive? Compare various Bible versions on that point. According to chapter 18, what difference does our answer to the question of how forgiving we are make? With the use of a concordance, look up Jesus' other counsel on forgiveness in Matthew. How does that counsel line up with our present passage?**
3. **Summarize the major points that Jesus makes in His counsel on divorce in 19:1-12. Use your marginal references to find and read the other place in Matthew where Jesus speaks to the issue of 19:3. What are the Old Testament references for the allusions in 19:4, 5? What are the implications of the final words in verse 5 ("the two will become one flesh") for the argument? What are the implications of that phrase for the Bible's rather confusing teaching on polygamy?**

■ Exploring the Word

With chapter 18 we come to the fourth of Christ's teaching discourses in the first Gospel. This one covers personal relationships in the kingdom and contributes significantly to our understanding of Christian ethics.

Whereas chapter 10 (the sermon on discipleship) was concerned with the outward (missionary) orientation of the kingdom, chapter 18 is a collection of teachings devoted to internal relationships—relationships between members that make churches into successes or failures. Jesus' teaching on divorce (19:1-12) has been included in the chapter because it also deals with internal ethical relations in the kingdom. This entire section of Matthew, running from 18:1 to 19:12, can be viewed in terms of Christian living in the light of the cross.

Greatness in Light of the Cross

Matthew 18 opens with a treatment of children and little ones. Verses 1 to 5 focus on greatness, verses 6 to 9 on offenses, and verses 10 to 14 on lost sheep. The fourteen verses are held together as a section by two Greek words signifying children and little ones, with a subtle shift from literal children to "unimportant" believers (the "little ones") at verse 6.

The passage begins with a question that greatly troubles the disciples: "Who is the greatest in the kingdom of heaven?" Mark tells us that prior to the question of 18:1, the disciples had been "arguing," on the road, about who was the greatest (Mark 9:33, 34). Perhaps the stimulus for the argument was Jesus' blessing of Peter in 16:17, but at a deeper level, the question resides at the center of the sinful human heart. The desire for egocentric greatness fuels the world's stunning accomplishments and its great sins. The desire to stand out, to be superior, to have people look at and admire "me," is part of the great rebellion of human beings against God. It was also the root of Lucifer's sin in heaven. He had said in his heart, " 'I will raise my throne above the stars of God. . . . I will make myself like the Most High' " (Isa. 14:13, 14). We saw in our treatment of Matthew 16:24 that the desire to be the god of our own lives forms the foundation of sin. We also noted that the only solution to that problem is the cross—that is, the death of our selves and the born-again experience in Christ.

In verses 2 to 5 Jesus tells the disciples that the greatest in the kingdom will be like little children. We need to understand that children were of little account in antiquity. Jesus turns the wisdom of the world on its head and suggests that true greatness is not found in accomplishments and worldly sophistication but in the humility and transparentness of children. That humility is an important qualification for entering the kingdom.

Unfortunately, like so many of Jesus' lessons, this one had not up to now stuck in the minds of the disciples. Matthew 20:20-28 finds John and James, along with their mother, still maneuvering for the choicest places in the kingdom. Luke tells us that the disciples were even debating which of them was the greatest on the way to the cross (Luke 22:24). Such is the depth of the root of sin and the human aversion to crucifying the all-important self.

The tone and topic of the passage shifts in verse 6. The tone moves from promise to warning, while the topic shifts from humility to the seriousness of causing "unimportant" believers (the "little ones") to stumble in their Christian walk. In verses 8 and 9 the warning tone remains, but now it is connected with causing oneself to stumble.

The overall message of verses 6 to 9 is that it is better to have a millstone around one's neck and be drowned than to lead a weak Christian astray. Likewise, it is better for a Christian to cut off a foot than to let it carry him or her into sin.

While the warnings are clear, we need to recognize that the language is figurative rather than literal. Unfortunately, some Christians down through the ages have applied it literally. Origen (c. A.D. 185–c. 254), for example, castrated himself out of literal obedience to these verses (and 19:12) in order to show his seriousness with regard to lustful thoughts. Be that as it may, the intention of Jesus' words is not self-mutilation, but that Christians must violently put sin away from themselves and refuse to dwell on those things that lead them into sin. The logical extreme of the literalistic interpretation would be suicide for the sake of the kingdom of heaven. After all, dead people don't sin at all!

God wants death, but it is the death of the willful sinful nature. Fortunately, God's empowering grace enables His children to overcome through perseverance. Meanwhile, the figurative language catches our attention and helps us see the seriousness of sinful activities.

In verses 10 to 14 the tone and the topic shift again. This time the tone is neither one of promise nor of warning but of concern. That concern is for all believers, especially the "unimportant" or weak ones and children. Not only is the Father concerned with every one of His earthly children, but they each have a special angel who watches over them. (The New English Bible supplies *guardian* before *angel*, but such an addition is not in the Greek, even though it may be implied.) The natural conclusion to verses 10 to 14 is that we as church members should be just as caring for other people as are God and His angels. In the light of the cross, all of our relationships will be more caring, especially as we Christians come to see greatness in terms of humble service to others rather than as domination of them.

Luke 15 has a similar passage about lost sheep, but there the purpose of the story is evangelistic (saving lost souls), while here it is pastoral (helping believers to remain faithful). That pastoral concern continues on into verses 15 to 17.

Forgiveness in the Light of the Cross

The Christian who is humble, caring, and concerned (vss. 1-14), will also be forgiving (vss. 15-35). Matthew's treatment of forgiveness in this chapter has three sections. The first (vss. 15-20) outlines the method of working with another Christian who has sinned. The second (vss. 21, 22) calls for unlimited forgiveness. And the third (vss. 23-35) is a parable illustrating that the forgiven Christian must pass on the blessing he or she has received by forgiving others.

Verses 15 to 20 set down rules for dealing with trouble between two Christians. If these rules were followed more often, the church would certainly be happier and healthier. First, says Jesus, try to settle the problem privately, " 'just between the two of you.' " It never helps to bring sin out in the open if the problem can be solved in private. Nor does it help to sit around and grumble to one's self or to others about another person. Note that Jesus commands the offended one to take the initiative—"go." That is a command to be like the God who sent His own Son to make reconciliation with His enemies (see Gen. 3:8, 9; Luke 15:4, 8, 20, 28; Rom. 5:6, 8).

If that personal visit does not solve the problem, then the injured person is to take one or two other Christians along with him so that there will be witnesses both to the arguments on both sides of the problem and to the sincerity put forth to heal the wound (vs. 16).

If this effort doesn't resolve the issue, then the matter must be brought to the church in its binding and loosing function (vss. 17, 18). As we saw in 16:19, that function has to do with setting standards and regulating conduct. In the present case, the church must decide whether the offending action is permissible or forbidden. Both parties are expected to abide by the decision of the church, recognizing that a just decision made under the guidance of the Holy Spirit will also be ratified in heaven (vs. 18). But if a just decision is rejected by the offender, his or her objectionable activity and unrepentant attitude excludes that individual from the fellowship (vs. 17).

The second segment on forgiveness (vss. 21, 22) finds Peter asking how many times he should forgive his neighbor. Although phrased as a question, Peter probably considered his suggestion of seven times to be quite a generous statement. After all, to forgive a person seven times is a great deal of forgiveness, especially since the rabbis taught that one must not forgive more than three times.

Thus Rabbi Jose ben Hanina claimed that "he who begs forgiveness from his neighbour must not do so more than three times," and Rabbi Jose ben Jehuda said, "If a man commits an offense once, they forgive him; if he commits an offense a second time, they forgive him; if he commits an offense a third time, they forgive him; the fourth time they do not forgive" (see Barclay, 2:213).

The biblical basis for this ruling was found in the opening chapters of Amos, where the rabbis concluded from the oft-repeated "for three sins" of various nations "even for four," that the limit of God's forgiveness was three times. Thus Peter, in an act of exceptional generosity, doubles the accepted Jewish quota and adds one more for good measure. He undoubtedly expects warm commendation for his graciousness. The thought of the blessing he had received at Caesarea Philippi (16:17-19) in front of the rest of the disciples still warms his heart. After all, despite Jesus' recent talk on the topic of humility, Peter still pictures himself as the front contender for being the greatest in the kingdom. He undoubtedly thinks his generous answer is a further demonstration of that greatness.

Jesus answers Peter in two parts. First, Jesus says, the correct number is not seven but "seventy times seven" (RSV and NIV margin), or 490. Now, that is a lot of forgiveness (even if it is a mere seventy-seven times, as suggested by the NIV)—so much that a person would lose count before transgression number 491 (or even 78) had arrived. However, Jesus is not teaching a lesson on the arithmetic of forgiveness but rather that there is no limit to forgiveness.

This is not the answer Peter expects, for Peter, like the rest of us, is really more interested in the limit of Christian love and forbearance than in its extent. After all, it is reassuring to know at what point I can stop loving my neighbor with a good conscience, to know when I have fulfilled my moral quota of love and forgiveness, so that I can with a clear conscience let people have what they deserve. The all-too-human question underlying Peter's query is, "When can I let go? When do I have a right to explode?"

Jesus' frustrating reply is, Never. For the Christian, there is no limit to forbearance and forgiveness.

The second part of Jesus' answer is given in the parable of the unmerciful servant (vss. 23-35). That parable has three main characters: the king (God), a servant forgiven an unbelievably large debt (me), and a servant (my neighbor) who owes the first servant (me) a relatively insignificant debt.

The parable has three scenes. In scene number one, the first servant is in the king's audience chamber, where he is forgiven a large debt. The second scene shows the recently forgiven servant out on the street, where he meets a neighbor who owes him a relatively small debt that he refuses to forgive. In the third scene, the unmerciful servant is thrown in jail (hell) until he pays off his impossible debt (vs. 34).

The moral of the story: We need to be just as forgiving to others as God has been to us (vs. 33). We need to learn how to forgive others from our heart (vs. 35). We found the same lesson earlier in the Sermon on the Mount, in which Jesus said, " 'If you do not forgive men their sins, your Father will not forgive your sins' " (6:15).

Many attempts have been made to moderate the parable or explain why its sharp contrasts cannot be genuine. But it is these very contrasts that help us understand not only the wideness of God's mercy but the mercy He expects of us as Christians.

The ten thousand-talent debt (vs. 24) was unbelievably large. A talent equalled six thousand denarii, or six thousand days' wages (20:2). At today's minimum wage of $4.25 per hour calculated on an eight-hour day, one talent would be worth $204,000, and ten thousand talents would be worth the incredible sum of $2,040,000,000. By contrast, the one hundred-denarii debt would be one hundred days' wages or $3,400. To put the matter another way, it would take one hundred days to work off the one hundred-denarii debt but (at seven days per week) 164,384 years to work off the ten thousand talents. While the smaller debt is not insignificant, the larger one is unbelievably large. After all, the annual budget for the province of Galilee was only three hundred talents.

William Barclay sums up the meaning of the contrast nicely when he pens that "the point is that nothing that men can do to us can in any way compare with what we have done to God; and if God has forgiven us the debt we owe Him, we must forgive our fellow-men the debts they owe to us" (Barclay, 2:214). Thus we are left without excuse if we fail to pass on the forgiveness that God has so graciously extended to us.

Divorce in the Light of the Cross

While in many ways Jesus' teachings on divorce in 19:3-12 do not fit in with the discourse of chapter 18, in other ways, the two sections are definitely related. For example, both sections deal with human relationships; divorce and remarriage certainly need to be seen in terms of God's unmerited forgiveness; and a Christian approach to divorce and remarriage *must* be seen in light of the cross.

In 19:1 we find the significant statement that Jesus has entered Judea for what turns out to be the last major journey of His ministry. In Judea He finds not only the usual crowds (vs. 2), but also His Pharisaic antagonists. As usual, they are seeking to find some fault with Him, this time in the area of divorce.

By their question of whether it is " 'lawful for a man to divorce his wife for any and every reason' " (vs. 3), the Pharisees are hoping to draw Jesus into a contemporary Jewish argument regarding divorce. The controversy is over the proper interpretation of Deuteronomy 24:1, which permits a man to divorce his wife if "he finds something indecent about her." The school of Shammai interpreted that phrase to mean adultery, while those scribes following Hillel viewed it as embracing a multitude of less serious things. At the very least, the Pharisees hope to force Jesus to take sides in the issue and thus alienate a portion of the crowd that is following Him.

But Jesus once again avoids their ploy. He avoids the contemporary Jewish debate altogether by using a rabbinic method of disputation that built upon the premise that "the more original, the weightier." Jesus took the argument back to Genesis, implying that what happened as early as Creation is weightier than what Moses legislated considerably later. While this form of argument did not do away with the Mosaic regulation, it did mean that Moses must be interpreted in light of the earlier statement.

Michael Green (181, 182) points out that Jesus made six strong points about marriage in His reply to the Pharisees. First, marriage was designed by God. It is a God-given ordinance, rather than a mere social contract.

Second, marriage is an ordinance between the sexes. God " 'made them male and female.' " God's intention was not a unisex world. As Green puts it, "There is a God-ordained difference and complementarity between the sexes. That is so obvious that it only needs to be stated in this late twentieth century when homosexuality has come to be seen as an equally valid alternative to marriage."

Third, marriage is intended to be permanent: " 'The two will become one flesh.' " It was never intended that the marriage relationship ever be broken by any "indecency," whether that expression be interpreted by Shammai, Hillel, or anyone else. Any deviation from the perpetuity of marriage is a declension from the ideal.

Fourth, marriage is exclusive. The two—not three, four, or five—are to become one flesh. One man and one woman are to be joined together. That ideal rules out the convenient "affairs" of so many modern people and the polygamy of the ancients. Apparently, God's allowance for polygamy in the Old Testament was a less-than-ideal concession to entrenched custom and human weakness. Beyond that, it provided security for females in cultures where they had no rights as independent citizens and where there were not enough males to go around.

Fifth, marriage creates a nuclear family unit. It includes both leaving one's parents and uniting with a spouse. Thus marriage becomes the strongest and most important of all human relationships.

Sixth, marriage is not for everybody. That is implied in verses 10 to 12. The disciples are shocked by the rigor of Jesus' exposition on the nature of marriage. He has been tougher than even Shammai. Therefore, the disciples suggest that if it is impossible to get out of marriage, perhaps it is best not to get into it in the first place.

While Jesus does not forthrightly deny this suggestion, He does say that not everyone can accept it. Then He adds that some will renounce their right to marriage "because of the kingdom of heaven" (vs. 12). Such was the status of Jesus Himself, John the Baptist, and apparently Paul in his mature years.

Jesus' words leave no doubt about divorce as an act that falls short of God's ideal. Thus Jesus agrees with the Old Testament, where God said, " 'I hate divorce' " (Mal. 2:16).

But divorces do take place in a less-than-perfect world, as do remarriages. However, second unions, says Jesus, are certainly less than God's ideal under any circumstances. He refers to them as acts of adultery, since they break the one-man-one-woman ideal. The only exception to adulterous remarriage in Matthew is given in chapter 19, when that ideal has already been shattered by the other partner (vs:9).

This is not a happy thought for those who have done all they could to save a marriage that failed yet feel the God-given urge to be in a marriage relationship. Fortunately, *divorce and remarriage are not unpardonable sins*, though some saints strive hard to make them that. We must never forget that just as Jesus' teaching on divorce and remarriage in verses 1 to 12 stands in the shadow of His teachings on forgiveness in chapter 18, so do men and women caught in the hopeless web of divorce and remarriage stand in the light of the cross. Divorce and remarriage, like any other sin (except hardness toward the Holy Spirit [12:30-32]), can be forgiven. But for that forgiveness to take place, men and women in such circumstances must confess that they have fallen short of God's ideal and stand in need of His cleansing grace. Such individuals can and will be forgiven.

Individuals caught in the problem of divorce and remarriage for whatever reason need the compassion of the church as well as the forgiving grace of God. Matthew 18 sets forth not only God's forgiveness for such individuals but also the *duty* of humans to forgive. And beyond forgiveness, Matthew 18:10-14 commands compassion for such hurting, repenting individuals. Those who are overly critical of their sincerely repentant brothers and sisters have forgotten God's forgiveness that has been extended to them. These critics are liable for the reward of the unjust servant of 18:32-34 and the millstone of 18:6. The lesson of the cross is that we need to constantly remember the understanding mercy that God has shown us, and then, through His grace, we are to extend the same mercy to others.

■ Getting Into the Word

Matthew 19:16–20:34

Read 19:16 to 20:34 twice. Then examine the following questions and issues.

1. **Compare the passages parallel to 19:16-27 in the other Gospels to see what additional facts you can glean about the identity of the man who interacts with Jesus in these verses. Write out your first impression to his question in 19:16. Carefully note Jesus' list of commandments in verses 18 and 19. What do they have in common? What do you notice about the order of the list? What types of commandments are missing from that list? Taking verses 18 to 22 as a group, describe the man's basic problem. Summarize the meaning of verses 23 to 26.**
2. **Matthew 19:27-30 lies between the story of the young man and the parable of the vineyard. How do these verses relate to the story of 19:16-26? How do they relate to the parable of 20:1-16? In what ways do verses 27 to 30 tie the story and the parable together? Why do you think 19:30 is repeated in 20:16? In light of 19:26-30, summarize the meaning of the parable of the vineyard.**
3. **In 20:20-28 we find the mother of James and John seeking the highest places in the kingdom for her sons. What is there about human nature that makes this topic so attractive in spite of everything that Jesus has said against it thus far in Matthew? Summarize in your own language the main points in 20:24-28 and the implications of those points.**
4. **Matthew 20:29-34 tells of Jesus providing sight for the**

blind. Compare that miracle with the parallel passage in Mark 10:46-52 and Luke 18:35-43. What major difference do you find between the accounts? How would you explain the discrepancy? Write out your answers in your Matthew notebook.

■ Exploring the Word

The Inadequacy of Self-Sufficiency: Avoiding the Way of the Cross

In 19:16 a man comes to Jesus with a question. Matthew notes that he is young (vs. 20) and rich (vss. 22, 23), while Luke says that he is a ruler (Luke 18:18). Mark adds to our knowledge by claiming that he runs up to Jesus and falls on his knees, thereby implying that he is both eager and devout (Mark 10:17). The rich young ruler's question concerns what he must do to have eternal life.

This man obviously believes that salvation can be achieved through rigorous action and behavior. From what follows, we know that he has already worked hard at religion, but he must feel that his efforts have not been spectacular enough. He may expect Jesus to announce that he needs to perform some spectacular act.

Jesus answers the young man on his own terms. " 'If you would enter life,' " He suggests, " 'keep the commandments' " (vs. 17, RSV). When the man asks which ones, Jesus mentions several commandments from the Decalogue.

We should note at least four things about this list. First, the commandments mentioned are all from the second table of the law and deal with the way people treat others. This gives us a hint as to the man's problem.

Second, Jesus lists the commandments in order: the sixth, seventh, eighth, and ninth. But then, to our surprise, he lists the fifth after the ninth! Why? Undoubtedly to call attention to it. The rich young ruler may have been among those Jesus condemned in 15:1-6 for using man-made tradition to avoid caring for his parents and showing them due respect.

A third thing to note about Jesus' list is that the tenth command (dealing with covetousness) is not mentioned at all. It will soon be evident, however, that this issue lies at the very center of the man's spiritual problem (vss. 22, 23).

Finally, Jesus adds a quotation from Leviticus 19:18 (" 'love your neighbor as yourself' ") to the commands to be kept. Once again, Jesus uses a text that was important in Judaism and is close to the core of the young man's problem.

In confidence the young man replies that he has kept all of those commands. He apparently is not at all embarrassed by this claim. He truly does seem to be a shining example of a certain type of moral person. But he is soon to discover that mere morality is not enough to gain entry into the kingdom of heaven. Jesus probes a bit further, demonstrating that the man's obedience is outward and legal rather than inward and spiritual.

In verse 21 Jesus drops His bomb: " 'If you would be perfect [or complete],' " He says, " 'go, sell what you possess and give to the poor, and you will have treasure in heaven; and come, follow me' " (RSV). With this suggestion, Jesus cuts to the heart of the rich man's problem. Matthew tells us that when the young man heard Jesus' words, "he went away sorrowful; for he had great possessions" (vs. 22, RSV). He was more in love with things and money than he was with people. Thus he was transgressing commandment number ten. His reaction also demonstrated that he loved things more than God, and thus he was also transgressing the first commandment of the Decalogue.

Here is a man who refused to submit to the cross. He refused to give up all so that he might find the eternal life for which he longed (16:24-26). His obedience was based on outward behavior rather than on conversion—on a legalistic obedience to the letter of the law rather than on death of the old self and resurrection to a new way of life in Jesus (see Rom. 6:1-10; John 3:3, 5). He was depending on conformity to the expectations of his peers rather than on the transformation demanded by the gospel (Rom. 12:2).

Jesus' invitation to him is to " 'come, follow me' " (vs. 21). He offered that same invitation to the fishermen at their nets in 4:19

and to Matthew at his place of work in 9:9. Those disciples gave up all and followed Jesus. But this apparently outstanding young man refuses to follow the way of the cross.

It is important to understand that his riches were not the problem, but rather his *love* of those riches. Other wealthy men (such as Zacchaeus, Joseph of Arimathaea, and Nicodemus) eventually followed Jesus without Jesus telling them that they needed to give up all their possessions. Each person has something in his or her life that tempts him or her to hold back from full surrender. For some it may be wealth, for others it may be pride of beauty or of their preaching ability. No matter what our idol, though, it must be put away. In the end, the commandment still holds true: We are to have no other gods before Yahweh (Exod. 20:3). The way of the cross is the only way to eternal life.

After the young man refuses the cross, Jesus turns to His disciples and tells them that it will be hard for the rich to enter the kingdom (vs. 23). He goes on to tell them that it will not only be hard but impossible—just as impossible as it would be for a camel (the largest animal in Palestine) to go through the eye of a sewing needle (vs. 24).

This statement catches the disciples off guard. They, like other Jews, see the wealthy as blessed of God. Who, they ask, can make it into the kingdom if it is impossible for the blessed rich (vs. 25)?

" 'With man,' " Jesus replies, " 'this is impossible, but with God all things are possible' " (vs. 26). And with these words, Jesus sets us up for the great parable of grace in chapter 20.

The "Unjust" Nature of Grace

To say the least, Peter is shocked by Jesus' answer about the "impossibility" of the rich entering the kingdom, and he responds with a very human question. After noting that, unlike the rich young ruler, he and the other disciples *have* left everything to follow Him, he asks " 'What then will there be for us?' " (vs. 27). In other words, "What will we get for our sacrifices?"

It would have been all too easy for Jesus to answer Peter with an impatient rebuke. He could have told Peter that his question was unspiritual and suggested that he and the rest of the disciples move beyond such egocentric questions as Who is the greatest? and What do we get? But Jesus doesn't follow this very natural path. Rather, He answers Peter with both delicacy and respect—after all, the disciples really *have* given up everything.

Jesus' reply comes in two parts. The first is a straightforward answer that meets Peter on his own ground, while the second is a parable that does contain a somewhat veiled rebuke.

In the straightforward part of His answer, Jesus tells Peter and the disciples that they will indeed be rewarded for their faithfulness. At the second advent, they will "sit on twelve thrones, judging the twelve tribes of Israel" (vs. 28). That judging probably does not mean passing judgment, but rather, as in the Old Testament, taking part in governance. (The Old Testament judges were rulers.) It is impossible to determine from this passage the exact nature of the disciples' reward and how theirs will differ from the rewards of other Christians, but Jesus' point is that the disciples have followed Christ and will receive a reward.

Before moving away from this verse, we should note one thing about trying to make Bible sayings so literal that every jot and tittle becomes a proof for some theological opinion. It should be obvious that the twelve disciples will not sit as rulers on twelve thrones. For one thing, Judas will be missing. The lesson here is that we ought to read the Bible for the main point in each passage, rather than trying to make inspiration verbally infallible. Read for the central message, not for some exciting "new truth" around the edges. All too many Christians follow the latter route with some very less-than-sanctified results.

In verse 29 Jesus turns the topic to all Christians. Not only the disciples, but all who have followed Him will receive their reward. Once again, we must try not to be too literal. After all, it is impossible to have a hundred fathers! Jesus' point is that the reward will be much greater than the sacrifice.

Beginning in 19:30 and running through 20:16, we find the second part of Jesus' answer to Peter: It is the parable of the vineyard. The parable begins and ends with the statement that " 'many who are first will be last, and many who are last will be first' " (19:30), except that 20:16 is in reverse order. The repetition and reversing the order are Jesus' subtle warning and rebuke to Peter and his fellows.

The parable is about a householder (God) who goes out to hire day labor for his vineyard. (Israel is often referred to as God's vineyard—see Isa. 5:1-7.) At the beginning of the twelve-hour workday, the landlord makes a formal agreement with the available workers to pay a denarius for a full day's labor.

But the farmer is desperate, because when grapes ripen, they must be harvested immediately, or many of them will spoil. So the farmer returns repeatedly to hire more workers. His final trip is at the eleventh hour, when the day is almost over. The implication is that these later workers can't be too ambitious, or they would have been employed earlier. But they still must eat, so they show up for work anyway. However, only to the first workers did the landlord state the exact amount he would pay for a day's labor.

The story takes on special interest in 20:8 when, at the end of the day, the landlord lines the workers up in the reverse order from which he hired them and pays them. Thus the last are paid first. Then, in plain view of the others, he pays these one-hour workers one denarius—a full day's pay (vs. 9).

Now what do you think is going on in the minds of those who worked all day? They started multiplying (20:10). Anyone who has worked on fruit farms or in construction knows how the laborer's mind operates: "If those guys got one day's pay for one hour's work," the logic runs, "we deserve twelve days' pay—that is two weeks' earnings, if you subtract the Sabbaths. At last," they rejoice, "we have discovered an employer who will allow us to get ahead!" Their concern, in other words, is Peter's question of 19:27—"What do we get?"

Then comes the bombshell. Everyone gets exactly the same pay! No wonder they grumble (vs. 11). I was a young construction worker when I first read Matthew 20, and I grumbled with them. To me, it was a travesty of justice.

Verses 13 to 15 develop the main point of the story. The farmer has been perfectly fair. He has given those who have worked all day the amount they agreed on, and he has given the others more than they deserve. Giving people more good things than they deserve is an act of grace. Thus the laborers who were called first are really complaining about God's graciousness. They are upset because the farmer is generous (vs. 15).

In verse 16 Jesus repeats in reverse order the saying with which He began the parable: " 'So the last will be first, and the first will be last.' " A very real implication of the parable is that the first won't be in the kingdom at all unless they get over their grumbling about God's graciousness and move away from too much concern with their own rewards. It is important to recognize that human love gives people what they *deserve*, but God in His grace gives them what they *need*. Jesus wants His followers to develop that same gracious attitude. In the meantime, we ought to be thankful that God doesn't give us what we deserve.

Before moving away from Jesus' first-shall-be-last statement, we need to ask who it was aimed at. Peter and the disciples certainly come to mind, since Peter's question provided the immediate reason for Jesus to give the parable. The disciples are in danger of adopting the attitude of the first workers. Then again, some Bible interpreters see the parable as a reference to the Jewish people as they saw Gentiles coming into the kingdom. In our day it could apply to those who have served Jesus all their lives in contrast to those who are converted in old age, or those long-time members of a congregation who helped finance and build the local church in contrast to later members who may be rising to positions of leadership.

We actually need to see the message of the parable as universal. None of us are so good and holy that we can grumble about God's grace to others. Doing so may leave us in the unenviable position of being last, even if we started first. And if we compare this "surprise" with some of Christ's other parables that deal with judgment surprises, being last could be equated with receiving something besides eternal life (see, for example, 25:46).

Some People Still Don't Understand the Nature of the Kingdom

Matthew 19:1 told us that Jesus had entered Judea. In 20:17 He is ready to go "up to Jerusalem," which gives Him another opportunity to warn His disciples of His approaching death and resurrection (see also 16:21; 17:9, 12, 22, 23). With the event at hand, Jesus this time adds several details not mentioned earlier. He informs His disciples that the Jewish leaders, after condemning Him to death, "will turn him over to the Gentiles." Other first-time details are the manner of His suffering—mocking and flogging—and the manner of His death—crucifixion (20:18,19). "The effect," pens R. T. France, "is to emphasize not only the totality of the rejection (Jewish leaders and Gentiles), but also the humiliation and the harrowing pain; this is to be no glorious martyrdom, but an ugly, sordid butchery. It is thus all the more striking to read yet again here that *he will be raised on the third day*" (France, *Gospel According to Matthew*, 291).

One of the wonders of the Gospels is that the disciples were caught off guard at Jesus' death in spite of his many warnings of what was coming. From the context, a probable explanation for their blindness is that they were too preoccupied with their own rewards and their own greatness in the coming kingdom to focus on what He was so earnestly trying to tell them. Jesus did all He could to warn them, but the events shortly to take place still found them unprepared.

Another sign of their unpreparedness and lack of understanding is found in verses 20 to 23. In this passage we find James and John's mother asking that the two foremost places in the kingdom be given to her sons. In 19:28 Jesus had told the disciples that they would have twelve thrones. Now the mother of the Zebedee brothers moves in to request for James and John the two closest places to Jesus—the thrones immediately to His right and left. So we are back to the familiar problem of who will be the greatest.

It is not surprising that James and John make the move for supremacy at this point. After all, these two brothers, along with

Peter, made up the privileged inner circle at the Transfiguration. Furthermore, hadn't Peter been plainly rebuked in 16:23? And hadn't he received an implied rebuke in 19:30? Now is their chance! So they come with their mother, who states their request.

She probably has excellent reasons to expect her request to be granted. Comparing 27:56 with Mark 15:40, we discover that her name is Salome, and John's account of the same scene provides evidence that she was the sister of Jesus' mother (John 19:25). That would make James and John full first cousins of Jesus, and helps to explain why Jesus on the cross committed His mother to the care of John (John 19:26, 27). These identifications cannot be proven beyond the shadow of a doubt, but they are quite probable. They certainly help us understand Salome's aggressive request if it is a family matter. But family matter or not, Jesus refuses to grant it (20:23).

The power play, however, puts the other ten disciples in an uproar (vs. 24). Unfortunately, the uproar is not because the ten somehow grasp the error in the Zebedees' request, but because each of the ten wants the top spot in the kingdom for himself. With such thoughts running through their minds, it is little wonder that they cannot understand Jesus' repeated effort to tell them about His death and resurrection. They are so concerned with their personal thrones that they cannot see (or do not want to see) His cross.

Because of their utter misconception, Jesus calls them together to once again try to help them understand that the principles of the kingdom of heaven that He has been seeking to impress on them since the Sermon on the Mount are upside down from the principles of the kingdoms of this earth.

In verses 25 to 28 Jesus makes a major frontal assault on their value system. Unlike in the world, where the greatest are rulers, in the kingdom of heaven, the "*great*" (referring back to the Zebedees' request) are servants (*diakonos*) and the "*first*" (referring back to the vineyard parable) will be slaves (*doulos*). Jesus concludes by telling them that He Himself has not come to be served but to serve. Not only has He come in the role of servant, but He will soon " 'give his life as a ransom for many' " (vs. 28).

Jesus could not have outlined the concept of servant leadership more clearly. How unfortunate that down through history church leaders and Christians in general have not been any more drawn to that concept than were the disciples. The reason is simple: The servant leadership model goes against human nature. Its successful implementation demands both conversion and transformation.

Chapter 20 closes with the last act in Matthew's account of Jesus' itinerant ministry. In healing the two despised blind men (vss. 29-34), He demonstrates the humble servant role He has just described to the disciples. Even on the way to the cross, when His mind could have understandably been on His own troubles, He is motivated by compassion (vs. 34). Such was the Servant Messiah. Such, also, should the followers of such a One be.

■ Applying the Word

Matthew 18:1–20:34

1. What is my view of greatness? Have I put that view into operation in my daily life? In what specific ways can I improve that implementation?

2. How have I exemplified mercy this past week to children and to the "little ones" in my church and neighborhood? What specific actions can I list that will improve my ministry in that line?

3. When I have a problem with my neighbor or fellow church member, do I follow the counsel of 18:15-17, or do I rely on gossip, faultfinding, and "spiritual assassination" to handle my problems? What evidence can I supply for my answer?

4. In what ways have I demonstrated that I am as enthusiastic about forgiving as I am about being forgiven?

5. What is my equivalent of the rich young ruler's problem? What should I do about it? When?

■ Researching the Word

1. Matthew 18:10 brought to our attention the thought of guardian angels. Through the use of your concordance, discover what you can about the work and ministry of angels in both testaments. List their various duties in relation to humans, God, etc. After completing your Bible study, it will be helpful to compare your findings with the article on angels in a Bible dictionary.
2. Matthew 20:28 uses the word *ransom* to describe Jesus' death. With a concordance, check the few other uses of this word. Then examine the treatment of the word in the *Seventh-day Adventist Bible Commentary* for 20:28 and in a Bible dictionary. In what ways is the ransom metaphor helpful in understanding Jesus' work? In what ways does it fall short?

■ Further Study of the Word

1. For general insight, see E. G. White, *The Desire of Ages*, 432-442, 511-523, 547-551; E. G. White, *Christ's Object Lessons*, 390-404.
2. For an informative summary on divorce in the Gospels, see J. B. Green and S. McKnight, eds., *Dictionary of Jesus and the Gospels*, 192-199.
3. For a helpful treatment of the parable of the vineyard, see L. Morris, *The Gospel According to Matthew*, 498-505.

CHAPTER TEN

Kingdoms in Conflict: Moving Toward the Cross

Matthew 21–23

Beginning with 16:21, when Jesus first announced His death and resurrection, Matthew has been preparing his readers for Jesus' climactic visit to Jerusalem. In 19:1 he has Jesus leaving Galilee and entering Judea. Then in 20:17 he has Jesus "going up to Jerusalem." The entry finally takes place in 21:1-11.

In that entry we sense a change in Jesus. No longer is He operating as if His identity is to be kept a secret. To the contrary, the way He rides into the city (21:1-11) and His dispute with the Jewish authorities at the temple (21:12-17) are open and confrontational. The conflict is carried on throughout the rest of chapter 21 and continues through all of chapter 22, coming to a head in Matthew 23 with Jesus' public condemnation of the Jewish leaders. He concludes by saying that their house will be left desolate (23:38). At that point, everything is in place for the Jewish leaders to make their final drive to remove the "troublemaker" once and for all.

Matthew 21 to 23 plays a crucial role in the sequential development of the first Gospel, not only by getting Jesus into Jerusalem, but also by picturing the escalating struggle between Jesus and the Jewish leaders as that struggle moves toward its irreversible breaking point. Whereas previously the relationship between Jesus and the Jewish leaders had been filled with increasing tension, now it has become intoterable for them. These chapters truly outline the kingdom of heaven in conflict with the kingdoms of this earth.

■ Getting Into the Word

Matthew 21:1–22:14

Read Matthew 21 to 23 one time, trying to identify its major theme(s). Next read 21:1 to 22:14 through again. How does it fit into the three chapters taken as a whole? Then reflect on the following questions and exercises:

1. What is the significance of the triumphal entry in 21:1-11? List any words or phrases that highlight that significance. In formulating your list, it will be helpful to compare 21:8 with 2 Kings 9:13. How do you think the Jewish leaders felt regarding Jesus' entry and the people's enthusiasm? In what ways would the cleansing of the temple have affected those feelings?
2. Use your marginal references to discover the Old Testament references behind 21:5. What do those references contribute to our knowledge of why Jesus chose a young donkey to make His entry into Jerusalem? What is the symbolism involved in riding a donkey? What kind of king would He be? What would have been the symbolism had Jesus ridden a horse rather than a donkey? (Compare Revelation 19:11-16 for help with that last question.)
3. How does the story of the withered fig tree fit into the sequence of events in chapters 21 to 23? Compare Mark's parallel treatment of the fig tree and temple sequences. What is different between the two treatments of the sequence? Given the problems that Jesus is facing with the Jews in the temple in particular and in chapters 21 to 23 in general, write a paragraph on what you see as the symbolism of the withered fig tree.
4. Matthew 21:28–22:14 contains three parables. Summarize in a few sentences the main lesson of each parable. How are they alike in their lessons? How are they different? Describe the composite understanding that you get from the three taken as a block of teaching.

■ Exploring the Word

Challenging the Existing Kingdom

In Matthew 21:1-11 we learn of Jesus' triumphal entry into Jerusalem. He is not alone. To the contrary, He is accompanied by "a very large crowd" (vs. 8) that is giving Him the red-carpet treatment by spreading branches and cloaks on the road for Him to ride over. This is no ordinary occasion. They are shouting, " 'Hosanna to the Son of David!' " a title with unmistakable Messianic significance (vs. 9). And when they enter the city, the crowds identify Jesus as " 'the prophet from Nazareth' " (vs. 11). "The prophet" is most likely another allusion to the great prophet, like Moses, who was to arrive in the latter times (Deut. 18:15, 18).

Two questions need to be asked at this time: Where did the crowds come from? and Why the enthusiasm? To answer these questions we need to keep several factors in mind. First, it is Passover season, and the roads are literally teeming with people headed for Jerusalem from all over the Jewish world. Thus there are thousands of Galilean pilgrims arriving by the same route as Jesus. Among the Galileans and others, there must surely be large numbers who have been impressed with Jesus' teaching and miracles.

Second, as the Gospel of John indicates (11; 12:12-19), the raising of Lazarus from the dead has just taken place. That outstanding miracle has caused widespread excitement in Jerusalem and the surrounding territory, causing many people to put their faith in Jesus. Because of this, the Jewish authorities are planning to kill Lazarus also (John 12:1-11). It was one thing for Jesus to perform miracles in the backwoods of Galilee but quite another to raise a person from the dead in Bethany—Jerusalem's backyard.

The already existant excitement is being fanned to white-hot flame by the *manner* in which Jesus chooses to enter the city. Matthew tells us that He rides into town on the colt of a donkey (vss. 2-7). That is an interesting move for a man who has just walked all the way from Galilee. Certainly there is no physical need for Him to ride the last two miles. Furthermore, Jesus has always walked. This is the only time we find the adult Jesus riding in any of the Gospels. What He is doing is obviously deliberate.

That deliberateness is guided by the prophecy of Zechariah 9:9, which says that Jerusalem's "king comes to you, righteous and having salvation, gentle and riding on a donkey, on a colt, the foal of a donkey." Jesus is making a very definite Messianic claim through His mode of entry, and the crowd does not miss the point. Their excitement is without bounds. The Jewish leaders do not miss the implication either, but to them, it is a challenge rather than something to be joyful about.

One other thing should be noted about Jesus' deliberate fulfillment of Zechariah 9:9. The prophecy specified that the Messianic King would be "gentle," rather than the warlike leader expected by the Jews. Entrance on a horse would have signified a warlike leader, but entrance on a donkey's colt symbolized the peaceful arrival of the Messiah as the "Prince of Peace" (Isa. 9:6).

At His second coming Jesus will make His entry on a horse. Then He will come as the conquering Messiah the Jews expected at His first advent (Rev. 19:11-21).

If the manner in which Jesus enters Jerusalem is a Messianic statement, the cleansing of the temple is just as much a statement that He is the Christ. Beyond that, both are a challenge to the Jewish leaders. As Barclay puts it, "If the entry into Jerusalem had been defiance, here is defiance added to defiance" (Barclay, 2:268).

With the cleansing of the temple, Jesus takes the battle to the very heart of the enemy camp. His demonstration in the temple is no burst of enthusiasm or righteous anger stirred up by the momentary excitement of the triumphal entry. A reading of Matthew could give that impression, but Mark tells us that it was the "next day" after the entry when the cleansing took place (Mark 11:12). That is a significant bit of knowledge, since it definitely indicates that this was not some spur-of-the-moment challenge to the Jewish authorities. To the contrary, the fact that a night passes between the entry and the cleansing indicates that we are dealing with a premeditated challenge whose purpose is to forcefully call the attention of the Jews to Jesus' mission. Thus in the cleansing we find Jesus making His Messianic claim and exerting His Messianic authority at the very heart of Judaism.

The challenge is now impossible for either the leaders or the common people to ignore. The common people flock to Jesus in the temple and shout Messianic praises to the "Son of David" as He heals the blind and lame outcasts (vss. 14, 15). The chief priests and the scribes react to all the celebration with indignation (vs. 15). The enthusiasm of the crowds was bad enough out in the city, but now it has entered their own special territory and cast their lucrative temple trade in an extremely bad light.

In the episode at the temple, we find a turning point in the description of Jesus' enemies. Heretofore in Matthew's Gospel, the high priests have been mentioned only three times, but in the rest of the Gospel they will be mentioned another thirty-two times. In cleansing the temple, Jesus has challenged the formal religious power structure. From now on, the high priests will make common cause with the scribes and Pharisees to get rid of Him with a determination that was not present before. In cleansing the temple, He has truly proved Himself to be a dangerous enemy.

The acted parable of the fig tree (vss. 18-22) should be seen as a symbolic sequel to Jesus' experiences with the Jewish leaders in the temple story of verses 12 to 17. The relationship between the events is more evident in Mark, which says that the tree episode took place over two days, with the temple cleansing occurring between the two halves of the fig-tree story (Mark 11:12-21).

Thus the meaning of the parable of the fig tree seems clear, even though neither Gospel makes it explicit. Just as it was with the fig tree, which seemingly promised life but produced none, so it is with the aborted promise of the Jewish nation and its temple worship. The barrenness of the tree foreshadows Jesus' declaration of the desolation of the temple (23:38; see also 24:1, 2).

After the fig-tree story, we find a group of high-level dignitaries coming to Jesus in the temple to question the source of His authority. That is an important question, since He has obviously assumed authority (even Messianic authority) in both the temple cleansing and in the triumphal entry.

Jesus' authority has been evident in Matthew's Gospel ever since the close of the Sermon on the Mount, where Matthew noted that the people were "amazed . . . because he taught as one who had authority, and not as their teachers of the law" (7:28, 29). The people were certainly correct that Jesus was different from the learned Jewish scribes. They cited the rulings of earlier rabbis as their authoritative base for making interpretations, while He spoke as one having authority in Himself. "You have heard it said. . . . But I tell you" (5:27, 28, 31, 32).

Jesus' authority had been questioned on previous occasions because He had not studied under a learned rabbi (13:54-57; John 7:15), but He had not been seen as much of a threat then. Now, however, His triumphal entry into Jerusalem and His cleansing of the temple have changed that perception. The result: His authority is being challenged by the very people who pass out Jewish teaching credentials (21:23).

With His counterquestion Jesus refers them back to the source of John the Baptist's authority: "Was it from heaven, or from men?" (vs. 25). This is not a diversionary tactic. After all, Jesus' authority is closely tied to that of John, who had pointed Him out as the One who would come after him (3:11).

Having already rejected the ministry of John, their honest answer is obvious. But the Jews have opted for diplomacy rather than honesty (since the common people are listening), saying they do not know the source of John's authority.

Jesus then replies to them on the basis of their own response to Him. If they will not answer His question regarding the source of John's authority, He has no obligation to answer theirs as to the source of His authority (vs. 27). Such astute maneuvering on Jesus' part, of course, does little to endear Him to the religious leaders.

The Fruit of Rejecting the Father and the Son

By the middle of chapter 21, Jesus has performed two provocative and symbolic actions (the triumphal entry and the cleansing of the temple), both of which highlight His Messianic role and indicate the growing rift between the Jewish leaders and their followers. The leaders are pictured as rejecting Jesus, while the latter group repeatedly demonstrate enthusiasm for Him.

Following these actions, Matthew has Jesus teaching and dialoging in the temple courts (vs. 23). The first installment in this dialog is the question of Jesus' authority in verses 23 to 27. That episode is followed in Matthew by three confrontational parables. Each parable has its own lesson, and together they have a cumulative effect. All three parables are aimed at the Jewish leaders, and all are concerned with who is acceptable to God. These three parables pick up a theme more prominent in Matthew than in the other Gospels—the failure of official Israel to accept Jesus as the Messiah and the resultant rejection of Israel by God. That theme was first made explicit by John the Baptist in 3:7-10, where he referred to the Jewish leaders as "vipers" and proclaimed that "every tree that does not produce good fruit will be cut down and thrown into the fire." Coupled with that statement was one implying that God could raise up children of Abraham from the stones if necessary.

That dual theme of official Israel's rejection and the outcasts' acceptance of the Messiah was repeated in such texts as 8:11, 12; 12:38-42; 13:10-17; 15:1-9; and 16:5-12. The three parables running from 21:28 to 22:14 each take up the theme and push it home to its natural conclusion.

The first parable is that of a father (God) and two sons (21:28-32). The first son (who represents the tax collectors, prostitutes, and other outcasts) verbally refuses to work in the father's vineyard but repents and works anyway. The second son (who represents the Jewish leaders) verbally agrees to obey but doesn't put his words into practice.

Jesus, using an excellent teaching technique, involves His audience in arriving at the parable's lesson. Which, He asks His hearers, did what the father wanted? The answer is obvious. It is also an answer that we find driven home elsewhere in the first Gospel. "Not everyone who says to me, 'Lord, Lord,' will enter the kingdom of heaven, but only he who *does* the will of my Father," Jesus remarked in His Sermon on the Mount (Matt. 7:21). In Matthew's Gospel it is not the hearers but the doers of the word who enter the kingdom. Righteousness is not passive acceptance but active obedience. Faith is belief that acts. Belief is demonstrated in daily life. It should be noted that this is not a message of salvation by works but rather a suggestion that love for God and other people flows naturally from the heart of a person who has met Jesus.

Thus Jesus' words stand against the so-called gospel of emotional revivalism that looks for mere verbal acceptance rather than a transformed life. Likewise, this parable puts the lid on the falsehood that suggests that believing certain doctrinal truths is the way of salvation. And again, the parable of the two sons strikes at the heart of those forms of Christian assurance that tend to equate salvation with accepting Jesus at the point of justification. Matthew's teaching on assurance of salvation is based on both accepting Jesus and living the Christlike life. Such a teaching never separates action from commitment. Also, repeatedly in Matthew, the Christian life is pictured as being subject to future judgment (7:21-23; 16:27; 18:23-35; 22:1-14; 25:14-46).

Obedience in Matthew's Gospel is not a surface thing. It must be from the heart. As Ellen White puts it, "Many today claim to obey the commandments of God, but they have not the love of God in their hearts to flow forth to others" (White, *Christ's Object Lessons*, 279). One must not only go to work in the Lord's vineyard, but go in the right spirit. That is clear from Jesus' teaching on the law in the Sermon on the Mount, and it will become even clearer in His teaching regarding the "greatest commandment" in 22:36-40.

The second confrontational parable is that of the tenants (vss. 33-44). This parable takes the sequence a giant step forward. Whereas the parable of the two sons pictured Jewish resistance to God in a passive mode, this one shows that resistance to be active—so active that it points both to rejecting the prophets and to killing the Son.

It would be almost impossible for any Jewish hearer to miss the allusion to God's much beloved Israel in the description of the vineyard. That vineyard is described in quite similar terms in Isaiah 5:1-7. But in Isaiah the fault lies with the vines, whereas here it is with the tenants. In both cases, the result of failure is divine judgment.

We can learn several lessons from the parable of the tenants. The first is the long-suffering of God. He does not send just one time, but keeps on sending. The landowner (God) not only does everything He can for His vineyard (see also Isa. 5:4), but He also sends servant (prophet) after servant, even though the tenants repeatedly disappoint Him by mistreating them. The story has a great deal to say about the persistent love and care of the Landowner.

The parable's second lesson is just as obvious—the perversity of the tenants (the Jews and their leaders). If the major theme of the gospel is God's love, a counterbalancing theme is humanity's rejection of that love. The tragedy of both the parable and history is that so often it has been God's own chosen people who have resisted His overtures.

The third lesson in the parable is the centrality and finality of sending the Son (see also Heb. 1:1, 2). "This parable," notes William Barclay, "contains one of the clearest claims which Jesus ever made to be unique; and to be different from even the greatest of those who went before" (Barclay, 2:291). Yet in spite of that clarity, the tenants, in keeping with their prior character, kill the Son. The parable pictures that act as the final one in bringing judgment on the tenants.

The fourth lesson growing out of the parable of the tenants is that even though God's judgment may be long in coming, it is nonetheless certain and irreversible. The judgment of the particular tenants of Matthew 21 will come with the destruction of Jerusalem (see chap. 24).

The parable's fifth lesson is the transfer of God's kingdom from the nation of Israel to a new people. " 'I tell you,' " Jesus says in His most explicit statement in Matthew on the topic, " 'that the kingdom of God will be taken away from you [literal Israel] and given to a people [nation, RSV] who will produce its fruit' " (vs. 43). That "nation" would be the Christian church, made up of both Jews and Gentiles. As noted earlier, the church is an important element in Matthew's theology.

But at this point it is crucial that the church also pay careful attention. The promise to the church is not irrevocable. It must not make the same mistake as Israel. It must "produce its fruit" (vs. 43). That is, it cannot play the part of the barren fig tree any more successfully than could ancient Israel (vss. 18-22). The church must be the son who does God's will and not merely the one who acclaims Jesus verbally. Fruit producing is always a crucial element in the lives of both God's church and its individual members.

The final parable in the trilogy is that of the wedding banquet (22:1-14). As in the other two, this one also ends in judgment for those who reject the Father or the Son.

The parable of the wedding banquet naturally divides into two parts. The first deals with Jesus' historic call to the Jews and ends with an explicit allusion to the destruction of Jerusalem in verse 7. This part of the parable replays many of the themes in the parable of the tenants, including the repeated sending of messengers, the perversity and violence of the Jews, and the king's judgment on them.

But at verse 8, the parable makes a shift as it moves beyond the Jews to those not initially invited to the banquet. Verses 8 to 10 foreshadow the gospel invitation moving from its earlier preoccupation with the Jews (vss. 3-7) to concern for Gentiles in the larger world. Verse 9 begins with a close parallel to the great gospel commission of 28:19, 20—"Go ye therefore . . ." (KJV). The command to preach to "both good and bad" (22:10) is a reflection of Christ's own preaching ministry. The Gospel of Matthew has repeatedly emphasized the nondiscriminatory nature of grace as Jesus preaches to outcasts and failures. By contrast, in the Qumran community, the flawed were not allowed into meetings. Thus the blind, deaf, dumb, crippled, and paralyzed were barred from the communal blessings. It is not to be that way in Jesus' kingdom. The gospel is truly the "good news" that *everyone* is invited to the wedding.

But only the cooperative can remain at the wedding. They must be in harmony with the King, who has commanded everyone to wear a wedding garment (vss. 11, 12). Those without the garment are judged unfit to remain at the feast. Thus not only are the Jews of verses 1 to 7 subject to judgment, but so are the members of the Christian church.

A great deal of discussion has taken place as to the exact nature of the wedding garment. It seems to me that F. D. Bruner is correct when he writes that "the wedding garment in the context of Matthew's Gospel is not passive, imputed (Pauline) righteousness; it is active, moral (Matthean) righteousness (5:20 . . .); it is doing God's will (7:21; 12:50 . . .); it is evidence of repentance by law-abiding discipleship (3:7-10 . . .)" (Bruner, 2:776). That interpretation is in line with Revelation 19:8, which tells us that the fine linen of the redeemed "is the righteous deeds of the saints" (RSV).

But Bruner is careful to caution us that the wedding garment must not be confused with a dreary legalism. "It should also be noted," he writes, "that the wedding garment of personal righteousness was not necessary in order *to be invited* to the party—both good and bad were invited (v 10)—but the garment of personal righteousness was necessary in order *to stay* in the party (v 13 . . .)" (Bruner, 2:777).

Once again in Matthew we find that doing God's will is important. A person in a faith relationship with Jesus will be a doer of God's will. Faith is not mere mental ascent that Jesus is Lord. It is living the Christ life.

The parable closes with a note of warning that "many are invited, but few are chosen" (vs. 14). It has become popular in certain sectors of the church to preach that it is difficult to be lost, but this certainly doesn't seem to be the message of Matthew's Jesus. In fact, the parable of the narrow gate (7:13, 14), the parable of the sower (13:1-23), and Jesus' prediction that "many will turn away" (24:10), give just the opposite impression. They line up with the "few" of 22:14.

■ Getting Into the Word

Matthew 22:15–23:39

Read 22:15 to 23:39 through two times; then work out the following exercises in your Matthew notebook.

1. **List what a Christian can learn from 22:15-22 regarding responsibility to human government. Are a Christian's duties to God and Caesar equal, as some conclude from 22:21? If not, which one comes first? How do you know? What does a reading of Romans 13:1-7 add to your understanding of 22:21? What does Acts 5:17-29 add?**
2. **Use the marginal references in your Bible to discover the two Old Testament sources for the two great commandments of 22:37-39. Use a concordance to discover how Jesus redefined and broadened the term *neighbor* for His hearers. Summarize your findings, and refer to the most important texts that help us understand Jesus' definition of the term.**
3. **Outline Matthew 23. Summarize Jesus' meaning in each paragraph. Explain the significance of 23:37-39. What is the connection between that passage and chapter 24? Why do you believe the characteristically "meek and mild" Jesus comes out so strong in chapter 23? How does that change fit into the progressive flow of His ministry in the first Gospel?**

■ Exploring the Word

The Jewish Leaders Counterattack

In the last three sections, we found Jesus on the attack. In three parables He has condemned the Jewish leaders as unsatisfactory sons, wicked husbandmen, and condemned guests. Beginning in 22:15, we find the Jewish leaders launching their counterattack in the form of three carefully formulated questions designed to trap and discredit Jesus in a public forum.

The first question deals with the payment of taxes to Caesar (vss. 15-22)—a loaded question in occupied Palestine. It presents Jesus with a dilemma. After all, if He says it is unlawful to pay taxes to Caesar, He will promptly be reported to the Roman authorities, and arrest will quickly follow. On the other hand, if He approves the lawfulness of paying taxes to Caesar, He will lose influence in the eyes of His people. The Jews held that God alone was King and that to pay taxes to any earthly king was to admit the validity of that kingship and thus insult God. Thus, whatever answer Jesus gives to His detractors will open Him to trouble.

The trickiness of the situation is also evident from the fact that the Pharisees and the Herodians have collaborated in this question. These two groups stood on opposite sides of the Jewish political fence and generally were in bitter opposition to each other. The Pharisees were vigorously orthodox and resented the taxes demanded by the Roman authorities, while the Herodians were of the party of Herod, the Roman governor.

Jesus' answer is both unique and wise. He asks to see one of their coins, and after getting them to admit that it has Caesar's portrait on it, He sets forth the maxim that both Caesar and God are to be paid their due (vs. 21). That remarkable answer ends the attack. The Jewish leaders quickly see that Jesus has escaped from the inescapable trap they so carefully laid for Him.

Perhaps the most remarkable thing about Jesus' answer is His point that Caesar's realm can be separated from God's. Up to this time in world history, there had been no separation of church and state. The two went hand in hand everywhere. Kings were viewed as representatives of the Divine. Jesus steers His followers in a new direction and opens the way for new ideas about church and state. Since His kingdom is not of this earth, Jesus' followers are to hold dual citizenship before His second coming. They will be citizens of a particular nation and also citizens of the kingdom of heaven.

Unfortunately, in a less-than-perfect world, a Christian's responsibility to these two realms comes into conflict from time to time. Matthew 22 does not tell us whether God's kingdom has priority over Caesar's or vice versa, or whether the two are equal. That problem was worked out by the early church. While Paul and Peter agreed that the rulers of earthly governments ought to be obeyed since they are God's agents (Rom. 13:1-7; 1 Pet. 2:13, 14), the New Testament also makes it clear that when the dictates of an earthly ruler come into conflict with God's commands, the Christian "must obey God rather than men" (Acts 5:29).

The second question in the Jewish counterattack against Jesus comes from the Sadducees (vss. 23-33)—the traditional enemies of the Pharisees. This group has not only lined themselves up with the Roman rulers, but they rejected all Scripture except the Pentateuch (the five books of Moses). They had also made significant concessions to Greek philosophy in their theology. According to Josephus, the Sadducees held that "souls die with the bodies" (*Antiquities*, 18:1.4). Thus they denied both immortality and the resurrection of the dead.

These rejections undergird their question to Jesus in verses 25 to 28 about the woman who, according to levirate marriage custom (Deut. 25:5, 6), had seven husbands but no children. The Sadducees want Jesus to tell them publicly whose wife she will be in the resurrection. Being far from sincere, their question is really aimed at making light of the very idea of a resurrection. At an even deeper level, it is obviously aimed at embarrassing Jesus in public.

But once again, Jesus turns the argument against His detractors. His reply focuses on two points. First, He suggests that their question is flawed, because it is founded on error. Not knowing the Scripture, He claims, they also fail to understand God and His power. They need to realize that the future existence cannot be measured in terms of the present one. God's new kingdom will be along different lines. As a result, the condition of marriage will not be the same, and jealousy will no longer exist. Resurrected people will be like the angels (vss. 29, 30).

The second part of Jesus' answer comes from Exodus 3:6, a

section of the Jewish Bible the Sadducees accepted. Jesus claims that they are even ignorant of that part of Scripture. After all, didn't God tell Moses that He was " 'the God of Abraham, the God of Isaac, and the God of Jacob,' " and that He was therefore the God of the living (vss. 31, 32)? In other words, the God of Israel has not forgotten His covenant with the patriarchs. They did not enter the realm of nonexistence at death. To the contrary, the resurrection proves that God is the God of the living. The great patriarchs are alive to God (Luke 20:38) and await the resurrection at the end of time (see 1 Cor. 15:51-55; 1 Thess. 4:16, 17; Heb. 11:39, 40). As Floyd Filson notes, "Jesus assumes that God will renew all things and provide a fitting place for the eternal life of his people with him, and he therefore takes it as certain that these men will be raised and given their place in that perfect eternal Kingdom" (Filson, 236, 237).

Matthew tells us that the crowds are astonished at Jesus' reply to the Sadducees (vs. 33). And well they might be, since Jesus has proved to their satisfaction a point that had eluded the Pharisees in their contention with the skeptical priestly class about the resurrection. Luke tells us that at the conclusion of Jesus' remarks, even some of the Pharisaic scribes were impressed. " 'Well said, teacher!' " was their word to Him (Luke 20:39).

With verse 34 the action shifts back to the Pharisees for the third question in Matthew's portrayal of the counterattack. This time one of the Pharisaic scribes puts forth a question to "test" (RSV) Jesus. " 'Which,' " the scribe asked, " 'is the greatest commandment in the Law?' "

Like the two previous questions, this one is loaded, and almost any answer is bound to end up in controversy. To the rabbis, it was obvious that some commands were more important than others. For example, the commandment not to murder was held to be more important than the command not to boil a kid in its mother's milk (Deut. 14:21). They divided the commandments into the light and weighty, and they speculated about which of the 613 scriptural commandments was the greatest of all. Thus the lawyer's question to Jesus has a background.

Most of the bystanders probably expect Jesus to select one of the Ten Commandments, but He bypasses the Decalogue for one of the most familiar texts in Jewish culture. Deuteronomy 6:5 was part of the Shema (the Jewish confession of faith). It opened every Jewish service and formed a part of the Jews' morning prayer. In effect, Jesus' answer defines the heart of religion as loving God with one's total being (vs. 37).

That answer alone would be satisfactory, but Jesus chooses to mention a second great commandment. This time He quotes from Leviticus 19:18, with its injunction to love one's neighbor. The underlying assumption of both this passage and of Jesus' entire teaching is that it is impossible to truly love God without loving other people. The apostle John put the matter succinctly when he wrote that "if anyone says, 'I love God,' yet hates his brother, he is a liar. For anyone who does not love his brother, whom he has seen, cannot love God, whom he has not seen" (1 John 4:20).

Jesus goes on to note that the two commands to love form the very undergirding of the Old Testament (vs. 40). It should also be obvious that the two great commandments sum up the two tables of the Decalogue. The command to love God forms the basis of the first four commandments, and the command to love one's neighbor is the motivation for the last six (see Exod. 20:2-17; compare Rom. 13:8-10; Gal. 5:14; James 2:8).

Before moving away from the two great commands, we should note that Jesus gave a definition of the word *neighbor* that greatly transcended the perspective of His Jewish hearers. To Jesus, a person's neighbor was not merely another Jew of orthodox stature; rather, the term included one's enemies and those still in rebellion against God. *Neighbor* even included Gentiles (5:43-47; Luke 10:29-37).

Jesus' reply to the question about the law is so convincing that it cuts short the anticipated discussion regarding the greatest commandment. Jesus takes advantage of the lull to put forth His own questions in verses 42, 43, and 45. While the argumentation in this passage is complex, it is also of crucial importance.

The answer to Jesus' first question (Whose son is the Messiah?) is obviously David, and the Jewish leaders say so. Jesus agrees with them but notes that this answer poses a problem. Quoting from Psalm 110 (the Old Testament passage most often quoted in the New Testament), Jesus points out that David calls the Messiah "Lord," and then poses His second question. How can it be, He asks, that a father can refer to his son as Lord? The answer must be that, contrary to conventional Jewish wisdom, the son is greater than the father.

This fact, Jesus implies, gives the Messiah the right to transcend the traditionally accepted role of Messiah that was inspired by the image of David as a conquering general. "At the very least," claims Filson, "Jesus declares the freedom of the Messiah to establish the Kingdom by another path than the political and military methods of David. The Messiah can be and will be the Suffering Servant rather than the military conqueror and earthly king" (Filson, 240).

This series of questions leaves the Jewish leaders speechless. They are trapped by Jesus' logic. The unlearned Galilean has beat them at their own game, and "from that day on no one dared to ask him any more questions" (vs. 46).

Jesus Confronts the Scribes and Pharisees

The verbal climax of Jesus' struggle with the scribes and Pharisees takes place in Matthew 23. Up to this point in the first Gospel, He has done all He can to wake them up, but to no avail. Now the time for soft words and roundabout tactics is over. In His love, Jesus now makes a frontal assault. His time is running out, and they still have not heard Him.

Matthew 23 falls into three sections that run along a unified theme. Verses 1 to 12 are given in the third person and present five characteristics for which the scribes and Pharisees are rebuked. But before presenting the characteristics, Jesus highlights the importance of the office of the scribes and Pharisees. They "sit in Moses' seat" (vs. 2). That is, they have the high privilege and responsibility of teaching God's Word to His people. It is in light of that sacred and weighty responsibility that their shortcomings must be viewed. Their faults are all the more serious because of their position.

Before looking at the negative characteristics described in this chapter, we need to recognize that not all Pharisees were as bad as those described here. The Pharisees themselves had some of the same condemnations for their less-responsible fellows as did Jesus.

Another thing we should recognize is that the characteristics of the Pharisees are often emulated by Christian leaders and laypeople. The Pharisees were a historic party in Judaism, but their spirit is rooted in human nature. Thus Christians need to read the criticism in Matthew 23 with themselves in mind as well as to gain information about the Jews who lived in Jesus' era.

The first characteristic of the Pharisees that is given in verses 1 to 12 is that they do not practice what they preach (vs. 3). Second, they are unwilling to carry out in their own lives what they prescribe for others (vs. 4). Third, they love the show-off value of their religious activities (vs. 5). Fourth, they revel in honorific titles and in being shown respect (vss. 6-10). And fifth, they misunderstand ministry by failing to realize that it calls them to a place of sacrificial service rather than to a place of executive exaltation (vss. 11, 12).

The second section of Matthew 23 runs from verses 13 to 32 and is presented in the second person. The condemnations in this section are enumerated in the form of seven "woes." Another characteristic of this section is that the scribes and Pharisees are called "blind" five times and "hypocrites" (play actors) six times. And, once again, lest we get too critical with the ancient Jews, we need to realize that their faults tend to be endemic among those who like to "play church"—both clergy and laity. There is a great deal of difference between playing church and living the religion of Jesus.

Like the five characteristics of verses 1 to 12, the seven woes are all too familiar to be read as abstractions. They speak to universal human characteristics. The first is the failure to enter the kingdom while at the same time blocking others from entering (vs. 13). That blocking can take place by discouraging others through playing the part of the hypocrite, by perverting the teachings of Scripture, or by living a loveless life. Unfortunately, it doesn't take much skill or dedication to be a stumbling block to others.

The second woe focuses on those self-sacrificing types who do all they can to convert people to their legalistic ways. The upshot is that such converts are more miserable than before they found the missionaries' perverted view of religion (vs. 15).

The third woe is aimed at the false use of oaths and the legalistic arguments surrounding such practices (vss. 16-22). The fourth woe deals with a perverted sense of values (vss. 23, 24). The very people who are so particular in the minor matters of religion are failing altogether in practicing the kind of love and justice that stand at the center of both the law (see 22:37-40) and true religion (see 5:17-48; 25:31-46). Jesus compares them to people who go to great extremes to avoid swallowing the smallest of insects while mindlessly swallowing the largest unclean animal of the Near East.

The fifth and sixth woes pick up from the fourth and focus on the failure to distinguish between external correctness and internal purity (vss. 25-28). The lesson is clear that purity of the inner life rather than external rigor is the substance of true religion. In fact, the external without the internal is a deadly deception.

The final woe hits directly at the "monument keeping" of much organized religion. Though the scribes and Pharisees fancy themselves to be heirs of the prophets because they have built memorials in their memory, Jesus implies that they are really partaking of the spirit that killed the ancient prophets (vss. 29-32). After all, are not they at that very time planning His own death? The greatest monument to true religion is not some celebration of the great religious events and personages of the past, but the spirit of the prophets living in our own lives in the present.

The final section of Matthew 23 is verses 33 to 39. Verse 33 finds Jesus picking up on the words of John the Baptist in 3:7 ("You snakes! You brood of vipers!"). This is followed by a condemnation of human resistance to God's messengers from Abel (Gen. 4:8) to Zechariah, who was stoned to death in the courtyard of the temple (2 Chron. 24:20-22; Zech. 1:1). Since 2 Chronicles (which reports Zechariah's death) is the last book in the Hebrew Bible and Genesis (which reports Abel's death) is the first, the phrase "from Abel to Zechariah" is Jesus' shorthand for all those in the Old Testament who were martyred for their faith. He says that those martyrdoms were caused by the same spirit that motivates the scribes and Pharisees who oppose Him.

But all is not condemnation. Matthew 23:37 finds some of Christ's tenderest words toward His fellow Jews. He wants to protect them, as does a mother hen when danger approaches. We get the impression from this passage that even Jesus' rebukes are given in love. Chapter 23 can be seen as an illustration of "tough love," a love that uses desperate tactics in its attempt to break through to its hearers before it is too late.

But one of the great tragedies of the Gospel story is that Christ failed to break through to the Jewish leaders of His day. Matthew 23 closes with a pronouncement of Jewish desolation and a hint at the second coming (vss. 38, 39). These leads provide the entrance for the topics of chapters 24 and 25.

■ Applying the Word

Matthew 21–23

1. **How is my fruit bearing? What items can I list that make me different from the fruitless fig tree? In what ways could I become more fruitful in my Christian walk?**
2. **Which of the two sons most characterizes my relationship with God? In what ways am I like the son who agreed to work but didn't? In what ways am I like the other son?**
3. **How is my relationship to the Landowner and the King? How could that relationship improve?**
4. **What about my relationship to Caesar? Am I always honest in my rendering unto Caesar? What about my render-**

ing unto God? In what ways am I satisfied with the adequacy of my duty to each? How might I improve?
5. If I had two paragraphs to summarize how I live the two great commandments, what are the most important things I could say?

■ Researching the Word

1. Using an exhaustive concordance, study the concept of wedding feast in the New Testament. (Those using a concordance based on the KJV will have to look up both wedding and marriage.) What can be learned about the kingdom of heaven from such a study? Examine the comments for the main passages on the heavenly wedding feast from the *Seventh-day Adventist Bible Commentary*. Describe how that added study fills out your knowledge of the topic.
2. Love is not only the basis of the law; it is also an important topic throughout Matthew. Using an exhaustive concordance, look up every reference in which Matthew uses *love*. Then use the system in your concordance for finding the Greek word underlying each occurrence of *love*. Next, summarize your conclusions regarding Matthew's use of love stemming from *agapē*, *agapaō*, and *agapētos*.

■ Further Study of the Word

1. For general insight, see E. G. White, *Christ's Object Lessons*, 272-319; E. G. White, *The Desire of Ages*, 601-620.
2. For a helpful discussion of the meaning of *love* in the Bible, see L. Morris, *Testaments of Love*.
3. For informative treatments on the triumphal entry and the cleansing of the temple, see J. B. Green and S. McKnight, eds., *Dictionary of Jesus and the Gospels*, 817-821, 854-859.

CHAPTER ELEVEN

The Return of the King and the Coming of the Kingdom

Matthew 24, 25

Matthew 21 to 23 presented the triumphal entry of Jesus into Jerusalem and the climax of His verbal battle with the Jewish leaders. Chapters 26 to 28 pick up the story and relate the betrayal, death, and resurrection of Jesus. Tucked in between those two narrative sections is Jesus' fifth and final teaching discourse in Matthew 24 and 25. These chapters focus on His second coming and judgment.

While there is a sense in which the kingdom of heaven came at the first advent of Jesus, it was not consummated in its fullness at that time. The fullness of the kingdom awaits the second coming at the end of earthly history. Thus Jesus taught His disciples to pray, "Your kingdom come" (6:10). It had arrived but not yet in its fullness.

In the meantime, Christians are citizens of two kingdoms. They belong both to a kingdom in this world and to the kingdom of heaven; they belong to both the present age and the age to come. But the present age and the present world are not their ultimate goal. Christians look forward to the end of the present world and the present age. Matthew 24 and 25 present Jesus' most extended teaching on the topic of end things.

Chapter 24 is largely taken up with Jesus' answer to the disciples' question regarding the destruction of Jerusalem and the end of the age (vs. 3). Then follow five parables dealing with preparedness for the kingdom. The parables of chapter 25—the virgins, the talents, and the sheep and the goats—are some of Jesus' best-known parables.

■ Getting Into the Word

Matthew 24:1-41

Read chapters 24 and 25 through once to get a feel for the unity of Jesus' entire discourse on the second advent. Then read 24:1-41 through twice, and examine the following questions and exercises. Keep your Matthew notebook close by for any thoughts you may want to write down.

1. What exact questions do the disciples ask in 24:3? List them in your Matthew notebook. How is their query related to chapter 23?
2. Can you clearly discern Jesus' answers to the various questions? Which signs refer to the fall of Jerusalem? Which refer to the second advent? Which refer to both events? Do you find the answers to these questions to be less than clear? If yes, discuss why you think Jesus would provide a less than clear answer.
3. Did Jesus teach that the end of the world was near at hand to His own time or to some more remote time in the future? Provide a list of texts for both positions. (The parables in 24:42–25:46 also provide information for answering this question.)
4. List all the "signs" of the times that you find in this chapter. What is the meaning of verses 6 and 8 in terms of signs? Are most of the signs unique events in history, or do they recur in each generation? If they do recur, how can they be signs? There seem to be two or three signs that can only be one-time events. List these along with their references.
5. Compare and contrast the messages of 24:32, 33 and 24:36-41. Can the meaning of the two passages be harmonized? If so, how?
6. List the lessons about the second coming that we can learn from 24:1-41.

■ Exploring the Word

The Fall of Jerusalem and the Return of the King

Matthew 24:1 has Jesus leaving the temple for the last time. In 23:38 He told the Jewish leaders that their house would be desolate, and in 24:2 He shocks the disciples by telling them in the most emphatic terms that the massive temple, one of the architectural wonders of the ancient world, will be totally destroyed.

The disciples, seeking clarification, later ask Jesus to expand on His remark. In verse 3 we find them asking three questions: (1) When will the temple be destroyed? (2) What will be the sign of His return? and (3) What will be the sign of the end of the age?

The disciples undoubtedly thought of the destruction of the temple, the end of the world, and the second coming as one event. To them, the temple was the center of earthly existence. It was impossible for them to think of a world without the great Jerusalem temple. Time, of course, has disproven their view that these events would all occur at the same time, but this was not obvious to them at the time.

Jesus, however, does not see fit to correct their false understanding. His answer mixes the two events and their signs to such an extent that it is well nigh impossible to disentangle them. The result has been a chapter that has proven very difficult to interpret, at least as far as its details are concerned. D. A. Carson has pointed out that "few chapters of the Bible have called forth more disagreement among interpreters than Matthew 24" (Carson, 488). The interpretive problems are rooted more deeply than in mere differences of theologies of the second coming. They seem to be built into the very structure of the chapter itself. That is, they seem to be deliberate. That thought, of course, leads us to question why Jesus the Master Teacher should present us with such a "garbled lesson."

There seem to be excellent reasons for His strategy. Foremost among them is that in this discourse, Jesus is not so much seeking to tell us *when* the end will come as to alert His hearers that they *must live in a state of continual expectancy* as they look for the end. That aim becomes clearer as chapter 24 nears its end and enters into the watch-and-be-ready counsels. The great parables of chapter 25 continue to drive home the lessons of faithful waiting and responsible working as Christ's followers look for the end of the age.

A second reason for Christ's less-than-precise teaching strategy is that the very lack of precision leads readers to continually rethink His teachings regarding the second coming as they seek to penetrate His meaning. This teaching technique is similar in some ways to His use of parables in chapter 13. There, He intimated that He taught in parables rather than in straightforward language because such teaching would drive those who were truly interested to wrestle with the ultimate meaning of what He said and make it their own (vss. 10-15). So it appears to be in Matthew 24. The very lack of precision in some of His statements has driven readers to struggle with the significance of the topic. The result has been a continued awareness of and an ongoing interest in the second coming. Such a technique has aided people to identify with the major point of the chapter—to watch and be ready, because they truly know not the hour of the Master's returning.

The Role of Signs

The request for a miraculous sign has been repeatedly brought up in Matthew. In prior chapters, the request was always made by the Jewish leaders (12:38, 39; 16:1, 4), but Jesus had refused to offer them any, except the sign of Jonah, who spent three days buried in a fish before his "resurrection" (12:39; 16:4).

But in chapter 24, the disciples finally ask Jesus for a sign. They want to know the sign for the destruction of Jerusalem, the second coming, and the end of the age (vs. 3). Jesus gives them a long list of signs, beginning in verse 5. His list includes false christs, wars and rumors of wars, nation rising against nation, famines, and earthquakes (vss. 5-8).

Unfortunately, these signs don't give us much specific information about the end of the age. After all, there have always been false messiahs, earthquakes, famines, and wars. What are we to make of such signs, especially in light of the oft-overlooked statements in verses 6 and 8? Verse 6 says that such signs should not alarm us. They belong to the course of nature, "but the end is not yet" (RSV). In other words, they are signs that the end is coming, but they are not the real signs of *the* end. That thought is reinforced by verse 8, which says that "all these [signs] are the *beginning* of birth pains."

It appears that these signs and most others in this chapter are similar to the sign of the rainbow that God gave to Noah as a remembrance of His covenant after the Flood. Thus every time Noah saw the rainbow he would remember the faithfulness of God, who had promised to never again destroy the earth by a flood. It was a sign that God was faithful to His promise (Gen. 9:12-16).

So it is with wars, famines, and earthquakes. Each one is a remembrance of the earth's sickness and a sign that the faithful, covenant-keeping God has not yet finished the plan of salvation. Each of these signs is a promise that Christ will come again to complete the saving of "his people from their sins" (1:21). The same can be said for most of the other signs of Matthew 24—persecution, false prophets, betrayal, the cooling of love (vss. 9-13), lunar and solar eclipses (dark days), and falling stars (vs. 29). Every falling star, every eclipse, every betrayal of trust, is a sign that Christ will come again, because His work is not yet finished.

A careful reading of the text, however, indicates that at least three signs in Matthew 24 are much more precise in their connection to the second coming. The first is found in verse 14, which claims that "this gospel of the kingdom will be preached in the whole world as a testimony to all nations, and then the end will come." That must have sounded like an impossible challenge to the few Galileans who first heard it, but the Christian church rapidly spread throughout the Roman Empire and beyond. And since the birth of modern missions two hundred years ago, Christianity has become the most outreach-oriented of all faiths. It has permeated the far corners of the earth. Yet its missionary task still is not complete. R. H. Mounce appears to be correct when he states that "only when the church has completed its worldwide mission of evangelization will the Parousia [second coming] no longer be delayed" (Mounce, 231).

The second concrete sign of the end is found in verse 27: "As the lightning that comes from the east is visible even in the west, so will be the coming of the Son of Man." That sign, of course, will not be that the end is near. Rather, it is a sign that it is taking place.

The only sign that is actually called a sign in Matthew 24 is found in verses 30 and 31—"the sign of the Son of Man" appearing in the sky. Once again, this is not a sign of the nearness of Jesus' coming, because it will take place as Jesus comes in the clouds "with power and great glory," accompanied by "his angels" and the blast of "a loud trumpet call," the resurrection of the dead, and the ascension of living believers (see also 1 Thess. 4:16, 17; 1 Cor. 15:51-54).

Thus the pattern of Matthew 24 appears to be that the *real* signs are not signs of nearness but signs of coming. The less precise signs are to encourage believers to keep watching, waiting, and working.

The Sign of Jerusalem

It should be noted that Matthew 24 has one other sign with a great deal of precision—the sign of the destruction of Jerusalem and the temple, judgment of which is a foreshadowing of the judgment and destruction of the entire world at the second coming.

Jesus has predicted that the destruction of the temple will be complete—"not one stone here will be left on another" (vs. 2). Josephus, the Jewish historian who lived through the destruction of Jerusalem, describes the almost unimaginable hardships during the final six-month siege. Not only does he claim that more than a million Jews died, but that nearly one hundred thousand more were taken captive. The famine was so bad that a mother was reported to have slain, roasted, and eaten her own child (Josephus, *Wars*, 6.3.4; see also Matt. 24:21). The Roman general Titus eventually ordered the entire city, including the temple complex, razed to the ground, thus bringing to fulfillment Christ's prediction of verse 2.

Christian believers, however, did not suffer the same fate as those Jews who had rejected Jesus as the Messiah. Christians had the counsel of Christ that we now find in Matthew 24. Verses 15 to 22 appear to be specifically directed toward the fall of Jerusalem and give directions for when Christians were to make their escape.

The Christians in Jerusalem were not only alerted to the coming crisis of the destruction of Jerusalem by the general sign of wars and rumors of wars, but they had specific counsel that when they saw "standing in the holy place 'the abomination that causes desolation,' spoken of through the prophet Daniel [9:27]," then those in Judea were to flee to the mountains (vs. 15). Luke's rendering of this passage makes the meaning clearer: "When you see Jerusalem being surrounded by armies, you will know that its desolation is near. Then let those who are in Judea flee to the mountains, let those in the city get out, and let those in the country not enter the city. For this is the time of punishment in fulfillment of all that has been written" (Luke 21:20-22).

The course of events allowed the Christians to heed Jesus' warnings. In August of A.D. 66, Cestius (Rome's legate in Syria) attacked Jerusalem and then withdrew for some unknown reason, even though victory was within his grasp. Then in 67 and 68 Vespasian subdued Galilee and Judea, but delayed the siege of Jerusalem because of Emperor Nero's death. It was not until the spring and summer of A.D. 70 that Jerusalem was put under siege and destroyed by Vespasian's son Titus. Sometime in the interval between the trouble of A.D. 66 and the destruction of A.D. 70, Eusebius (A.D. 263–339) tells us that "the members of the Jerusalem church, by means of an oracle given by revelation to acceptable persons there, were ordered to leave the City before the war began [in earnest] and settle in a town in Perea called Pella. To

Pella those who believed in Christ migrated from Jerusalem" (Eusebius, *Ecclesiastical History*, 3.5.3).

Thus the Christians, following the warning of Christ in Matthew 24 and the unnamed prophet noted by Eusebius, fled the city and avoided its destruction. Both that destruction and the salvation of Christians from the catastrophe were signs of great significance concerning the second coming of Jesus and the end of the world. In the context of Matthew 24, they function as guarantees of the final destruction of a sinful world and the ultimate salvation of those who believe in Jesus. Ellen White summarizes it nicely when she writes that "the Saviour's prophecy concerning the visitation of judgments upon Jerusalem is to have another fulfillment, of which that terrible desolation was but a faint shadow. In the fate of the chosen city we may behold the doom of a world that has rejected God's mercy. . . . But in that day, as in the time of Jerusalem's destruction, God's people will be delivered" (White, *Great Controversy*, 36, 37).

In verses 32 to 36, Jesus gives us two great truths about human knowledge of the second advent. The first is the lesson of the fig tree—one of the minority of trees in first-century Palestine that lost its leaves for the winter. Just as the appearance of new leaves on the fig tree indicates that spring is near, so sensitive Christians can tell when Christ's appearance is near at hand (vs. 33). On the other hand, they can never know the exact time of that appearance (vs. 36).

Jesus goes on to give the illustration of Noah. Just as people "were eating and drinking, marrying and giving in marriage, up to the day Noah entered the ark," so will it be with the coming of the Son of Man (vss. 37-39). Most interpretations of that text imply that the sign of Noah will be great wickedness in the world, but that may or may not be true.

The great-wickedness interpretation harks back to Genesis 6:5, which states that in Noah's time, "*the Lord saw* that the wickedness of man was great in the earth, and that every imagination of the thoughts of his heart was only evil continually" (RSV). Note, however, that Genesis 6:5 is from God's perspective. Matthew

24:37-39 can also be read from the human point of view. From that vantage point, the text simply says that life near the end of time will go on as usual in the eyes of most people. After all, eating, drinking, and marrying are normal activities. It is only the excesses of Noah's time and those implied just before the second advent that make them irregular. But most people, including those in the churches, will undoubtedly focus on the normality of life just before the advent rather than its abnormality. Life will appear to be going on as usual until the great second-advent surprise.

That interpretation ties in nicely with those texts that liken the second advent to the coming of a thief (see for example 1 Thess. 5:2). That interpretation also harmonizes with verses 40 and 41, which indicate the suddenness of the separation of the saved and the lost.

Some get their secret-rapture teaching from verses 40 and 41, but the context implies nothing secret at all. Christ's coming will be seen and heard by all as He and His angels descend with trumpets blaring (vss. 30, 31, 27). At that time, the saints will be raptured to meet Christ in the air (1 Thess. 4:16, 17), but the wicked will be destroyed by the brightness of His coming (2 Thess. 2:8). Rapture, yes. Secret, no.

The point of 24:37-41 is the absolute certainty and suddenness of the second advent. Neither the saints nor the wicked can predict the exact moment of the event. Both are to some extent surprised as to its exact timing, but true believers have at least had the level of their awareness raised by Jesus' counsel in the signs. However, they constantly need to watch and be prepared. That is the message of the five parables that we find in 24:42 to 25:46.

Before turning to those parables, however, we should summarize the lessons that can be gleaned from verses 1 to 41. Michael Green (232, 233) has summed up the lessons of Matthew 24 in a helpful manner. First, he notes, the return of Christ will be personal as well as certain.

Second, history is going somewhere. It is not meaningless, random, or eternal. Nor is it an endless cycle. "There will be a real end just as there was a real beginning. And at the end we shall find none other than Jesus Christ."

Third, the return of Christ points to the triumph of good over evil, the triumph of God's purpose over human and cosmic rebellion.

Fourth, the return spells restoration. "There will be a new creation, a new heaven and earth, in which only goodness dwells" (see 2 Pet. 3:11-13; Rev. 21:1-5).

Fifth, the return of Jesus points to judgment and separation. Some will be taken and some left (vss. 40, 41). It will be a time when the secret thoughts of the heart and the innermost character become known to all.

Sixth, the return of Christ will be decisive. Signaling the end of the age, it ushers in the fullness of the kingdom. The time for repentance and change will be forever past.

Seventh, the return will be as sudden and unexpected as a flash of lightning in the sky (vs. 27). "It will come out of the blue upon a heedless world."

Last, the return of Jesus will come at a time known only to God the Father (vs. 36). Preachers don't know the time, nor did the disciples. Even Jesus in His incarnate state did not know the time. God in His wisdom knows when it will be best to end earthly history. In the meantime, Christians are to be faithful in the face of hardships (vs. 13) and watchful as they await the return of their Saviour (vs. 42).

It is to the topic of watchfulness that we now turn. How ought Christians to live in light of Jesus' certain return?

■ Exploring the Word

Matthew 24:42–25:46

Read 24:42 to 25:46 twice. Then do the following exercises.

1. **This section consists of five parables. The first one is found in Matthew 24:42-44. Summarize the lesson(s) in that parable in a few sentences. Then describe the relationship of**

that parable to 24:1-42.

2. **Verses 45 to 51 contain the second parable. It is similar to the first but adds several bits of understanding. List the new elements contributed by this parable.**
3. **The third parable is that of the ten virgins (25:1-13). Enumerate the lessons that can be learned from this story.**
4. **The fourth is the parable of the talents (25:14-30). The teaching of this parable adds several elements not present in the story of the virgins. Enumerate those elements, and explain how they help us know how to behave while awaiting the coming of Jesus.**
5. **In many ways, the parable of the sheep and goats (25:31-46) is the climax to the entire sequence found in Matthew 24 and 25. In what ways is it a climax? What does it add to our understanding of what was begun in the first four parables? What is the basis of the judgment in this parable? How does that basis of judgment relate to faith and salvation by grace alone?**

■ Getting Into the Word

Watching for the Coming King

With verse 42 we come to the practical outcome of what has gone before in Matthew 24. If no one knows the time of the advent except the Father (vs. 36), then it behooves Christians to "watch," because they do not know what hour their Lord will return (vs. 42).

Then in verse 43 Jesus gives a short parable urging His followers to be constantly expectant. They are to be as expectant as a householder who expects his house to be broken into. A constant state of watchfulness and readiness for the Lord's return is the message of this short parable. After all, "the Son of Man will come at an hour when you do not expect him" (vs. 44). Down through history, the time when Christ is least expected to return is today.

Barclay relates the fable of three apprentice devils who were coming to earth to complete their training. Each presented his plan to Satan for the ruination of humanity. The first proposed to tell people that there was no God. Satan replied that that would not delude many, since most have a gut feeling to the contrary. The second said he would proclaim that there was no hell. Satan rejected this tactic also, since most people have a sense that sin will receive its just deserts. "The third said, 'I will tell men that there is no hurry.' 'Go,' said Satan, 'and you will ruin men by the thousand' " (Barclay, 2:350, 351).

The most dangerous delusion is that time will go on indefinitely. *Tomorrow* can be a dangerous word. It is against this attitude that Christ warns us in the first of His five parables on watchfulness and readiness.

The second parable (vss. 45-51) continues the theme of urgency and watchfulness, but with several added nuances. This parable sets forth the idea that Christians have duties and ethical responsibilities as they wait and watch. Their waiting is not to be done in idleness. Also in this story, the householder's return is delayed for reasons of which the servants know nothing.

Unfortunately, delay can lead to bad behavior. Since the servants are on their own in an uncertain situation, one of them allows his baser passions to rise to the surface. He begins being unkind to others and living a loose life, thinking that he has plenty of time.

But at that point, the lesson of the first parable is reiterated: "The master of that servant will come on a day when he does not expect him and at an hour he is not aware of" (vs. 50). Then Jesus gives an added lesson—one that will surface again in the conclusion of parables four and five (25:30, 46). Unfaithful servants will lose their heavenly reward and will receive, instead, the same reward as the unfaithful Jews (8:12), wicked people in general (13:42, 50), and the scribes and Pharisees (23:13, 15, 23, 25, 27, 29). Thus the concept of faithfulness and watchfulness is driven home in a more complete way than in the first parable.

The third parable (25:1-13) carries on the theme of waiting in watchful expectation that was begun in the first two, but once again, the complexity of the message is increased. The scene of the parable is a Palestinian wedding—a ceremony that was typically a drawn-out affair lasting for a week or more. The entire community was involved, and, unlike Western custom, the newlyweds did not go on a honeymoon. Rather, they stayed at home and kept open house.

Even though the parable of the ten virgins has a Palestinian wedding feast as its backdrop, it is not necessary to understand all the ancient wedding customs to catch the major lessons of the story. However, one detail of crucial importance is that Jesus, as in 9:15, is the Bridegroom. That in itself is a bold claim, since the Old Testament frequently describes God (rather than the Messiah) as the Bridegroom and Israel as the bride (see, for example, Isa. 54:4, 5; Jer. 2:2; Hos. 1–3).

Beyond the coming of the Bridegroom, the focus of the parable is on the ten virgins and their lamps (vs. 2). In fact, the primary focus is really on the division between the virgins. Five are described as wise and five as foolish. The difference between the two groups is determined by the preparation they have made for the coming of the Bridegroom. All have lamps, but only half of them have brought sufficient oil.

Note that all ten are outwardly Christians, for all ten are awaiting the coming of the Bridegroom. Also note that all ten become drowsy and fall asleep (vs. 5). Thus we are not dealing in this parable with believers and nonbelievers. All claim to be believers.

A major point in the parable is that the Bridegroom is "a *long time* in coming" (vs. 5). This is why the virgins all sleep. Earthly necessities go on, even while Christ's followers await His return. No one can exist in a constant state of high-pitched alert. The theme of Christ's delayed return has already appeared in 24:48, and it will show up a third time in 25:19. The delay was undoubtedly already becoming a problem for some believers when Matthew wrote his Gospel in the third or so decade after Jesus' ascension.

The difference between the wise and foolish believers, as we noted above, is not whether they sleep. They all do. But not all have prepared for the summons. Some have left their preparation to the last minute, when it is too late. Jesus says that they pay deeply for their neglect. The "door was shut" (25:10), their probation is closed (see also Rev. 22:10, 11), and they miss the great "wedding supper of the Lamb" that takes place at the second advent (vss. 11, 12; see also Rev. 19:9).

The moral of the story is given in verse 13: "Keep watch, because you do not know the day or the hour." That moral, of course, has also been the undergirding rationale of the first two parables in this series. But this one adds that it will be a "long" delay before the Parousia (second coming) and that no individual can rely on another person's preparedness. In the judgment of God, we each stand as individuals.

It should be pointed out that the parable of the virgins does not indicate how we are to prepare for the Bridegroom's coming. That will be the topic of the last two parables in the series.

Working While Waiting and Watching

The parable of the talents (vss. 14-30), in common with the three preceding parables, continues to stress being ready for the Master's return. But it seeks to answer a question previously not answered: What is readiness?

The meaning of readiness is the contribution of the story of the talents. The story line is quite simple. A man (Christ) goes away and gives each of his servants talents. To one, he gives five; to another, two; and to the last, one talent.

The first two put their talents to work and increase their master's investment, but the third merely buries his in the ground for safekeeping. It should be noted that in the ancient world, burying money wasn't such a bad idea if one desired only security. Of course, a person needed to remember where it was buried. The practice of burying valuables undergirded the parable of the hidden treasure in 13:44.

But the master desires more than security from his investment; he expects the talents to be used for profit. This becomes evident when, "after a *long time*" (note the similarity on this point to the previous two parables—24:48; 25:5), the master returns and demands an accounting to determine the faithfulness of his servants in his absence (vs. 19).

In the judgment scene that follows, he rewards the two servants who have been faithful in meeting their responsibilities during his absence, but he punishes the one who has done nothing, even though he knows he was expected to be responsible (vs. 24). The irresponsible servant not only receives no reward, but what he has is taken away from him. In the opinion of the master, he fails to qualify for entry into the kingdom (vss. 28-30).

The lesson is clear. Readiness for the return of Christ does not mean passively waiting for the event. Rather, readiness is responsible activity that produces results for the kingdom of heaven—results that can be seen and approved by the Master.

We can also learn from this parable that God doesn't expect the same results from everybody. Christians have varying levels of ability (vs. 15). However, it is not the amount of a person's ability that is evaluated in the judgment, but whether he or she has put to use the full range of abilities that God has given. People are not equal in ability, but they can be equal in effort. God expects good interest on His investment from each of us.

Another lesson from the parable of the talents is that faithful people are "rewarded, not with a well-endowed pension, but with even greater responsibility" (Schweizer, 471). Greatness based on service (20:26-28) will continue into the age to come. It is an eternal principle of the kingdom of heaven. Ellen White captures the concept nicely when she writes that true education "prepares the student for the joy of service in this world and for the higher joy of wider service in the world to come" (White, *Education*, 13).

The Essential Work of the Waiting Ones

The parable of the sheep and the goats (which is technically more of an apocalyptic judgment scene than a parable) brings the judgment theme that began in chapter 23 to a climax. It also brings to completion Jesus' developing teaching on readiness. Whereas the first three parables in the present sequence placed the emphasis on watching (24:42–25:13), and the fourth emphasized working while watching (25:14-30), this one (25:31-46) is explicit as to the essential nature of that working.

The story of the sheep and goats is a vivid word picture of the final separation that will take place when Jesus comes in the clouds of heaven. It is a picture that allows for no middle ground or any second chances. One is either a sheep (a standard Old Testament symbol for God's people) *or* a goat. One is either assigned to the right (the symbol of favor) *or* the left (the symbol of disfavor). There is no middle ground. Nor is the decision of the judgment open to appeal. The scene is one of finality. Those individuals failing to utilize the waiting and watching time appropriately before the second advent are eternally lost from the kingdom (vs. 46).

A crucial element in the parable is that of surprise. Both the sheep and the goats are surprised at the king's verdict in their particular cases. Both groups question that verdict (vss. 37-39, 44).

The reason for the surprise stems from the false interpretation of true religion (see also James 1:27; Rom. 13:8-10) that is held by most people. The average person sees the heart of true religion as believing in right doctrines or as practicing certain ritual and lifestyle duties.

But that is not the biblical position. In one of the great Old Testament texts, God says through Micah that what is required of His children is not outward behavior or ritual obedience but " 'to act justly and to love mercy and to walk humbly with your God' " (Mic. 6:6-8). Jesus has already quoted that text three times in Matthew (9:13; 12:7; 23:23), each time in the context of verses dealing with a false understanding of true religion. And the rest of the New Testament picks up on that same theme. Thus James can write: "Religion that God our Father accepts as pure and faultless is this: to look after orphans and widows in their distress and to keep oneself from being polluted by the world" (James 1:27). And

Paul can write that "he who loves his fellow man has fulfilled the law" (Rom. 13:8-10; see also Gal. 5:14).

Nor has the first Gospel been silent on the topic of true religion and its rewards. Jesus put it most plainly when He claimed that " 'if anyone gives even a cup of cold water to one of these little ones because he is my disciple, I tell you the truth, he will certainly not lose his reward' " (10:42). Again, Jesus noted that the two great commandments can be summed up as love to God and neighbor; He defined perfection in terms of being merciful to one's enemies (5:43-48; Luke 6:36); and He explicitly told the behaviorally oriented, rich young ruler that if he would be perfect, he should sell his " 'possessions and give to the poor.' " His reward would be treasure in heaven (19:21).

These teachings come to a climactic point in 25:31-46. Here, the standard of judgment is set forth in unequaled clarity. People are not asked what they believe or whether they have kept the Sabbath, paid tithe, or taken good care of their health. While these things are important, one can practice them rigorously and still be totally lost (23:23). The real point of the judgment is whether individuals have shown tangible love to their neighbors.

While that point is crystal clear in the first Gospel, Ellen White sums it up nicely. Commenting on 25:31-46, she writes that Jesus "pictured to His disciples the scene of the great judgment day. And He represented its decision as turning upon one point. When the nations are gathered before Him, there will be but two classes, and their eternal destiny will be determined by what they have done or have neglected to do for Him in the person of the poor and the suffering" (White, *The Desire of Ages*, 637).

Some have held that verses 31 to 46 teach salvation by works, but this is not the case. The passage speaks to the standard of the last judgment rather than to how one is saved. Underlying the entire first Gospel is the assumption that Christ paid the penalty for sin in His great mission of saving His people from their sin (20:28; 1:21). The point in verses 31 to 46 is the tangible evidence as to whether an individual has been saved. If people have been saved, their lives will produce evidence that they have internalized the grace and love of God by their willingness to pass on His gifts to others. Thus Joachim Jeremias can write that "at the Last Judgment God will look for faith that has been lived out" (Jeremias, 209). In like manner, Leon Morris tells us that "we must bear in mind that it is common to the whole scriptural picture that we are saved by grace and judged by works. . . . The works we do are the evidence either of the grace of God at work in us or of our rejection of that grace" (Morris, *Matthew*, 634).

An important lesson from the story of the sheep and goats is that the works that really count are simple and uncalculating. They are as simple as feeding the poor and visiting the sick. And they are uncalculating in the sense that those who perform them do not do so to heap up merit but because the love of God exists in their hearts and naturally overflows to others. Helpfulness and mercy have become natural for them. They have internalized the love of God, and it shows up in their daily lives, even though they are not conscious of that virtue.

On the other hand, the whole attitude of those deemed to be goats is that if they had known the sick and poor were important persons, they would have been the first to help them. They have had their eyes on prestige, reward, and recognition and have failed to internalize the love of God. Thus they have missed the thing in religion that really counts. Their religion is really a form of disguised selfishness.

To all such followers, Jesus says: " 'I don't know you' " (vs. 12). " 'Not everyone who says to me, "Lord, Lord," will enter the kingdom of heaven, but only he who *does* the will of my Father who is in heaven. Many will say to me on that day, "Lord, Lord, did we not prophesy in your name, and in your name drive out demons and perform many miracles?" Then I will tell them plainly, "I never knew you. Away from me, you evildoers" ' " (7:21-23).

It is the unconscious internalization of God's love and its expression in daily life that is the one essential qualification for the kingdom of heaven. Such people have begun to live the principle of servanthood and greatness that has come up again and again in Matthew's Gospel. Such people are safe to save for eternity, because they have internalized the principle of love, *the* principle of the kingdom. Such people have developed through grace that "righteousness [which] surpasses that of the Pharisees and the teachers of the law." Thus they are prepared to "enter the kingdom of heaven" (5:20).

■ Applying the Word

Matthew 24, 25

1. **Too often, the approach of some preachers and evangelists has been to get people into the church through hyped-up sermons on the signs of the times. Is that approach a true reflection of Jesus' teaching in Matthew 24 and 25? What can I do in my church to create a healthier atmosphere that is based more on solid faith than on trumped-up sensationalism?**
2. **Has the nearness of the second coming become a meaningless cliché to me? What evidence do I have for my answer? What specific steps can I take to revitalize my faith in and desire for the second coming of Christ?**
3. **What abilities and responsibilities (talents) has God given me? How can I better put them to use as I await my Lord?**
4. **In examining my religion, what evidence do I have that I have a meaningful experience? What evidence do I have as to whether I am a sheep or a goat in my family, on my job, in my church, and in my community?**

■ Researching the Word

1. **Christ's discourse on the second coming has parallels in Mark 13 and Luke 21:5-36. Divide a clean sheet of paper into three columns, then outline the presentation in each of the three Gospels. Last, compare the three presentations. How are they the same? How do they differ? What is the unique contribution of each?**

2. Using an exhaustive concordance, examine every Bible text that speaks of the final judgment. Divide your findings into their natural categories, and write a short essay on your conclusions.

■ Further Study of the Word

1. For general insight, see E. G. White, *The Desire of Ages*, 627-641; E. G. White, *Christ's Object Lessons*, 325-365, 405-421.
2. For more on the destruction of Jerusalem, see Josephus, *Wars of the Jews*, 5.9.1–6.4.8; G. W. Bromiley, ed., *International Standard Bible Encyclopedia*, 2:1029, 1030; F. F. Bruce, *New Testament History*, 368-392; J. B. Green and S. McKnight, eds., *Dictionary of Jesus and the Gospels*, 172-176; E. G. White, *The Great Controversy*, 17-38.
3. For an overview of the Gospels' teaching on eschatology, see J. B. Green and S. McKnight, eds., *Dictionary of Jesus and the Gospels*, 206-209; for a broader perspective that deals with eschatological issues in the entire Bible, see G. W. Bromiley, ed., *International Standard Bible Encyclopedia*, 2:130-143.

CHAPTER TWELVE

The King Rejected

Matthew 26:1–27:44

Ever since 16:21, Matthew has been moving us toward the cross, the great climax of his Gospel. The story of Jesus' death is not an epilogue or an appendix to Christ's life. To the contrary, it is His death that makes His life meaningful. After all, Jesus came to this earth so that He could "give his life as a ransom for many" (20:28). His blood was to be "poured out for many for the forgiveness of sins" (26:28). And it was through His death and resurrection that He would "save his people from their sins" (1:21). The King's death is the focal point of the first Gospel. Thus Martin Kähler's definition of the four Gospels as "passion narratives with extended introductions" puts the emphasis in the right place, even though it suffers a bit from exaggeration.

Matthew 26 and 27 take us to the end of King Jesus' earthly life, but chapter 28 brings us to the Resurrection, in which victory is snatched out of the grasping hands of defeat. Thus the end turns out to be a beginning.

Matthew 26:1 to 27:44 presents a Jesus whose teaching ministry is largely over. We find few words from His mouth outside of His teaching at the Last Supper and His prayer in Gethsemane. Rather, we watch the drama as the Jews, with the aid of their Roman adversaries, put their Messiah on the cross. Beyond that, these chapters highlight human responsibility in the face of the cross, as individuals are forced to make decisions for and against Jesus. The theme of responses to Jesus began in chapter 2 and provides one of the threads that runs all the way through the first Gospel. In these verses, the issue of the responsibility of human choice comes to its apex, not only for the various disciples, Jews, and Romans, but for Jesus Himself as He faces the cross.

■ Getting Into the Word

Matthew 26:1-56

Read 26:1-56 through two times. Then turn to the following exercises.

1. **List those statements (and their references) that indicate Jesus was in control of the events leading up to the cross. Include verses 57 to 68 in this exercise. Write a few sentences discussing the implications of that control for the meaning of the cross.**
2. **Up to this time, Judas has been a minor player in the first Gospel. But in verse 14 he moves toward center stage. Enumerate what we can learn about Judas in verses 1 to 56 and in 27:1-10. What additional facts can be gleaned from the parallel passages in Mark 14, Luke 22, and John 13? What connections are there, if any, between 26:14-16 and 26:6-12? What conclusions can be drawn from the information you have collected about Judas?**
3. **Outline the Gethsemane experience. Discuss in a paragraph or two the essence of the temptation Jesus was struggling with. Do you see any connection between that struggle, the core temptation of 4:1-10, and the problem of 16:21-26? If so, what is it?**
4. **Outline Peter's experience in verses 1 to 56 and 57 to 75. List his high points and his low points. What kind of character profile can you develop for Peter in these chapters? Evaluate Peter's experience in John 21 in light of Matthew 26. From this viewpoint, what does John 21 teach us about Jesus (and God)? About Peter?**

■ Exploring the Word

Responses to King Jesus

Matthew 26:1-16 highlights the polarization that takes place as men and women are confronted by the claims of Christ. On the one hand, we find the Jewish leaders and Judas Iscariot. On the other is the woman with the alabaster jar. Varied response to Jesus has been a theme of Matthew's Gospel. This was so at the time of His birth (chapter 2), and it continues to be so at the time of His death. As the implications of Christ's message crystalize in human minds, people are either against Him or for Him (see, for example, 12:30). There is no middle ground, once the implications of Jesus and His message are realized. When an individual comes face to face with Jesus, he or she is forced to make a choice either for Jesus and the self-sacrificing cross or against them; either for the principles of the kingdom of heaven or for the principles of the kingdom of this world.

But before exploring the examples of polarization in this passage, it is important to note that Matthew does not present Jesus facing the cross as a pawn of events beyond His control. To the contrary, Jesus is in command of events.

His dominance over events is evident from 26:2 onward. In that verse He is well aware that He will "be handed over to be crucified." He has repeatedly emphasized that He knows His future (9:15; 16:21-24; 17:9-12, 22, 23; 20:22, 28; 21:33-45). Jesus is not blindly walking into a trap. He has a choice, and He has full knowledge of the events about to transpire. He knows one of the twelve will betray Him (vs. 21), and He knows which one it will be (vss. 23-25). He knows the rest of the disciples will forsake Him that very night (vs. 31), and He knows that Peter will deny Him (vs. 34). But Jesus also knows that He will be victorious over death through His resurrection (vs. 32), that He will sit at the right hand of God, and that He will eventually come again in the clouds of heaven to rescue His followers (vs. 64).

Far from being a pawn of blind fate, Jesus knows that if He

should choose to defend Himself, He can call on His Father, and God will instantly put twelve legions of angels (seventy-two thousand) at His disposal (vs. 53). But that is one of the major points of Matthew 26. Even though Jesus is in command of events and could escape the cross, He chooses not to do so in order that "the Scriptures [might be] fulfilled that say it must happen in this way"—the way of the cross (vs. 54).

Matthew's picture of Jesus as being in command of events is in harmony with that of John, who has Jesus saying, " 'I lay down my life, that I may take it again. No one takes it from me, but I lay it down of my own accord' " (John 10:17, 18, RSV; see also John 15:13).

But just because Jesus is in control and has knowledge of what is transpiring does not mean that other forces are not maneuvering to bring about their own desired end. Chief among those forces are Judaism's high priest (Caiaphas), the other leading priests, and the elders of the people (important laymen). At the very least, Matthew appears to be referring to a powerful subcommittee of the Sanhedrin—the highest judicial body of the Jews. Matthew is telling us that "official" Judaism has rejected Jesus and desires His death (vss. 3, 4).

But these leaders are faced with several serious problems. First, they dare not risk an open move against Jesus, because the masses are favorable to Him (vs. 5). Yet they are under the pressure of time. After all, if they delay their move until after the Passover, Jesus will presumably leave the city and thus elude their grasp.

Aid for their cause comes from a most unexpected source—an almost unbelievable source: the defection of one of Jesus' twelve disciples. Judas Iscariot agrees to work as an inside man for thirty pieces of silver, the price of a slave (Exod. 21:32; see also Zech. 11:12). Judas volunteers to arrange an opportune time for the Jewish leaders to arrest Jesus (vss. 14-16).

The Gospels all report Judas's betrayal, but none of them provides a reason for the action, though many reasons have been set forth. Some Bible students have conjectured that Judas wanted to put Jesus in a position where He would be forced to use His unusual powers to destroy the opposition and establish the kingdom that so many Jews expected. A second view sees Judas as disillusioned with Jesus. According to this line of thought, the disillusionment stemmed from Judas's discovery that Jesus was a Man of peace rather than a military Messiah who would overthrow the Romans. Thus the betrayal was an act aimed at getting rid of Jesus. According to a third view, Judas saw Jesus as a failure. Thus Judas betrayed Him to save himself.

The only motive mentioned in the New Testament for Judas's betrayal is money. It is no accident that Matthew places the story of the woman who anointed Jesus' feet with expensive perfume (vss. 6-13) between the story of the frustrated plotting of Caiaphas and the Jewish leaders (vss. 3-5) and the story of Judas's volunteering to aid them (vss. 14-16).

The fourth Gospel helps us here. It tells us that Judas was especially upset with the anointing because of the "wasted" perfume's value (three hundred denarii, or almost a year's wages) and that he was stealing from the disciples' communal moneybag, which he carried (John 12:4-6). Thus Judas saw personal loss in the anointing.

But selfishness alone does not provide us with a sufficient explanation for Judas's about face, especially since he still expects an earthly Messianic kingdom in which he will be a foremost (and presumably wealthy) leader. Thus it seems that the best explanation for Judas's betrayal is that the "wasted" money at the anointing serves merely as a stimulus for putting into operation his plan to force Jesus to act against the Jews and the Romans. Thus, from Judas's perspective, the slow-moving Jesus will be compelled to act in setting up His kingdom. Of all the possible constructions behind Judas's betrayal, this one best suits all the facts. And it also explains why Judas committed suicide when his plans went wrong (27:1-5).

Matthew appears to have deliberately placed the story of the anointing between the plots of Caiaphas and Judas, even though he had to take the event out of its chronological setting to do so. (See John 12:1-12, which puts the anointing "six days before the

Passover" and the triumphal entry the "next day.")

Yet the story is not included in the first Gospel merely to help explain Judas's actions. To the contrary, Mary's anointing has a message of its own. It is a message of immense devotion that symbolizes Mary's gratitude to Jesus. In sharp contrast to the Jewish leaders' and Judas's responses to Jesus in the story's immediate context, Mary demonstrates her love for the One who has done so much for her personally and who has brought her brother (Lazarus) back to life (John 11:1-44). Mary's was a positive response to Jesus.

Beyond that, the anointing is rich in symbolism. After all, the very meaning of *Messiah* is the "anointed one." Just as kings were anointed in the Old Testament (see for example 2 Kings 9:6), so Mary anointed Jesus.

Perhaps the most surprising part of the anointing story is Jesus' explanation in verse 12 that Mary's deed is to prepare Him for burial. This statement indicates, once again, that Jesus is in control of His situation. After all, customarily, bodies were not anointed for burial before they were dead. Anointing was traditionally performed on corpses, not on living people, except in the case of criminals. Thus Jesus' interpretation of Mary's act seems to assume (correctly) that His death will be that of a criminal, whose body will be buried without proper ceremony.

New Meaning for an Old Symbol

Matthew 26:17-30 sets forth Jesus' last supper with His disciples. Even though it is a Passover meal, Jesus and the disciples eat it the evening before the regular Passover meal (see John 13:1; 18:28; 19:14). Thus, even though the regular Passover meal took place on Friday evening that year, Jesus and His disciples celebrate it on Thursday evening. In Jesus' case this is a necessity, because He is aware that He will be dead by Friday evening.

The early Passover meal explains why there is no mention of the lamb at the Last Supper, whereas the other parts of the meal are all in place. The Passover lambs were slain in the temple on

Friday afternoon, the very time that Jesus also died. This timing is important, since, as Paul put it, Jesus is "a Passover lamb sacrificed for us" (1 Cor. 5:7, Phillips). Even Jewish tradition indicates that Jesus was executed "on the eve of the Passover" (Sanhedrin, 43a). Jesus, knowing He will be dead before the regular meal, provides for a special meal a day early.

On that Thursday evening, Jesus for the first time indicates that a member of His own inner circle will betray Him (vs. 21). Prior to this time, He has indicated that He will die, but never has He tied one of the disciples to the event.

The effect on the twelve is traumatic. Verse 22 tells us that they are "exceeding sorrowful" (KJV), "in great distress" (NEB), or "deeply grieved" (NASB). No matter how the Greek is translated, it indicates violent emotion, and even shock.

The revelation shakes up the disciples even to the point of self-doubt. Each in turn inquires, " 'Surely not I, Lord?' " Notice that the very way they phrase the question indicates that they expect a negative reply (vs. 22).

It is of interest to note that Judas must have covered his tracks quite carefully. After all, no one asks, "Is it Judas?"

Yet Judas knows. Caught off guard, he does not immediately participate with the other disciples in asking Jesus if it is him. But he soon comes to his senses, realizing that if he fails to participate in the query, he will be identified as the culprit. Thus he also says, " 'Surely not I, Rabbi?' " (vs. 25). Judas does not refer to Jesus as "Lord," as do the other disciples, but rather as "Rabbi"—a term of address appropriate for any Jewish teacher and a form of address not used at all by the other disciples in the first Gospel (see 26:49 for another example of Judas's use of the term).

Jesus does not respond to the queries of the other disciples, but He indicates to Judas His awareness that he will indeed be the betrayer (vs. 25). At this point, Judas knows he has been found out. He also knows that he will have to act quickly if he is to successfully carry out his plan. It is at about this time, John tells us, that "Satan entered" Judas. Jesus told him that what he had to do should be done "quickly," and Judas "went out" to put his plan into action (John 13:27-30).

Then Matthew has Jesus set forth a new meaning for an old symbol. The old meaning of the Passover meal centered on God's deliverance of His people from Egyptian bondage (Exod. 12:1-30). The new meaning has to do with God's deliverance from sin through the sacrifice of Christ. The new meal thus symbolizes an even greater deliverance than the old.

As Jesus breaks the bread and passes it to His disciples, He says, " 'Take and eat; this is my body' " (26:26). He could easily have added "which will be broken for you" without doing violence to His intent (see Luke 22:19; 1 Cor. 11:24). He next takes the cup, indicating that it is His " 'blood of the covenant, which is poured out for many for the forgiveness of sins' " (vss. 27, 28). Just as the Old Testament covenants between God and His people were ratified by blood, so will the new covenant prophesied in Jeremiah 31:31-34.

Jesus will die "for many." Thus His death should be seen as a substitutionary death. He bore our sins to the cross and died in our place. He took the condemnation that was ours so that those who accept Him can participate in the life that is His (see 2 Cor. 5:21; 1 Pet. 2:22; Heb. 9:28; Gal. 3:13; Isa. 53:5, 6, 11). He will die as our substitute. His blood will be poured out for the "forgiveness of [our] sins" (vs. 28).

But at this point, Jesus once again indicates to His disciples that He is in control of events. He knows His death is at hand, but He also knows that He will rise to victory and that in the future He will drink of the vine again with His faithful disciples " 'in my Father's kingdom' " (vs. 29). These words express the assurance of His faith in both His resurrection and His second coming, at which time His disciples will also be resurrected (1 Thess. 4:16).

Christians of all persuasions, although differing over the exact symbolic meaning of the elements of the Last Supper, have made it a major event in their worship experience. The Communion supper is a remembrance of their Saviour, who died for each of them (1 Cor. 11:25). The meaning of the service is best captured by Paul, who penned: "Whenever you eat this bread and drink this cup, you proclaim the Lord's death until he comes" (1 Cor. 11:26). Thus the new symbolism of the first Christian Passover supper points in two directions at the same time: backward to the death of Christ and forward to His return in the clouds of heaven to bring His kingdom into its fullness.

At the end of the service, Matthew tells us, they sang a hymn and went out to the Mount of Olives. That hymn was probably Psalms 115 to 118, which were traditionally sung at the end of the Passover meal.

Struggles in Gethsemane and the Ultimate Kingly Choice

Jesus may have known the future, but that does not mean that He had no choices to make regarding bringing about that future. Just as Caiaphas and Judas had to make their choice about the part they would play in the final events of Christ's life, so Jesus also had to make a choice. He could still back out. The cross was not inevitable. He could still turn from the cross and walk away. His final decision to go through with the most excruciating part of the plan of salvation had yet to be made. That is the significance of His struggle in Gethsemane.

But before we get to Jesus' momentous decision, Matthew gives us one more glimpse of His "support group," the eleven remaining disciples. Unfortunately for both Jesus and the disciples, they will not be very helpful in their support. In fact, Jesus predicts that they will " '*all* fall away on account' " of Him (vs. 31). They will fall away because of His ordeal. Beyond any fears of personal safety, they have yet to grasp the very purpose of His sufferings. They still visualize messiahship in the framework of a conquering King rather than a suffering Servant. Such a misconception serves to disorient them at the time of crisis.

Next, Jesus indicates once again that He is not stumbling toward the cross blindly. He knows what He is doing. He even knows that He will rise again to meet His followers in Galilee (vs. 32). That prediction is picked up again in 28:6, 7, where an angel instructs the disciples that the risen Christ will meet them in Galilee, and yet again in 28:16-20, where the eleven meet to worship their risen Lord and receive the gospel commission.

Meanwhile, Peter tells Jesus that he will never fall away, even if he has to die with Him. The rest of the disciples make the same affirmation. But Jesus knows better. He knows that they are not yet to the place in their understanding and experience that they can withstand the magnitude and shock of the crisis that is soon to fall upon Him (vss. 33-35).

Jesus Himself is not quite ready either, even though He is not burdened with the disciples' false concept of the Messiah's role. His final preparation will take place in Gethsemane.

Apparently the Garden of Gethsemane (on the slopes of the Mount of Olives) had been a place frequented by Jesus and the disciples. After all, Judas knows where to find them when he arrives for the betrayal.

It is at that familiar spot that Jesus chooses to spend His last hours as a free Man. Leaving most of the disciples a distance behind, Matthew tells us that Jesus, "overwhelmed with sorrow to the point of death," takes Peter and the sons of Zebedee to strengthen Him as He prays (vss. 36-38). Jesus expects them to pray also, but they repeatedly fall asleep (vss. 40, 43, 45). That failure is a foretaste of their larger failure yet to come that night in their desertion of Him (vs. 56).

Moving somewhat beyond His three disciples, Jesus "fell with his face to the ground and prayed, 'My Father, if it is possible, may this cup be taken from me. Yet not as I will, but as you will' " (vs. 39). Returning twice to His sleeping disciples, Jesus goes away, both times to repeat essentially the same prayer (vss. 42, 44).

One thing is clear from this experience: Jesus dreads His "cup" of suffering. Many writers have recognized a sharp contrast between Christ's fear of His impending death on the cross and the reaction of other famous martyrs down through history.

Not only did such ancients as Socrates, believing they had nothing to fear from death, face the end of their lives with calmness, but Christian martyrs also faced death serenely, and even ecstatically at times. For example, when Polycarp (c. A.D. 69–155), the second-century bishop of Smyrna, faced the proconsul who would soon take his life, he told his persecutor to get on with the job. In a letter written soon after his martyrdom in A.D. 155 or 156, we are told that facing his death, "he was inspired with courage and joy, and his face was filled with grace, so that not only did he not collapse in fright at the things which were said to him," but he expressed a joyful reaction (*The Martyrdom of Polycarp*, 12). Such has been the experience of many martyrs down through history. Knowing they were right with God, they have had no fear of death.

With so many tranquil deaths in history, we are forced to ask why Jesus so fearfully anticipated His. Did He love the world too much? Did He lack faith? Or was He just plain afraid of pain?

The answer seems to lie in another direction. It has to do with the nature of the "cup" He had to drink. In the Old Testament, the "cup" has associations with the wrath (or judgment) of God (Isa. 51:17; Ezek. 23:33, 34). Christ's cup, John Stott points out, "symbolized neither the physical pain of being flogged and crucified, nor the mental distress of being despised and rejected . . . , but rather the spiritual agony of bearing the sins of the world, in other words, of enduring the divine judgment which those sins deserved" (Stott, *The Cross of Christ*, 76). Jesus' apprehensiveness of the cross is due to the fact that on it He will drink for humanity the cup of God's judgment against sin.

Jesus' dread in Gethsemane stems from His realization of God's hatred of sin. It is almost unbearable to Him that He must become "a curse for us" and become "sin" in God's eyes (Gal. 3:13; 2 Cor. 5:21). "He felt that by sin," Ellen White penned, "He was being separated from His Father. The gulf was so broad, so black, so deep, that His spirit shuddered before it. This agony He must not exert His divine power to escape. As man He must suffer the consequences of man's sin. As man He must endure the wrath of God against transgression" (White, *The Desire of Ages*, 686).

In Gethsemane the moment of decision has come. Jesus must either move forward to the cross or give up His mission. The tempter, of course, is still at His side, pointing out that His closest friends can't even stay awake to support Him (vss. 40, 43, 45), one of His disciples is at that very moment on a mission to betray Him (vss. 14-16, 46), and the ungrateful people He will die for are soon to crucify Him (27:32-44).

Fighting the temptation to do His own will and back off from the cross, Jesus undergoes duress in Gethsemane that we can understand only faintly. In great agony and dread, He finally makes His decision: " 'My Father,' " He repeatedly prays, " 'if it is not possible for this cup to be taken away unless I drink it, may your will be done' " (vss. 42, 44).

The decision is finally made. Jesus, exuding a calmness missing throughout His garden experience, goes back to the disciples. His decision to go forward to the cross is irrevocably made. He awakens them, announcing that " 'the hour is near, and the Son of Man is betrayed into the hands of sinners. Rise, let us go! Here comes my betrayer!' " (vss. 45, 46).

At that point, Judas arrives with the large armed crowd sent by the Jewish leaders. Once again Jesus demonstrates that He is in full control of the situation by healing the ear that has been cut off by Peter from one of the ruffians sent to arrest Him (Luke 22:51; John 18:10). Jesus tells Peter that if He should ask, His Father would send seventy-two thousand angels to His rescue. He then goes on to tell Peter that He desires to fulfill the Scriptures " 'that say it must happen in this way' " (vss. 53, 54). Or, as John puts it, " 'Shall I not drink the cup the Father has given me?' " (John 18:11). The answer is obvious. Jesus has made His decision in Gethsemene.

The final act in Jesus' arrest is the desertion of "all" the disciples as He predicted (vss. 56, 31). In spite of their protestations to the contrary (vs. 35), not one of the disciples is prepared to suffer with Jesus. The shock has simply been too great, and Judas's surprise complicity hardly lessens their shock. Even Jesus, who could use His power to escape or defeat His enemies, does nothing but stand there and reason with them (vss. 55, 56). The cumulative events prove to be too much for the disciples' fragile faith. *All* of them flee.

■ Getting Into the Word

Matthew 26:57–27:44

Read 26:57 to 27:44 through at least two times. Then proceed to the following questions and exercises.

1. Matthew 26:57-67 tells us about Jesus' trial before the Sanhedrin. Outline the sequence of events in that trial as portrayed by Matthew. Write a paragraph on your general impressions of the trial.
2. In 26:69-75 we find a progressive series of denials by Peter. List the progressive element in each denial along with the implications of each denial.
3. Matthew 27:11-26 tells us about Jesus' trial before Pilate. List those texts and ideas that provide insight into Pilate's view of Jesus. Study the parallel passages of Jesus' Roman trial in the other Gospels. Why did Pilate finally cave in to the wishes of the Jewish leaders? Read the article on Pilate in a Bible dictionary. What ideas did you gain from that reading which shed light on Matthew's portrayal of him?
4. Chapter 27:32-34 tells us about Jesus' crucifixion. Read the entries under *cross* and *crucifixion* in a Bible dictionary. Write a short summary on how that information has helped you better understand Jesus' crucifixion.
5. In 27:32 we read of Simon of Cyrene carrying the cross. Using your Bible's maps, find the location of Cyrene. What was a Jew from such a far-off place doing in Jerusalem? See Deuteronomy 16:16, Acts 6:9, and the article on the "diaspora" (or "dispersion") in a Bible dictionary for possible answers. Mark 15:21 names Simon's two sons. What does that imply about Simon?
6. Make a list of all the insults heaped upon Jesus while He hung upon the cross (27:32-44). Then add to that list the insults directed at Him in 26:57 to 27:31. What impact do you think these combined insults had on Jesus as He moved toward the cross and hung upon it?

■ Exploring the Word

Five More Responses to the King

Matthew 26:57 to 27:31 can be viewed as five responses to Jesus as Messiah. The first response is that of the Sanhedrin. Their response is one of predetermined guilt. Jesus' trial before the high court of the Jews can hardly be considered a trial in the general sense of the term, since the leaders and most of the members have judged Him guilty before the hearing has begun (26:3, 4, 59).

The Sanhedrin's task is complex because they are seeking the death penalty, but that is not theirs to mete out. The Romans, while using local administration in conquered provinces whenever possible, kept the ultimate penalty in their own hands.

Thus the Jewish leaders are faced with a crucial problem. They want to have Jesus put to death for His Messianic claims, but the Romans did not accept blasphemy as a capital offense. As a result, the leaders of the Sanhedrin have a twofold task before them. First, they must develop an agreement among their own members on the need to have Jesus executed for blasphemy—a matter of Jewish law. Second, they must develop an appropriate strategy to induce the Roman governor to mete out the death penalty on the basis of Roman law.

After some less-than-successful maneuvering, the Jewish leaders finally fasten a charge on Jesus based on a misinterpretation of His predicted three days in the grave before the resurrection of His body temple (26:61; John 2:19-21). But that is not enough. Therefore, Caiaphas plainly asks Jesus if He is " 'the Christ [Messiah], the Son of God.' " Jesus not only replies in the affirmative, but goes on to say that in the future, the members of the Sanhedrin will see Him " 'sitting at the right hand of the Mighty One and coming on the clouds of heaven' " (26:63, 64; see also Rev. 1:7).

That answer is all Caiaphas needs. "Blasphemy!" he cries out. Blasphemy was a sin punishable in the Old Testament by stoning (vs. 65; Lev. 24:10-23). In the technical sense, of course, Jesus has not blasphemed, since He has not pronounced the divine name

(Sanhedrin, 7:5), but the Jewish high court is more interested in obtaining a conviction than it is in the accuracy of its accusations.

Thus the first task of Caiaphas and his followers has been accomplished. The task ahead is to transpose that Jewish accusation into a breach of Roman law serious enough to call for the death penalty. This task is picked up in 27:11. But before we get to the Roman trial, we need to deal with two of the disciples.

The second response to Christ in 26:57–27:31 is that of Peter. As foretold by Jesus, Peter's response is to deny Him.

Perhaps the most amazing thing about this response is that Peter has the courage to be anywhere near the courtyard of the high priest (vs. 58). After all, only a short time before, he had fled with the other disciples (vs. 56). It took courage to show up at the scene of the trial. Unfortunately, Peter's courage doesn't stand up to much pressure. He denies His Lord three times that night.

It is difficult to miss the contrast between Christ and Peter in verses 64 to 75. Jesus has boldly confessed who He is before the highest officials in the nation, while Peter denies before a band of servants that he even knows who Jesus is.

The progression of Peter's denials is also worth noting. Initially, he merely claims that he does not know what the servant girl is talking about when she suggests that he has been with Jesus (vss. 69, 70). But as the pressure gets heavier, Peter (contrary to Jesus' instruction in 5:34-37) denies with an oath and flatly lies in saying, " 'I don't know the man!' " (vss. 71, 72). When that doesn't prove satisfactory, he puts distance between himself and Jesus by cursing and swearing and again perjures himself by denying that he knows Jesus (vss. 73, 74). By that time Peter has made a comprehensive repudiation. He soon hears the cock crow, remembers Jesus' prediction, and weeps bitterly (vss. 75, 34).

A remarkable thing about Peter's experience is that it is recorded in the Bible at all. After all, at the time the Gospels were written, Peter was regarded as the leading apostle. The very presence of the story implies three conclusions. The first has to do with God's boundless grace in restoring Peter to the ministry (John 21:15-19). The second is Peter's transformation, since he must have shared his failure with the Gospel writers. The third is the transparent honesty of the Bible, which, unlike so many "churchly" biographies, does not hide the flaws of its heroes or the redeeming grace that heals those flaws.

The third response to Jesus in our passage is that of Judas. His response is one of utter frustration. Not only has he failed in his plan to force Jesus to exert His power against the Romans and set up His kingdom, but Judas has forfeited his place in the kingdom itself. In utter despair, he throws the money he received for the betrayal into the temple and goes away and hangs himself (27:3-5).

Meanwhile, the leaders of the Sanhedrin have delivered Jesus to Pilate, the Roman governor (27:1, 2). That brings us to the fourth response to Jesus, that of Pilate. The Roman governor seeks to wash his hands of Jesus and his part in His crucifixion (27:24), but such a tactic fails to absolve him of his guilt.

Matthew makes it clear that there was not much of a formal trial. But that was not strictly necessary, since a Roman governor had a great deal of authority in such matters and could pursue justice in almost any way he deemed best.

Because of his almost absolute power in such cases, Pilate was a key player in the plan of the Jewish leaders. Unfortunately for them, however, extrabiblical sources indicate that Pilate held both the Jews and their customs in contempt. Beyond that, Pilate is described by both Philo (c. 20 B.C.–A.D. 50) and Josephus (A.D. 37–c. 95) as being greedy, inflexible, cruel, and one who resorted to robbery and oppression (see Green and McKnight, 615). The Jews had to work with wisdom and care against such a man. Their task was not an easy one.

Pilate appears to see through the ploys of the Jewish leaders, and he has no inclination to play into their hands. To the contrary, he attempts to free Jesus by utilizing the custom of releasing a prisoner at Passover. But that attempt fails when the Jewish leaders prevail on the crowd to call for the release of Barabbas (an insurrectionist "who had committed murder" [Mark 15:7]) instead of Jesus (27:15-18, 21).

Pilate's resolve in favor of Jesus is strengthened by a message his wife sends him about her dream that Jesus is innocent. Pilate himself sees no crime calling for the death penalty in Jesus (vss. 19, 23). But the Jewish leaders intensify the pressure on him by inciting the crowd. That crowd, it should be noted, is most likely not the one that welcomed Jesus to Jerusalem a few days earlier at the triumphal entry. It is quite probable that the Jewish leaders have taken care to ensure that the crowd on this occasion will be sympathetic to their position.

Not only is the crowd in an uproar, but, according to John, the Jews are beginning to insinuate that unless Pilate puts Jesus to death, he will be accused before the Emperor Tiberius of harboring a man who claims to be king (John 19:12). With that move, the Jewish leaders hit Pilate at his weakest point. After all, the emperor cannot be expected to be merciful to a governor who condones treason in the face of many witnesses. Also, with their accusation, the Jewish leaders have bridged the gap between Jewish law and Roman law. Pilate now has a pretext for issuing the order for the death penalty, which he does, even though he sees through the thinly veiled Jewish plot. Realizing that the Jewish leaders have forced his hand, Pilate begrudgingly gives the crucifixion order (27:26).

The fifth response to Jesus in 26:57 to 27:31 is that of the Roman soldiers. Their response is one of crude mocking. After dressing Jesus up in a royal fashion "they knelt in front of him and mocked him," saying " 'Hail, king of the Jews!' " After that cruel sport they spit on Him, beat Him on the head, put his own clothes back on Him, and lead him away to be crucified (27:27-31).

The Ultimate Contradiction: A Crucified Messiah

Crucifixion! The very thought of it was enough to bring a case of chills to the hardiest inhabitants in the Roman world. A cruel form of capital punishment, crucifixion combined public shame with slow physical torture.

The public shame consisted of dragging the traverse beam of a cross through the streets to the place of public execution. In an era that lacked TV programs and movies to satiate the downward side of human desire for violence, crucifixions were often the "best show" in town for the bored and curious. The victims were stripped of all clothing and affixed to the cross in a manner that prohibited them from caring for their bodily needs or covering their nakedness from the taunts and indignities of spectators.

The physical torture of crucifixion ranged from the nails driven through hands (or wrists) and feet to the inescapable burning of the Palestinian sun. The victim was immobile and therefore unable to fend off heat, cold, or insects. Since crucifixion affected no vital organs, death from fatigue, cramped muscles, hunger, and thirst usually came slowly, often after many days.

According to Roman law, crucifixion was reserved for the punishment of slaves and foreigners who were considered criminals. It was often used as a public demonstration of the folly of rebelling against the empire. And Jesus, of course, was condemned before Pilate as a political rebel.

In Jewish understanding, anyone executed by crucifixion was rejected by his people, cursed by the law of God, and excluded from God's covenant with the Jewish people (Gal. 3:13; Deut. 21:23). To top it off, the Jews expected their Messiah to be a mighty conquering king, not a suffering criminal. No wonder Paul could refer to Christ's cross as "a stumbling block to Jews and foolishness to Gentiles" (1 Cor. 1:23).

"For the disciples who had followed Jesus to Jerusalem," penned Jürgen Moltmann, "his shameful death was not the consummation of his obedience to God nor a demonstration of martyrdom for his truth, but the rejection of his claim. It did not confirm their hopes in him, but . . . destroyed them" (Moltmann, 132).

The disciples are not the only ones who recognize the paradox of a crucified Messiah. Yet, unlike the disciples, the others are not silent on the topic. To the contrary, they heap insults on the suffering Jesus. Matthew mentions three distinct groups who do so.

First are the passersby. " '*If* you are the Son of God,' " they cry out (echoing the exact words of Satan in the first two wilderness temptations [4:3, 6]), " 'come down from the cross' " and " 'save yourself' " (vss. 39, 40). Second are the chief priests and scribes, who mock Him to one another and say: " 'He saved others . . . but he can't save himself! He's the king of Israel! Let him come down now from the cross, and we will believe in him' " (vss. 42, 43). Finally, even the criminals crucified on his right and left "also heaped insults on him" (vss. 44, 38).

How would you have responded to such treatment by the very people you were dying to save? Most of us probably would have gotten down from the cross, called fire from heaven to show them who we really were, and used the twelve legions of angels that Jesus claimed God was willing to put at His disposal to wreak havoc on such ungratefuls.

That is the temptation Jesus is faced with. All through His ministry, His great temptation has been to avoid the cross. Now His temptation is to come down from His cross—a very real possibility, since He can resume His godly powers any time He so chooses. But to do so would break the plan of salvation. The entire universe can be eternally grateful that Jesus resisted the great temptation. By staying on the cross, He demonstrated the truth that in order to save others, He could not save Himself. Thus the chief priests and scribes uttered a profound truth but knew it not (vs. 42). It was Jesus' death on the cross that enabled Him to "save his people from their sins" (1:21).

Some of the first to be saved witness the event itself. They have been impressed by the way Jesus handles Himself in the face of insult and injury. They are persuaded by the Holy Spirit that Jesus is truly the Saviour of the world.

One of the earliest to grasp that truth is one of the two criminals executed with Him. Jesus tells the repenting felon that he most certainly will be in the eternal kingdom (Luke 23:40-43). Apparently another convert from the cross event is Simon of Cyrene, who was forced to carry Jesus' cross partway to Golgotha. Evidence for Simon's conversion is found in Mark 15:21, which notes that he is "the father of Alexander and Rufus." The knowledge of their names is highly suggestive that the family became followers of Jesus. A third apparent convert at the cross is the centurion (and perhaps some of his soldiers) in charge of the crucifixion, who eventually exclaims, " 'Surely he was the Son of God!' " (vs. 54).

The crucified Messiah, while being the ultimate contradiction, has also proved to be one of the most powerful forces in world history. The convicting power of the cross has been a deciding point in the lives of men and women from that terrible day on Golgotha to the present. The victory of Jesus that day is still saving "his people from their sins" (1:21).

■ Applying the Word

Matthew 26:1–27:44

1. **Have I really thought seriously about the meaning of the Lord's Supper? In what specific ways can I make the experience more meaningful for myself and those with whom I worship?**
2. **There is a sense in which each of us has Gethsemane experiences that drive us to wrestle with the Lord to surrender our wills. What can I learn about the experience of Jesus that can make my surrender to God's will more full and complete?**
3. **There are two great temptations in life. The first is not to go to my cross. The second is to get down from the cross and give people what they really deserve. Is the cross firmly planted in my life? If not, what should I do about it? What experiences drive me to get off my cross and act like I did before I was converted? How can God and I work together for victory in each of these situations?**

■ Researching the Word

1. **Study carefully the Last Supper in each of the Synoptic Gospels and in 1 Corinthians 11. Then examine the relevant passages in John 13 and 6. Itemize the contribu-**

tions that Matthew makes to our understanding of the topic. Then make a list of any additional information supplied by the other passages.

2. Peter is one of the most interesting characters in the New Testament. Use a concordance (exhaustive, preferably) to study Peter in the Gospels. (Remember that he is sometimes referred to as Simon and even as Cephus.) Develop a character profile for him. List and discuss his major characteristics in the Gospels. Then do the same exercise for the rest of the New Testament. You may want to compare your findings with the article on Peter in a Bible dictionary *after* you have completed your Bible study on the topic.

■ Further Study of the Word

1. For general insight, see E. G. White, *The Desire of Ages*, 557-568, 652-661, 685-757.
2. For a helpful treatment of Jesus' last week before His death, see E. H. Kiehl, *The Passion of Our Lord*.
3. For an authoritative treatment of crucifixion, see M. Hengel, *Crucifixion in the Ancient World*.

CHAPTER THIRTEEN

The Kingdom Made Certain: The King's Death and Resurrection

Matthew 27:45–28:20

With this chapter, we have come to the end of our journey through Matthew's Gospel. Slowly but surely, our author has led us up to the three final movements in his drama: Jesus' death (27:45-56), His burial and resurrection (27:57–28:15), and His missionary commission to the disciples (28:16-20). The first two movements make certain the kingdom, while the third sets the direction for the work of the church that will grow out of the redemptive work of the resurrected Jesus.

■ Getting Into the Word

Read Matthew 27:45 to 28:20 two times; then respond to the following questions and exercises. Have your Matthew notebook handy.

1. **Compare the four Gospels in their discussion of Jesus' death. Make four columns on a clean page in your Matthew notebook. List each element that Matthew contributes to our knowledge of that event. Then in the other three columns, list the information added to Matthew's account by the other evangelists.**
2. **List the precautions taken regarding the safety of Jesus' tomb in 27:62-66. Then list the events that took place on the resurrection morning in 28:1-15. In light of the empty**

tomb, discuss what you believe might have been the actual effect of the precautions on the thinking of the various categories of people who had some knowledge of those precautions.

3. **Enumerate the elements in 28:16-20 that point to the divinity of Jesus. Also list the various elements in Jesus' great commission. What are the implications of each element? In a paragraph or two, indicate the relationship between the resurrection event and the great commission.**

■ Exploring the Word

The King's Death

Matthew tells us that between the sixth and ninth hours on the crucifixion day (from about 12 noon until 3:00 p.m.), the earth was covered with darkness (27:45). That darkness could not have been a lunar eclipse, since it was Passover and thus a time of full evening moon. The darkness was apparently of supernatural origin. In the Old Testament, darkness is several times linked with judgment (see, for example, Joel 3:14, 15; Isa. 5:30; 13:10, 11). With that in mind, it seems the best way to understand the darkness of 27:45 is that it is an indication of God's judgment on the sin Jesus was bearing on the cross.

That interpretation lines up with the one Jesus seems to have made near the time of His death, when He cries: " 'My God, my God, why have you forsaken me?' " As Jesus nears death as a "ransom for many" (20:28) and the bearer of the sins of the world (2 Cor. 5:21), He has the feeling that even God has forsaken Him. But that sense of abandonment is not total hopelessness. After all, He still addresses the Father as "my God." Yet Jesus' despair should not be minimized. After all, He is in the midst of drinking the "cup" of God's wrath that He had so dreaded in Gethsemane (26:39-44).

Matthew has only one more word for us from Jesus as He hangs on the cross, but he doesn't even tell us what Jesus said—only that just before He died, He "cried out again in a loud voice" (vs. 50). The other two Synoptics give us the same information (Mark 15:37; Luke 23:46). Only John provides us with the words themselves. According to John, just before Jesus' death, He cries, " 'It is finished' " (John 19:30).

That is undoubtedly the greatest single word (as it is in the Greek) ever uttered. "It is the cry," notes William Barclay, "of the man who has completed his task; it is the cry of the man who has won through the struggle; it is the cry of the man who has come out of the dark into the glory of the light, and who has grasped the crown. . . . *Jesus died a victor and a conqueror with a shout of triumph on His lips*" (Barclay, 2:408, italics supplied).

Jesus has completed the saving work He came to do. He has lived a perfect life, and now He is giving His life as "a ransom for many" (20:28). Matthew next tells us that Jesus "gave up his spirit," or died (27:50). At this point, Satan's defeat is forever sealed. The battle has been won.

One of the great visible symbols of that victory and the new order of things is that "the curtain of the temple was torn in two from top to bottom" (vs. 51). That tearing of the curtain separating the Holy from the Most Holy Place in the earthly temple signifies two things. First, the old system of ceremonies and sacrifices that pointed forward (Col. 2:17) to Jesus' sacrifice on the cross is a thing of the past. Now that the real sacrifice has taken place, the ceremonial system has served its purpose. The ripping of the curtain from top to bottom (indicating divine intervention, since a human tearing would have been from bottom to top) signifies that even the Holy of Holies of the earthly temple is no longer holy. The scene of action has shifted to heaven, where Jesus will minister as High Priest for those who believe in Him (Heb. 8:1, 2). Thus a second significance of the tearing of the curtain is that believers will now have direct access to the Father through the sacrifice of Jesus and through His postresurrection ministry in heaven (Rom. 8:34; Heb. 4:15; 7:25; 10:19-22).

The tearing of the curtain in the earthly temple may also be seen as a foreshadowing of more serious events to come in A.D.

70, when the temple itself will be destroyed along with Jerusalem (24:2). Divine rending of the curtain is the beginning of the fulfillment of Jesus' words that the Jewish house has truly been left desolate (23:38).

Another visible symbol indicating that Satan's defeat has been sealed with the death of Jesus is the great earthquake that opens many of the tombs of Old Testament believers. Matthew indicates that after Jesus' resurrection, they were also resurrected and appeared to many in Jerusalem (27:53).

Some of the bystanders are mightily impressed with the manner of Jesus' death and the events surrounding it. One such group is the Roman centurion and some of his soldiers, who are not only terrified, but exclaim, " 'Surely he was the Son of God!' " (vs. 54). Thus the Gentile witness about Jesus that was so strong in Matthew 2 and several other places in the first Gospel is also evident near its close. For a book written to and for Jews, Matthew's Gospel certainly has had a lot of good things to say about Gentile faith. That emphasis will be sounded again in the book's closing verses.

The Empty Tomb and the Death of Death

R. T. France (*Matthew*, 402) points out that 27:57 to 28:20 is based on a chiastic structure in which the account of the resurrection is the dramatic focal point:

27:57-61 Jesus dead and buried
  27:62-66 Setting of the guard
    28:1-10 The empty tomb and the risen Lord
  28:11-15 Report of the guard
28:16-20 Jesus alive and sovereign.

In the chiastic literary format (which is quite common in the Bible), the first and last items correspond with each other, the second and the second to the last with each other, and so on, with the central item being the focal point. Thus in the present passage, the resurrection of Jesus is of utmost importance. The same is true for the rest of the New Testament. Without the resurrection, there is no gospel or good news. New Testament faith is built on the reality of Jesus' resurrection from the dead. According to Paul, the gospel message is that "Christ died for our sins . . . , that he was buried, that he was raised on the third day" (1 Cor. 15:3,4). Again Paul emphasizes that "if Christ has not been raised, our preaching is useless and so is your faith. . . . And if Christ has not been raised, your faith is futile; you are still in your sins" (1 Cor. 15:14, 17). Just as it is in Matthew's chiasm, so it is in the rest of the New Testament: the resurrection is the central reality, the reality upon which all else rests.

But that reality is not in the disciples' thinking before it takes place, even though Jesus predicted it to them on numerous occasions during His ministry (16:21; 17:23; 20:19; 12:40). Their minds have been so fixated on the coming Messiah as conquering King that they have totally failed to understand Jesus' role as suffering Servant (see Ps. 22; Isa. 53). As a result, Jesus' death catches them off guard and puts them in the pit of despair. The hours spent by Jesus in Joseph of Arimathea's tomb are the darkest in the disciples' lives (vss. 57-61). They have lost all hope, because they have failed to hear and grasp Jesus' promise of His resurrection on the third day.

But, interestingly enough, not everyone forgets the prediction of resurrection. The Jewish leaders remember, even though they do not believe it will take place. Rather, they fear that the disciples will steal the body and *claim* a resurrection (vss. 62-64). In that case, the disciples' lie concerning Jesus' resurrection would be worse than His lie that He was the Messiah (vs. 64). The Jewish leaders are so concerned about the possibility of a renewed crisis that they take the unprecedented step of breaking their own extremely rigid Sabbath laws by visiting Pilate (an unclean Gentile) on their holy day to request a guard for Jesus' tomb (vs. 62). That breach of their usual practice indicates the depth of their fear of a hoax being perpetrated by the disciples.

Pilate, presumably thoroughly tired of the whole business,

readily agrees to cooperate with the troublesome leaders, since if he doesn't cooperate, and the body is gone on the third day, there will be no end to the problem. He thus grants the Jewish leaders a guard to seal the tomb and to watch over it (vss. 65, 66).

But in taking such precautions, Leon Morris points out, the Jewish leaders "did more than they knew. They ensured that there could be no nonsense about disciples stealing the body when in due course Jesus did rise from the dead. The precautions of his enemies would underline the truth of his resurrection" (Morris, *Matthew*, 732).

Matthew 28:1-10 brings us to the resurrection event. None of the New Testament writers describe the actual resurrection. Rather, they present an account of its effects along three lines: the empty tomb, the guards' fear, and Jesus' meeting with some of His followers.

It is of special interest that Matthew has the angel (vs. 5) and later Jesus (vs. 9) meeting first with two women. In the first Gospel, these women are the primary human witnesses to the resurrection. That is an important point regarding the historical validity of the account, since women were not accepted as witnesses in Jewish society. If Matthew had been inventing the story (as some have accused), he would hardly be expected to highlight the witness of the women if he wanted to convince his first-century audience.

The highlighting of the women is also of interest in the sense that Matthew is remaining true to his first chapter, where he took the rare step of including females in Jesus' genealogy. Thus the women in the resurrection account reinforce one of Matthew's great themes: the people Jesus came to save include females as well as Gentiles and other outcasts from Jewish society. The "his people" of 1:21 is much broader than traditional Judaism had been willing to admit.

Females have had a part in Christian ministry from the very beginning of the church. In 28:7-10 we find them being told to bear witness of the resurrection to the disciples.

Jesus' Sunday resurrection and the appearance of the angel affects various people differently. The Roman soldiers are "afraid . . . and [become] like dead men" (vs. 4), whereas the women appear to at first be surprised. They are later "filled with joy" and run to tell the disciples the good news (vs. 8).

Any believer who understands the significance of the resurrection will be filled with joy. It is Jesus' victory over death. In the long run, it signals the death of death itself. The resurrection is the great victory of God the Father and Jesus over Satan and the forces and power of death. The resurrection demonstrates that God is truly in control. Beyond its cosmic proportions, Jesus' resurrection also functions as a guarantee of the resurrection, at His second coming, of all who have died believing in Him (see 1 Cor. 15:20-23, 51-55; 1 Thess. 4:16).

The resurrection of Jesus is the key to understanding the New Testament from Acts through Revelation. His shameful death had been viewed as anything but a victory by the disciples. To the contrary, they viewed it as a public defeat and a rejection of His claims. If Jesus had not been raised, Christianity would have ended in a Palestinian grave.

Without the resurrection, Christianity would have nothing to offer the world but a few nice ideas. But with the resurrection, the disciples became transformed men who no longer feared the Jewish and Roman authorities. To the contrary, they became fearless crusaders who would push the gospel message everywhere. The core of their preaching in the book of Acts was, "You . . . put him to death by nailing him to the cross. But God raised him from the dead" (Acts 2:23, 24; see also 3:15; 4:10; etc.).

It is this great truth that the women of 28:7-10 are told to tell to the disciples. Jesus adds that the women are also to instruct the disciples to meet Him in Galilee (vs. 10), as He had predicted in 26:32. With that meeting, Matthew will close his Gospel. But first, he must deal with the guards' report concerning the angelic visitation and the empty tomb.

The empty tomb proves to be a problem for both the Roman guard and the Jewish leaders. The first thing the soldiers do is to send a delegation into Jerusalem to report to the Jewish leaders what has happened. The paradox of the record is that the very men who predicted deceit by Jesus' followers (27:63, 64) now turn to deceit themselves in order to cover up the resurrection. Even more astounding is that they instruct the guards to tell the very story of body theft that the guards had been ordered to prevent (28:13). The Jewish leaders are desperate and are willing to go to any lengths to obscure the facts.

The soldiers are also in a jam. Their basic problem is that they do not have the corpse they were sent to guard. But to say that they fell asleep is not much of a solution. After all, sleeping on guard duty was punishable by the most severe penalties, perhaps even death. But the alternative to reporting the missing body to their superiors also would bring severe punishment, since it would be a confession of their failure to carry out their duty. Of course, they could tell the truth. But what Roman officer would believe such an improbable story of angels, brightness, and a resurrection?

All in all, it seems best to the soldiers to accept the solution of the Jewish authorities and thus avoid, or at least delay, certain punishment. The move in that direction is sweetened by the bribe of "a large sum of money" (vs. 12) and by the promise of the Jewish leaders to "satisfy" Pilate (who will soon be leaving the city for his residence in Caesarea and may not hear of the problem) if the report reaches his ears (vs. 14).

Matthew tells us that the soldiers agree to the deception. And, notes Matthew, "this story has been widely circulated among the Jews to this very day" (vs. 15). In actual fact, the story continued to have circulation long after the death of the apostle. Justin Martyr (c. A.D. 100-165) tells us that in the middle of the second century, the Jews were still claiming the disciples had stolen the body (*Dialogue With Trypho*, 108).

Of course, the Jewish leaders didn't really have too many options. After all, they either had to stick by the lie, produce the body, or believe in the resurrection of Jesus. The last alternative was unacceptable. Thus, since they couldn't produce the body, they were stuck with the lie.

The King's Final Command and Promise

Matthew's concluding paragraph (vss. 16-20) finds the resurrected Jesus meeting with His disciples in Galilee. That meeting was one of the most momentous events in Christian history. As Sherman Johnson puts it, "the effect of this brief scene on the life of the Christian church has been incalculable. No part of the Bible, with the possible exception of the letter to the Romans, has done more to give Christians the vision of a world-wide church. It has sent them to all nations, bearing the message of salvation through Christ, with which are linked the responsibility and privilege of obeying his words" (Johnson, 7:620).

We should note several things in Matthew's final paragraph. First, the eleven disciples worship Jesus (vs. 17), just as the women did in verse 9. Worship is an understandable response on the part of those who now realize that the Jesus with whom they have fellowshiped for three years has overcome death itself and is alive again. They are coming to a fuller appreciation of what it means for Him to be the Son of God.

Second, "all authority in heaven and on earth" has been given to Jesus (vs. 18). Authority has been one of the issues all through Matthew's Gospel (7:29; 9:6, 8; 21:23), and world dominion was the issue in the third temptation, when Satan offered Jesus "all the kingdoms of the world and their splendor" if Jesus would only bow down and worship him (4:9, 10). But Jesus has chosen the way of the cross, the only genuine way to universal dominion. Because of His victorious life, death, and resurrection, He has won "*all* authority in heaven and on earth" (vs. 18) for dominion in "*all* nations" (vs. 19) for *all* time ("always," vs. 20). Jesus is truly Lord.

Third, Jesus delegates His authority to His followers for the express purpose of enabling them to go into all the world to make disciples and baptize them. In the first Gospel, a disciple is both a learner and a follower. Thus Jesus not only commissions His disciples to teach the theoretical truth of the kingdom but also to teach obedience to everything He has commanded (vss. 19, 20).

Discipleship in Matthew has never been mere belief or knowledge. Rather, the first Gospel has repeatedly stressed obedience to the will of God in the things of practical life (see for example 7:21; 25:31-46). Not only does Jesus instruct the disciples to teach, but they are also to baptize in the "name" (singular, indicating the basic unity of the Godhead) of the Trinity (vs. 19). We find the command to baptize being put into operation in the earliest records of the church after Jesus' ascension. Thus Peter on the day of Pentecost urges his hearers to "repent and be baptized" (Acts 2:37, 38).

Fourth, Jesus' presence will be with His followers always, even "to the very end of the age" (vs. 20). Thus Matthew's Gospel closes with one of the great themes of his first chapter—Jesus continues to be " 'God with us' " (1:23).

Fifth, and another theme from Matthew's first chapter, is the international scope of the gospel. The restriction given to the disciples in 10:5, 6 to preach only to Israel is now removed. The message of the risen Christ is to be preached to "all nations" (vs. 19). That international element is first found in the genealogy of chapter 1 and the adoration of the Magi in chapter 2.

Thus Matthew's Gospel is a unified book with several themes running across its twenty-eight chapters. We have come to the end, but have we? Not really. Jesus makes it sound like the beginning. While it is true that His personal teaching ministry has ended, it is also true that the universal teaching ministry of His church finds its beginning in 28:16-20. His followers are to go throughout the world, preaching the risen Saviour, who came to "save his people from their sins" (1:21). *In Matthew's Gospel the end is really the beginning.*

■ Applying the Word

1. **Have I taken full advantage of the open pathway into the throne room of God provided by the death of Jesus and His ministry as my personal High Priest? In what ways have I taken full advantage of my privilege? In what ways**

could I enrich my experience?

2. What does the resurrection of Jesus mean to me? In what ways does it inform, energize, and direct my daily Christian walk and my eternal hope?
3. Jesus' last words in the first Gospel to me as an individual Christian are found in the great commission. How can I apply the various commands and promises of that commission more fully in my daily experience? What specific activities would God like me to initiate or participate in as a response to Jesus' great sacrifice for me?

■ Researching the Word

1. Use a concordance to study the disciples' interpretation of Christ's resurrection. Look up all texts in the New Testament on the topic. Write a paragraph on what it meant for both their theology and their personal lives. Your study will be enriched if you think about the contrast in the disciples' lives before and after the resurrection as set forth in the Gospels and in the book of Acts. Write a paragraph on that contrast. Support your argument with specific scriptural texts.
2. Matthew 28:1-10 suggests that Jesus rose on the first day of the week (our Sunday). Some argue that His resurrection is the reason to keep Sunday instead of the biblical Sabbath (our Saturday). Using a concordance, look up each reference to the first day of the week in the New Testament. In your Matthew notebook, write down each reference. Next to each reference, write a few sentences concerning what can be learned about the first day from that text. How many of them suggest Sunday keeping as a memorial to the resurrection? Can you think of a New Testament symbol that God has given as a memorial of Jesus' resurrection? On that last point, you may want to read Romans 6:1-11. What light does that passage shed on the issue?

■ Further Study of the Word

1. For general insight, see E. G. White, *The Desire of Ages*, 741-835.
2. For a helpful study on Christ's resurrection, see M. C. Tenney, *The Reality of the Resurrection*.
3. For valuable insights into the implications of the great commission, see M. Warren, *I Believe in the Great Commission*.